THE HISTORY OF THE SALVATION ARMY

Volume VII

1946–1977

THE HISTORY OF THE SALVATION ARMY

The Weapons of Goodwill

Volume VII

1946–1977

Frederick Coutts

HODDER AND STOUGHTON
LONDON SYDNEY AUCKLAND TORONTO

British Library Cataloguing in Publication Data

Coutts, General Frederick
 The History of The Salvation Army.
 Vol. 7: 1946–1977
 1. Salvation Army – History
 I. Coutts, Frederick
 267'.15'09   BX9715

 ISBN 0-340-39087-5 (*cased*)
 ISBN 0-340-39086-7 (*paperback*)

CONTENTS

FOREWORD

Voltaire is quoted as having said: 'History is nought but a list of crime and calamity.' Edward Gibbon, the famous historian, expresses a similar opinion: 'History . . . is indeed little more than the register of the crimes, follies and misfortunes of mankind.' Happily that is only one side of the story. The history of mankind also contains records of unselfish and genuine love, of courage and compassion, of steadfastness and untiring service.

This latter view is certainly true about the history of The Salvation Army and not least about Volume VII which covers the years 1946 to 1977. During this period following the end of the Second World War the work was consolidated and the Army's international links were strengthened. The oneness of The Salvation Army in a divided world must strike the reader as a modern miracle.

Owing to political changes at this time in some countries a number of doors were closed. In several other countries new doors were opened and the Salvation Army ministry which started then continues to flourish today.

General Frederick Coutts (R), author of Volume VI of *The History of The Salvation Army*, is the writer of this new volume. For this demanding task he is eminently qualified, not only by his literary skill and his aptitude for research, but also through his personal involvement with the movement during a lifetime of dedicated ministry as a Salvation Army officer.

London   *Jarl Wahlström*
April 1986   ·   *General*

INTRODUCTION

The period covered by this seventh volume of *The History of The Salvation Army* reveals a movement which, though by repute occupied with healing the hurts of others, was perforce busy binding up its own wounds as well.

This was no new experience for Salvationists for it was not the first time for soldiers in an international army to find themselves on opposite sides of a national battle line. At the beginning of the century, during the Boer War, William Booth had described himself as 'a father with a divided household. My children [he said] are on both sides. Whoever wins I lose.'

His eldest son and successor faced the same test. Throughout the First World War General Bramwell Booth sought to retain unbroken his fellowship with those of his people who were on the opposite side of the western front. In the Army press he would not have them labelled 'enemies'. The word was taboo. Scraps of information about them brought to him through officers in neutral countries were thankfully received. It was one of his most momentous days when the German authorities agreed that Lieut.-Colonel Carl Treite, then the principal officer in Berlin, should come to Stockholm to talk with him.

The strain upon the Army's international ties was even more severe during the Second World War. General and Mrs Carpenter became virtual prisoners in the British Isles. Large tracts of Europe and East Asia became giant no-go areas. Salvationists had to believe in the loyalty and integrity of comrades with whom they could not communicate directly much less meet face to face. But they continued to beseech the God and Father of all men not that this or that side should win but that the will of the Lord should prevail.

As his biographer has stated, the single-minded General Carpenter incurred no small obloquy on this account. But when at last the dark night of war ended, long separated salvationists found to their great joy that, though parted, they had each been faithful to his creed, his calling and his comrades. Their confidence in God and in one another was not shattered but strengthened. As the sound and fury of battle died away they found that, as General Orsborn had written and they themselves had sung, they were still:

> One in faith and harmony,
> One in perfect charity.

What follows can be read as an account of how they sought to return thanks to God for His goodness.

Author's note

* The rank given to officers in this volume is that which was held at the time of the reference.
* (R) appearing after a name indicates 'Retired'.
* The author is grateful to his comrades serving in the editorial and literary departments (particularly the archives section) of International Headquarters for their unfailing help with information and correction.
* As 'all men are liable to error' further needful corrections will be welcomed.

PART ONE

THE SIXTH GENERAL: ALBERT ORSBORN

(June 21, 1946–June 30, 1954)

1 AS MEN THAT DREAMED

Only those who lived through the Second World War – and this applies to participants on both sides – can imagine the heartfelt relief which hailed the signing of the armistice agreement on Luneberg Heath on Monday, May 7, 1945. They were as men that dreamed. No longer did either soldier or civilian need to fear the terror by night nor the destruction at noonday. Earth and sea and sky were at peace. 'Unbounded joy in all our hearts and homes over the cessation of hostilities' cabled General Evangeline Booth from her retirement in Hartsdale (N.J.) to the Army's International Headquarters in London. Salvationists and friends crowding the Royal Albert Hall on the evening of Thursday, June 25, answered back by singing:

> To arms, Salvation Army!
>   Loud rings the clarion call,
> Nor weary in the conflict
>   Till Christ is Lord of all.

General George Lyndon Carpenter, who led this meeting of praise, was due to retire from active service in less than twelve months so that, at a time when long distance travel was still by sea, the notices summoning the next High Council to assemble at Sunbury Court on Thursday, April 25, 1946, had to be in the post by February 26. For would-be travellers even to secure a suitable booking was still something of a hazard at this time. Nor were the circumstances attending the election of the sixth Salvation Army General wholly propitious. The world powers themselves were exhausted – the victors by their all-out struggle to win; the vanquished by their frantic efforts to avoid defeat. The bill for the collective damage was not calculable in hard cash. Could the cost have been estimated in pounds and pence, the account might in due course have been met. But the expense of spirit in terms of human pain and woe had bankrupted both sides. As Sir Winston Churchill observed at the time: 'The vital springs of human inspiration are, for the moment, drained.'

Yet there were those who realised that the darker the night, the brighter the light of goodwill would shine and the farther could its beams carry. The international edition of the Army's *War Cry* was one example of this. From 1940 onward paper rationing in the United Kingdom had reduced its size to four pages, approximately 31 cm by 27 cm, using no type larger than eight point. This was by way of a brave attempt to solve the insoluble problem of accommodating a quart of news in a pint pot of space. But when this restriction was lifted in the autumn of 1946, the weekly circulation rose by more than twenty-five per cent – a figure which any commercial house might have envied. The editor, the gifted Brigadier A. J. Gilliard, was not slow to turn this increase to the healing of the world's distresses. The ink was hardly dry upon the armistice terms before *The War Cry* was carrying appeals for reinforcements to strengthen the first of the relief teams making ready to cross the Channel. With that spirit abroad the successor to General Carpenter, whoever he or she might be, had but to sound the call to speak comfortably to the desolated countries of Europe – and there would be an instant answer. The response must have been of the greatest encouragement to Commissioner Albert W. T. Orsborn when, on Thursday, May 9, 1946, he was elected by thirty-six votes out of forty-six to the international leadership of The Salvation Army.[1]

The new General was not yet turned sixty years of age and already had more than forty years' service as an officer to his credit, beginning with corps and divisional duty, followed by eight years on the staff of the International Training College as Chief Side Officer for men, leading to three as Chief Secretary in New Zealand with four in charge of the Army's evangelical work in Scotland and Ireland, and the next six with parallel responsibilities for the whole of the United Kingdom. He was possessed by a love of words which found expression in the richly devotional songs which he wrote for use in the Army's public worship, and by a love of the Word as was evidenced in his public preaching. Among the eight nominees who went to the ballot, he was the man for this particular hour.[2] The three main tasks to which he set his hand were (i) a continuing emphasis upon the gospel of Christ as the power of God unto man's salvation – body, mind and soul; (ii) a renewal of the Army's world fellowship, ravaged and savaged as it had been by six years of total war; and (iii) a serious consideration of the best way in which to broaden the base of the administrative authority of the General.

These three aims are not set down in any order of importance. In his first broadcast after his election the General referred to each of them, but the third required what in today's jargon is called research in depth. A study group of five commissioners – with Commissioner Catherine Bramwell-Booth in the chair and Colonel Walter Rushton as secretary – was appointed for this purpose, with instructions to have their report completed within six months. It was clear that the new General believed that the King's business required haste. In the event the Commission required no touch of the spur. Its recommendations were submitted on July 31, 1946 – with results which are set out below.

Meanwhile even before the General had been publicly installed in office, he joined 500 young people for a day's meeting in the Clapton Congress Hall on Sunday, June 23. Two days later, drawn by a commingling of sentiment and a sense of opportunity, he flew to Oslo. There, fifty-eight years previously, he had been carried as a child of two in his father's arms through a snowstorm from the dockside to the meeting where his parents, who had been appointed to help pioneer the Army's work in Norway, were to be welcomed. This time upwards of four thousand people packed the Calmeyergatan mission hall where the Founder, William Booth, had also been greeted on his final visit to the Norwegian capital in the spring of 1912. When the General addressed the company gathered at the airport to receive him the band replied with:

> In the ranks of the dear old Army,
> 'Neath the yellow, red and blue

– a declaration of a loyalty which had survived the harsh years of quisling rule.

The next port of call was Stockholm. The Scandinavian airlines had not then reached their present standards of elegance and comfort, and it was with an absence of any personal satisfaction that the General boarded the adapted Dakota with its metal seats ranged along the interior of the fuselage. But as the plane bumped and bucked along its way, clinging too closely to earth's contours for comfort, the traveller caught sight of an aircraft moving in the opposite direction and bearing the legend 'Swedish missionary services'. Overseas personnel were being repatriated and reinforcements sent out to replace them. To the observer these things were a parable – almost a sign from heaven – pointing to the way in which modern techniques could, and should, be harnessed to the service of the gospel. This was an object lesson of which the General made use in more than one meeting which followed – including his public welcome at the Westminster Central Hall, London. On this occasion the Lord President of the Council, the Rt. Hon. Herbert Morrison, said that 'the voluntary spirit, the urge to serve, without fee or reward, for the good of the community, must be preserved if we are to continue our way of life.'

This truth had already been illustrated that same afternoon when H.R.H. the Duchess of Kent had opened the reconstructed ward blocks at the Mothers' Hospital, Lower Clapton Road, which had suffered severe damage in an air raid on November 8, 1940. 'I believe', observed the Duchess, 'that this is the first hospital to be reconstructed and repaired since hostilities ceased, and I congratulate everyone associated with this great effort.' Bombs or no bombs, the Leader of the Women's Social Services in Great Britain and Ireland, Commissioner Phillis Taylor, could say that 2,000 babies had been born at the Mothers' Hospital and the associated centres at Willersley Castle and Bragborough Hall, during each of the war years.

This was not the only social service development in the country during the early days of General Orsborn's term of office. Wicksted Hall, a country property in Shropshire, was opened as an eventide home for men, as was the Sir Thomas Kelly memorial, 'Holywood', in Co. Down, and Netherfield Hall at Stansted Abbots (Essex), providing accommodation for another hundred senior citizens in all.

This crusade of determined helpfulness was seen to advantage outside the British Isles and against the background of wartime destruction. Like John Wesley, the Army looked upon the whole world as its parish. By this time the relief teams – which included a Swedish contingent – had fanned out across Europe from the English Channel to the Baltic, as far east as Friedland on the border of the Russian zone and as far north as Lapland. In the impoverished French capital the Palais de la Femme had proved a clearing house for literally tens of thousands of articles of clothing for necessitous families. The President of the 'Social Services for the Protection of Children in Paris' wrote:

> We have received a generous part of the superb clothing and layettes given by The Salvation Army in Canada. I cannot express how great is my gratitude. For many years we had stocks of clothing which enabled our health visitors to provide the needy with indispensable articles – but our cupboards were completely empty at the moment when poverty was greater than ever. The gift of The Salvation Army was inestimable.

The Salvation Army in Germany had shared the plight of the country. From 1937 onwards collections had been prohibited. The sale of *Der Kriegsruf* was first restricted and then banned. The use of Salvation Army ranks and symbols was forbidden. During the war thirteen of the Army's thirty homes and institutions in the Reich were destroyed and another five seriously damaged. Of eighty corps properties thirty-three were demolished and another eight needed major repair. It had been years since Die Heilsarmee had known so few soldiers, so few officers, so few usable properties, as at the conclusion of the Second World War. But though sadly diminished in numbers, looking inevitably the worse for wear, often hungry in body, Salvationists maintained a holy defiance in the service of their cause. The relief teams put new heart into their German comrades in so far as they were not ashamed to call them brethren. Even more, the technical expertise which they displayed when, for example, the administrative wing of a poison gas factory at Leese was transformed into a home and school for 200 boys and girls, commended the gospel which they preached.

This it was that captivated more than one German administrator – as when the Lord Mayor of Frankfurt, asking the Army to take over the running of a bunker hostel in the city, said that he welcomed not just its social but its religious work. One report of his speech made the point that the only activity to which he specifically referred was the visitation by Salvationists of the public houses where they sold their papers and sang of the love of God.

This goodwill which recognised with divine impartiality the needs of body and spirit was allowed still greater freedom of expression when, on the eve of Christmas, 1946, the British government allowed individual donors to send up to 7 lb of rationed food to addresses overseas. The Army's European Relief Department offered to facilitate the dispatch of such gifts but their intrinsic worth can be judged only against the situation on the domestic front. The spring of 1946 disclosed a world shortage of grain which led to the introduction of bread rationing in Britain in the following summer, and this lasted for two years. In the autumn the individual allowance of butter, bacon and meat in the United Kingdom was further reduced, and then potatoes were rationed for the first time. *The War Cry* – ever on the side of the angels but as practical as any housewife could wish – provided a list of foodstuffs which could not be donated. A second list set out the items which would require airtight packaging to survive the hazards of the post. A third list itemised what could be sent without risk – beginning with tinned preserves and ending with dried eggs and soap powders. Within the week young Salvationists from Andover (Hants.) had clubbed together to make a gift of their monthly sweet ration, and fifty officers in the Bristol division had each pledged themselves to send a 7 lb parcel. Another Salvationist couple mentioned the scheme to their immediate neighbours who in due course contributed 140 tins of food and 90 packets of tea. Interested friends in Jersey – doubtless remembering their own hardships during the occupation – joined in a similar gesture of goodwill.

To return now to the proceedings of the Commission which was considering the establishment of an Advisory Council to the General, those so appointed were among the most senior of Army leaders. The chairperson, Commissioner Catherine Bramwell-Booth, had been much in her father's counsel and for eleven and a half years had been Leader of the Women's Social Services. Commissioner Edgar Dibden, who had thirty-six years of active officership to his credit, was widely versed in the Army's financial needs. Commissioner Charles F. A. Mackenzie was an American officer who had served in India as well as in Britain. Commissioner Donald McMillan bore an honoured Army name and had been an officer since 1906. The names of Commissioner Frank Dyer (Managing Director, The Salvation Army Assurance Society) and Commissioner A. H. Barnett (a veteran missionary officer) were added so that the Commission might never lack a quorum.

Two points should be made clear. It must not be supposed that, prior to this date, the Army had been under the control of some one person who could do with it as seemed good to him. Even William Booth was bound by the aims which, under God, he himself had determined. He could not use the Army for any purposes other than those which, at his desire, had been embodied in legal form. From the days when he was in his prime there were boards and councils which saw to the smooth running of the Army's internal machinery. The most modest tea slip for working late of an evening required two verifying signatures as well as that of the recipient. How much more was any major decision given the widest possible consideration. Nevertheless the Commission wisely sought to remove the faintest shadow of personal favouritism from the administration. Even General Orsborn himself had circulated at the 1939 High Council some 'Notes for discussion of proposed legislative and administrative adjustments'.

Though the members of the Commission did not agree on every detail of their final submission of July 31, 1946 – two of them each presented a minority report – all were agreed that the proposed body should be advisory and would in no way impinge upon the General's exercise of his supreme responsibility for the direction of the Army's work. Rather would it act as an extension of his own powers to survey existing activities, to plan new developments, and to take account of the way in which the movement could better function in a changing world. It is significant that while each successive General has considered afresh the relationship between his own office and the work of the Advisory Council, none has made any attempt to dispense with its services.

As for its agenda, while the Commission recommended that this should be drawn up by the General, it also proposed that this could 'include matters submitted by the Chief of the Staff, the members of the Council and all territorial commanders. Other officers might submit, through their respective leaders, subjects for the General's consideration.' To illustrate: any proposals affecting the soul-saving work of the Army in any part of the world, the training of officers, changes in orders and regulations, statements of doctrine, consideration of the Army's legal basis in countries where the movement is at work, the content and production of the Army's literature, the appointment, promotion or retirement of officers which could affect the membership of any subsequent High Council, all come within the purview of the Advisory Council. All such discussions and consequent recommendations are treated as confidential by members of the Council yet, though its work is thus largely out of sight, it has become an integral part of the Army's international administration.

In the autumn of 1946 came the welcome news that contact had been restored with Salvationists in Japan. Since the Pacific fighting did not end until August 14, 1945, this was an undeniable tribute to the courage and the care with which Brigadier Charles Davidson had pursued the task given him by General Orsborn to report on conditions in Japan in so far as these affected the Army. The brigadier had served in the Far East prior to the war and was taken prisoner at the fall of Singapore. However, after liberation and homeland furlough – grievously shadowed by the passing of his wife – he returned, a lone envoy, on this 'faith and fact-finding mission'. At best the Army had never numbered more than a fraction of the population, seemingly always destined to be battling against odds. This Gideon's band undoubtedly exercised an influence greatly in excess of any head count, but the passions of war forcibly silenced their public witness – at least for the duration. The movement was proscribed, the use of the name forbidden, their symbols suppressed. But the brigadier first gathered together a company of some sixty 'officers' who lived in the Tokyo area and then, with infinite patience, was able to renew fellowship with another 200 drawn from various parts of the country. But to place the word 'officers' in quotation marks does not do them justice for, as soon as the government ban was lifted, meetings were renewed; carefully preserved uniforms were worn again; slowly – but certainly surely – Army properties were restored to their rightful purpose, and before the year was out the flag with the star in the centre was to be seen on the streets again.

In addition to making history in this very satisfactory fashion, the first volume of *The History of The Salvation Army* was now in its final stages of production. The foreword is dated December 1946, and perhaps the outstanding comment therein by General Orsborn is that 'much in this first volume may be surprising . . . even to Salvationists.' It is true that legend can gather round memorable personalities of the past, especially when they are figures as picturesque as William Booth. But the Founder was no legend. The truth as revealed by the historian only confirmed his greatness. However, General Orsborn himself made history by appointing the Chief of the Staff, Commissioner Charles Baugh, his second in command, as Territorial Commander for Canada. This has since become a recognised movement in leadership positions – witness the identical transfer of Commissioner Arnold Brown in mid-1974. But as no previous Chief of the Staff had reverted to a territorial appointment *The War Cry* carried the following explanatory paragraph:

> The General and the Chief of the Staff had both previously contemplated the possibility of advantage accruing to the Army in the position of the Chief of the Staff being terminable or interchangeable with that of a Commissioner in another appointment. Before and after the election of the General by the High Council the Chief of the Staff had expressed his willingness, under certain circumstances, to take another kind of appointment. These new appointments are being made with complete harmony and goodwill between our leaders.

A further appointment at this time was that of Commissioner William R. Dalziel as British Commissioner, with responsibility for the Army's evangelical work in Great Britain and Ireland, thus filling the office left vacant by the General's own election to the international leadership.

2   REPAIRERS OF THE BREACH

As there was no country in any continent which had not been affected to some extent by the Second World War, so there was no Salvation Army operation which was not in need of reinforcement or replacement or repair. Important as was the mending of the organisational structure, more important still was its manning – especially when it is remembered that at every level of Army activity leadership was, and is, a determining factor. Providentially the movement has long been staffed by men and women whose sense of vocation outweighs their love of comfort. Where duty calls or danger threatens they have rarely been found wanting.

From the numerous international changes which took place it can be noted that in 1947 Colonel and Mrs Arthur Ludbrook returned to Peiping to take charge of the remnant who, under the leadership of Major Su Chien-Chi – honoured the previous year for his loyalty by admission to the Order of the Founder – had remained faithful to the Army though all links with International Headquarters had been severed. Major and Mrs Clayson Thomas went back to Rangoon where they found a derelict property with no light by which to see nor chair on which to sit. Colonel and Mrs S. Carvosso Gauntlett arrived in the even more devastated city of Berlin where the Army's territorial headquarters had been gutted by fire in the thousand-bomber raid of February 2/3, 1945, where such filing cabinets as were in use bore a marked resemblance to orange boxes, and the half-dozen office rooms available were heated by an assorted collection of pot-bellied stoves on which water could be boiled for morning coffee or thin soup warmed for a midday meal. Lieut.-Commissioner and Mrs William A. Ebbs were appointed to South Africa with headquarters at Johannesburg, and the Norwegian Lieut.-Colonel and Mrs Alfred Salhus were transferred from the training of African cadets in the capital to the oversight of the work in Nigeria. The Swedish Lieut.-Colonel and Mrs Richard Jacobsen travelled to Santiago to take charge of the South America (West) Territory; the British-born Lieut.-Colonel Emma Davies of Ceylon; the Swedish Lieut.-Colonel and Mrs Ivar Palmer of the Madras and Telegu Territory in India; Lieut.-Commissioner and Mrs Albert E. Chesham of the USA Southern Territory and Lieut.-Commissioner and Mrs Claude Bates of the USA Western.

The appointment of the Australian-born Lieut.-Colonel and Mrs Roy L. Rust to the Eastern India Territory with headquarters in Calcutta was announced in the international *War Cry* for March 22, 1947, but the issue dated November 15 of the same year carried the unwelcome news that he had lost his life when, at a hairpin bend on a mountain road in the Lushai Hills, the trailer attached to his car had swung over the edge of the track and both vehicles had careered to their destruction. The colonel died soon after reaching the hospital at Aizawl, where later a memorial hall was built to honour his more than a quarter of a century's service as a missionary.

There were other Salvationists, however, who hardly needed to leave their own immediate neighbourhood to meet with men who were far from family and friends. One of these was Major Albert Goldsmith, serving in the Accounts Department of International Headquarters, to whom the door of opportunity opened wide when he found some Italian prisoners of war in a meeting at which he was present in the North Midlands. With the subsequent influx of German prisoners of war he sought – and obtained – permission from the British War Office to commence a regular ministry among them as well. What follows are sample news reports which began to appear from the autumn of 1946 onwards.

> Over a thousand prisoners in camps scattered in outlying districts of Kent enjoyed the music and the messages of the Bexleyheath band which, accompanied by Major Albert Goldsmith, led four meetings on Sunday. Huts were cleared and men crowded in by the hundreds . . . Songsters June Peach and Doreen Rutt who sang and played were some of the first women to visit the camps and were received with interest and courtesy . . .
>
> When Colonel and Mrs Albert Dalziel visited Kettering a group of German prisoners of war who were wandering aimlessly about

the streets were invited to the meeting. As Director of European Relief, the Colonel gave firsthand information about conditions in Germany and, in some cases, of their actual home areas . . .

When German prisoners of war attended the Sunday morning meeting at Bromley Temple, Victor Haines[1] gave the Bible address in German, which his wife translated into English for the benefit of the rest of the congregation . . .

When in the summer of 1947 prisoners of war in Britain were allowed to use public transport, the number of men attending Salvation Army meetings on Sundays increased still further, though none was happier than their English hosts when the British Prime Minister announced that the rate of repatriation was to be stepped up so that prisoners could expect to be home again by the middle of the following year. Till then numbers of lonely men continued to find spiritual fellowship in the Army hall and enjoyed the fellowship of the table with many an Army family as well. German Salvationists began to be discovered also – an officer in a Lincolnshire camp, a Czech comrade in Norfolk and a bandsman from Dortmund in Essex. There were happy memories for the lad who, on his twenty-first birthday, was given a Bible by the corps which he attended. Nor will another POW forget the Army hall where, after six years of separation, he was reunited with his mother – a displaced person from Lithuania who had been working in a Surrey hospital, to which she had been traced by the Army's 'Missing Persons' bureau.

A further boon and a blessing was the demobilisation camp at Munsterlager, run by the Army, through which passed a multitude of returned prisoners of war. The ten thousandth man was bewildered to be greeted personally by the reception officer, and still more to be kitted out afresh from head to toe – until he discovered his number on the repatriation roster. He was but one of many who benefited from the joint efforts of the camp staff and the German Red Cross service in restoring fathers to their families, husbands to their wives and sons to their parents.

Turning to the new world, the American continent must now take its turn in the ongoing post-war story. General Orsborn had already acknowledged its significant place in the international life of the Army by appointing a senior American officer, Commissioner John J. Allan, to be the Chief of the Staff, and by devoting the last three months of 1946 to campaigning in both the North and South American continents. In Canada he led the annual Congress meetings and made a point of visiting London (Ontario), the Army's birthplace in the Dominion. In twelve of the principal cities in the United States he was warmly greeted and attentively heard by large congregations. A widely circulated photograph of the period showed President Truman and the General chatting amiably together in the White House with Sir Oliver Franks, the British ambassador, smiling down upon them both like a referee who knows that his services will not be required at this meeting of rivals in goodwill.

Public gatherings were also addressed by the General in Jamaica, Trinidad and Panama, as well as in Buenos Aires, Rio de Janeiro, São Paulo, Santiago and Lima. At no point was there any lessening of interest in the work of the Army. On the contrary, in North America as in Britain, the return of so many servicemen to 'civvy street' meant an increase both in the size of the Army's presence on the streets and its variety of activities. When, for example, in the spring of 1946 the band of the Regent Hall played by royal command in the grounds of Buckingham Palace, there were fifty-three bandsmen present, twenty-five of them servicemen still wearing the uniform of their unit. Three months later, when flying was not the commercial commonplace that it is today, the band of the Los Angeles Congress Hall chartered a plane to fly to and from Phoenix in order to share in a local fund-raising drive. In the eastern states the place of the brass band in Christian evangelism was greatly strengthened when Captain Richard Holz, newly released from his duties as a military chaplain, was appointed head of the music department at the territorial headquarters in New York.

The following year saw an even weightier occasion, weightier in the sense that it bore a world-wide harvest, the opening of the first ever Brengle memorial institute.

Samuel Logan Brengle was promoted to Glory in 1936 and Commissioner Ernest Pugmire, by this time National Commander in the United States, seized the opportunity to set up to this apostle of personal holiness a memorial which would perpetuate his teaching. August 1947 saw the realisation of this dream. Fifty officers, drawn from all over the United States, met in conference for twenty-one days – ten at Camp Lake, Wisconsin, and eleven at the school for officers' training in Chicago. Both staff and delegates were well versed in the brand of practical Christianity practised by the Army. Brigadier and Mrs Albert G. Pepper acted as host and hostess. Major Mina Russell, who shared in this first occasion and who since has done much to spread the gospel according to Brengle in all five continents, wrote of this initial institute:

> The delegates were practical people with experience in everyday living as Salvation Army officers. They had known pressures from without, misunderstandings from within. They were concerned with the control of multiple programmes as well as with the problems of disturbed needy people. These were realities to be faced, but every person there realised that these very responsibilities made it all the more important that none of his own strengths should have to be diverted to the solving of his personal problems. He knew that to meet his own responsibilities as they should be met, he himself had to be freed from personal conflict, free to operate at God's level, the level of full surrender . . .
>
> But what about going back to work? . . . Would the experience stand the test of the daily routine in the corps, the institution, the office? There seemed to be little question about this in the minds of those who were there because they felt they had found the most practical thing in the world, a few for the first time in their lives. That they should work out the Army programme under the direction of the Holy Spirit, that they should be free from fears regarding place and position, that they should not have to cater for an attention-demanding self, all seemed to contribute to their idea of the most effective leadership possible for the complex problems of the day.[2]

And a further venture was under way on the American scene. In the thirties a Mexican evangelist and his wife, Alejandro and Isabel Guzman, were led to dedicate their lives for the salvation of the people of Mexico City who were untouched by the conventional activities of the Christian churches. Like attracted like, and it was not long before Guzman found himself surrounded by a small band whose hearts God had touched and who took the name of 'The Salvation Patrol'. As with William Booth and his early pioneers, the Patrol had to make use of whatever buildings were available, and they discovered a disused foundry which they rented for sixty-five pesos a month. In this way 163 Imprenta Street – a dirt street in a not-too-savoury quarter of the city – became their first centre. At a subsequent church convention in the north of the country Guzman spoke of the work which he was doing – and then was asked whether he had ever heard of The Salvation Army. He had not. He had never been outside Mexico and his only language was Spanish. But a copy of Hugh Redwood's *God in the Slums* fell into his hands – and his search for The Salvation Army became like the search for the Holy Grail. Eventually Guzman found his way to Dallas where his story found a ready listener in Major William Gilks, then divisional commander for Texas. He promptly took Guzman to Atlanta to meet Commissioner Ernest Pugmire, at that time leader of the Army in the southern states. The upshot was that when General Evangeline Booth visited Atlanta in October 1937, she enrolled Guzman – with four of his men and two of his women helpers – as Salvationists. It would be hard to say who were the more delighted – the welcoming crowd or the tiny group who were welcomed.

Guzman's evangelistic work prospered – prospered beyond the power of the former Patrol members effectively to supervise, even though ten of their number had by now been accepted as Salvation Army officers. They had pledged themselves to abide by the Army's faith and practice like any other officer – but Mexico City was a long way from Dallas, the nearest divisional centre. Sheep could not be shepherded by remote control – not even when their shepherds were as dedicated as Brigadier and Mrs Raymond Gearing. A division as large as Texas, with upwards of forty corps, not to mention Red Shield lodges and harbour light centres and Friendship Houses and youth clubs and community centres, was more than one man's work as it was. But this Macedonian cry could not be denied. A choice had to be made between Texas and Mexico. So the brigadier and his wife were appointed to Mexico and, leaving three of their four children behind them, they journeyed (in Mrs Gearing's words) 'to the land which God had showed them'. With Adjutant and Mrs Guzman (newly promoted to that rank) as their principal assistants, they were given the oversight of the Mexico City corps with its children's home and men's dormitories, an outpost in another part of the capital, two new openings in the townships of Monterrey and Pueblo and a home league at Nuevo Laredo in the far north.

They had not long to wait for their first emergency. On the last day of December 1946, 200 Polish refugees, released from detention centres in Siberia, arrived in Mexico City on their way to a colony which the American government was preparing for them in Vera Cruz. Their train was five and a half hours late in arriving, and the officer had waited until 10.30 before commencing his watch-night service. But when the tired travellers arrived the meeting was halted, tables were placed in position and piled high with nourishing food. Small wonder that the American ambassador afterwards wrote in acknowledgment: 'You . . . were particularly generous in receiving a large group of Polish refugees on the night of December 31, 1946 . . . For the efficient manner in which you arranged for their feeding, lodging and transportation, I want to thank you.'

The Salvation Army in Mexico City has continued as it began. Today it houses the territorial headquarters for a work which reaches from the Rio Grande in the north to Maracaibo on the eastern side of the Venezuelan border.[3]

Other advances on the North American continent were made through the initiative of individual Salvationists. One of the most outstanding of these was recognised when, at the 1946 Congress in Atlanta, General Orsborn announced the admission of Major Cecil Brown to the Order of the Founder[4]. She had (so the citation declared) 'carried on for many years an extraordinary ministry of teaching, practical aid and, above all, soul saving amid primitive conditions in the remote Smoky Mountains of her native North Carolina.'

An open-air meeting in Asheville (NC) was her introduction to The Salvation Army and, after having been commissioned as an officer, she asked to be allowed to minister to her own people who lived in the hills in their lonely wooden cabins, far from any place of worship and comparative strangers to any pastoral care. In 1935 her request was granted though, wrote one reporter at the time:

The Salvation Army was unknown to these people in their isolation, but this friendly young woman in this strange blue uniform was just 'one of the Brown girls', and therefore one of their own. They accepted her – if at first they did not receive her message.

It was not long, however, before patient hard work brought its own reward, and the mountain dwellers began to look forward to her visits, to set aside a little room for her pastoral work in their homes and to turn to her in any emergency, knowing that she would not fail them. Many a sick man or woman was taken in her car down the rough mountain tracks for hospital treatment in the nearest town, and the Captain often served as intermediary between a patient in the hills and the doctor in Waynesville . . .

Regular Salvation Army meetings were commenced in a number of centres and halls began to be erected. Converts were enlisted to fell timber and the Captain's own stalwart brothers directed building operations. The Army had come to stay.

At the time of her admission to the Order of the Founder the area for which the newly promoted Major Brown, with her officer assistant, was responsible covered some fifty square miles and included nine centres of Army activity.

There was need of such up and coming officers to take the place of those whose race was run – among whom were the Army's third, fourth and fifth Generals. On December 13, 1947, General Higgins was promoted to Glory at the age of eighty-three. Less than five months later, on April 9, 1948, he was followed by General Carpenter who was within sight of his seventy-sixth birthday. General Evangeline Booth passed away at the age of eighty-four – though this was not until July 7, 1950.

The service of these three leaders can be taken together for, whatever their differences in lifestyle, each made a distinctive contribution to the work of the Army. The biography which was subsequently written of General Higgins was entitled *Storm Pilot*, and there is no doubt that his supreme service to the Army vessel was to keep her on course despite the mini-gales and cross currents of the events associated with the first High Council. No pilot ever gave more thought to his ship and less to himself. General Carpenter was a man of the same pattern. He was ready to swear to his own hurt and change not – and time vindicated him without anyone having to jog time's elbow.

The election of both these men as General was accepted

as a fitting conclusion to their life's service. With General
Evangeline it was an international coda to her American years.
Time – and the Second World War – did not allow her to
stamp her name upon the world scene as she had done upon
the USA, but those comrades who had welcomed her at the
age of thirty-nine to the leadership of the Army in the land of
the brave and the free never abandoned their first love. One
writer has said that she 'could make a stirring little production
of walking from her car across the sidewalk of Fourteenth
Street to the front door of her headquarters'[5] and they liked
it that way. She was to be counted blessed in retirement
because she lived to see the greatest post-war development
made by the Army in the southern states.

There were already USO (United Service Organisation)
clubs for black servicemen in the south, and long before the
outbreak of the Second World War there had been black corps
– notably Washington 2 on Seventh and P Streets, but all
these were segregated. However, it was borne upon the heart
and mind of Adjutant Vincent Cunningham, then editor of
The War Cry published in Atlanta and circulating throughout
the south, that the wisest and most fruitful approach to an
unsegregated ministry would be by means of the Army's
open-air activities. Commendatory messages to this effect
were received from the Mayor of Atlanta, five state gover-
nors and also Senator J. Strom Thurmond, though the
latter hedged his approval with the qualification that
'segregation . . . be maintained in the south'. However, the
following news flash appeared in the international *War Cry*
for May 22, 1948.

A PROGRAMME FOR THE NEGRO
(Atlanta, Ga.) (Special)

Salvation Army evangelistic work among the Negro population of
the South was begun under the leadership of the Southern Territorial Commander, Lieut.-Commissioner Albert E. Chesham
when, with the training college principal, staff and cadets, he
conducted an open-air meeting at Auburn Avenue and Bell Street
in the heart of the Atlanta negro district.

What follows is an abbreviated account of the ensuing
open-air meeting which could well have won an 'Oscar' in any

newspaper on either side of the Atlantic. The caption read 'Making melody on Bell Street', and the by-line 'Major Raymond Brown'.

There was melody on Bell Street and somehow it was alive . . . Faint as it was it insinuated itself into the consciousness and gradually took complete possession. The group on Bell Street had this experience. One by one they fell silent and listened.

> When I remember that He died for me
> I'll never go back any more . . .

The group on Bell Street looked questioningly at one another, but none broke the silence. They listened until the chorus was over and the tall man in the grey coat said positively: 'The Salvation Army'.

'What they doin' here?'

'Dunno. Maybe they figure it's safe now that we've got Negro police.'[6] A scattering of laughter ran through the group.

The crap game was in full swing. The little pile of crumpled bills on the table showed that it was pay day. There were several of large denominations. The man with the dice was crooning to them lovingly. He had visions of the little pile of bills nestling in his pocket after the next pass. He cupped his hands about the bones and supplicated.

Through the fog of cigarette smoke the melody came stealing . . . streamers of melody curling langorously into the brain . . . working on the heart . . . The dice artist stopped crooning and looked around. The crowd and the table were thinning – rapidly. The money on the table went with its owners. The melody had done it. He put the dice in his pocket and made for the door.

Outside he stood . . . in front of the saloon. The melody caught him . . . reached out sinuous fingers and enveloped him. He saw again the little cabin, the streams of smoke rising lazily into the quiet air. The scent of wistaria was strong upon him. His mother was snapping beans and singing the old hymns of the church as only she could sing them.

He walked towards the Salvationists. He had forgotten the whisky. Somehow the melody had driven it from his mind. He thought instead of his wife. He made a decision. He would go home. He would tell her it was all his fault. Maybe between them they could straighten things out. His mind tasted the idea and found it good. Yes; he would go home, but first he had something to do. He reached the open-air ring. He knelt . . .

An old Negro took the tract offered him and said, hesitantly: 'We're only poor ignorant folk but we sure needs de Lawd. Why don't you come down often?'

The Salvationists did. They came again – and again – and again. And they have kept on coming!

3 FELLOWSHIP IN THE LORD

One significant fact about the corporate life of the Army in the mid-forties was that, as soon as the artificial restraints of war were removed, Salvationists began to draw together again. Not spiritually – for in aim and purpose they had never been parted. But it was as if some unseen power was compelling them to come together physically as well. They knew that this urge was born of the love of God shed abroad in their hearts, the outcome of an inward and invisible grace. At heart Salvationist had never been at war with Salvationist. 'We own no man as enemy' reads a line in his song book. He saw his leaders testifying to this basic Christian virtue as they travelled from country to country identifying themselves with the various national, racial and linguistic groupings which make up that part of the Body of Christ known as The Salvation Army. And the desire to demonstrate afresh this inherent one-ness gave rise to various spontaneous reactions within the movement itself – within Salvation Army bands, for example.

The Army band is one of the most public features of Salvation Army life. Within the context of a corps the band is a voluntary association of men – nowadays with an increasing proportion of women – who dedicate their musical skills to the service of the gospel. They pledge themselves to live by Christian standards. They receive no payment for their services. In addition to the support of their corps they contribute to the overhead costs of their activities as a band. They accept the corporate discipline necessary for the prosecution of their practical expertise, and all their service flows from their acceptance of Jesus as Saviour and Lord. Here are three examples of their desire to demonstrate the reality of their fellowship with their comrades.

In the autumn of 1946 the band of the Rotterdam 1 corps under Bandmaster Knippenberg visited the Regent Hall corps situated at 275 Oxford Street, London. Travel so soon after the war could still be more of a penance than a pleasure. Private hospitality was a drain upon the family rations. Both visitors and their hosts had known the hazards of armed conflict. The corps property in Rotterdam had suffered in the bombing which accompanied the fall of the city. Eighteen of the bandsmen had been taken for forced labour. The Regent Hall property had been damaged in the air raids on London and the homes of a number who worshipped there had been destroyed. But if an ordeal shared is an ordeal halved, then these two groups of Salvationists were able to encourage one another in the Lord.

It does not detract one iota from the superb musicianship displayed by the Tranås band under Bandmaster Borg when they visited London and the home counties during Eastertide, 1947, to say that their compatriots from Huskvanna, under Bandmaster Henning Peterson, were true encouragers of the brethren when they visited Bremen, Hamburg, Hanover and the Ruhr over Easter, 1948. Most of the men brought their rations with them and then left extras for the scanty cupboards of their hosts.

But perhaps the most electrifying of these exchanges was the visit of the Coventry City band, under Bandmaster J. F. Grieg, to Germany in June, 1950. This event was the brain child of the territory's first post-war leader – the British-born Lieut.-Commissioner S. Carvosso Gauntlett who between the wars had already served in Czechoslovakia, Denmark, Germany and Hungary. He knew what the name of Coventry meant on the continent – in the words of a Berlin paper: 'the hate-filled, victory-assured symbol of absolute destruction by bombs of an enemy city'. But when after having visited Hamburg, Kiel and Hanover, these English Midlands bandsmen arrived in Berlin at seven a.m. one weekday, the capital's Philharmonic brass orchestra, led by Hans Steinkopf, were on the station platform to greet them. Enthusiasm reached such a pitch that extra police had to be summoned to control the estimated crowd of 5,000 who made it difficult even for the bandsmen to reach their allotted places for the final outdoor festival. *Wiedersehen* was sung in such an emotional fashion that some of the Coventry men could hardly join in for their tears. The return journey was made by train via Bielefeld,

Wuppertaal, Bonn and Cologne, leaving the last named at three-thirty on Monday morning and reaching Coventry in the early hours of Tuesday morning. A Cologne paper spoke of 'this musical revenge'. A Bielefeld report concluded:

> The militarism of The Salvation Army is the only form of soldiering we could heartily accept. For its activity is humane, it brings love to all men and results in blessing. It seems symbolical that this invasion comes from Coventry, that stricken city, but this offensive is dedicated to the cause of Christian charity.

Back in the United Kingdom the youth department at National Headquarters was thinking hard how the new post-war educational opportunities for young people could be used to further the cause of Christ. Early in 1947 it was announced that an undergraduates' circle was being formed to provide mutual help and encouragement for those who were expecting to attend universities or university colleges. But this plan was bettered by an announcement in *The War Cry* for February 26, 1949, which read:

> The newly formed Salvation Army students' fellowship, launched recently at the Regent Hall by the British Commissioner (Commissioner Wm. R. Dalziel) meets a long felt and urgent need.
>
> Scholarships and grants now available make it possible for young people with the necessary ability to proceed to a university and to follow a course of study of their own choice. Many young Salvationists are availing themselves of these opportunities. In nearly all the universities of the United Kingdom and Northern Ireland are to be found young Salvationists pursuing a variety of studies such as law, medicine, languages and economics.
>
> To link up such comrades in a fellowship is obviously a desirable means of help to each of them. Moreover, the Fellowship aims to strengthen the corporate witness of Salvationists in university life . . . The conditions of membership are twofold – (a) that of a university or teacher training college and (b) soldiership of The Salvation Army.

By Easter of that same year thirty of the eighty-strong Fellowship gathered at 'Rosehill', near Reading, for a three-day conference on 'The Faith of the Salvationist' with Commissioner Wm. R. Dalziel as president and Mrs Lieut.-Colonel Bessie Coutts, BSc (Hons) as vice-president. The membership was drawn from the universities of Oxford, Cambridge, Durham, Sheffield, Bristol, London, Leicester and Southampton, and the General addressed the opening session. Even before this development in the United Kingdom, groups of Salvationist students had met for fellowship in Norway and Sweden, and this new activity was internationally recognised in 1950 – since when it has spread to all five continents.

Another current sign of the desire of Christian people to make common cause in the battle of the Lord, and for the Army to take its due place in that holy war, was the presence of a delegation of five senior officers at the first assembly of the World Council of Churches at Amsterdam in 1948. These were (in alphabetical order) Commissioner Marcel Allemand (Switzerland), Lieut.-Commissioner Arend Beekhuis (The Netherlands), Commissioner George Bowyer (Great Britain), Commissioner Alfred G. Cunningham (International Headquarters)[1] and Commissioner Ernest Pugmire (USA).

The date of the first assembly was originally planned for August 1941, but the outbreak of the Second World War made postponement inevitable until August 1948, when 1,400 delegates representing 140 Christian bodies in forty different countries met together. Briefly yet comprehensively the Army's press declared that 'the spirit and aim of the Assembly is to enter into such a relationship as will enable the people of God to take a united stand to combat the evils of the present time.' The non-sacramental principle observed by Quakers and Salvationists was vindicated once for all by Dean Douglas Horton, chairman of the Faith and Order Commission of the WCC, when he said, and was so quoted in *The Officer*, the official magazine privately circulated among all officers with a working knowledge of English, that 'to believe that they have given up communion with Christ and with one another is to misunderstand their manner of life. It is the bread of the Spirit on which they feed.'

One important event which must be mentioned without further delay was the marriage of General Albert Orsborn to Commissioner (Mrs) Phillis Taylor on Saturday, August 2, 1947. The husband–wife relationship has a peculiar value for the Army officer when it is remembered that both man and woman act, and are recognised, as ministers of the gospel. She is as 'called of God' to the ministry as he is. Both are commissioned to turn men from darkness to light and from the power of Satan unto God. The officer and the wife of the officer are one by virtue of their marriage vows and one in their spiritual calling as well. For such reasons those who had shared the General's grief when his wife died within a week of childbirth now greatly rejoiced with him on this happier occasion. 'Greatly rejoiced' are justified words – for Mrs Taylor had much to bring to this new partnership. She was the eldest daughter of General and Mrs Edward Higgins (R), and consequently had long been aware of the demands made both in and out of the public eye upon Salvation Army leaders. She had enjoyed the happiness of home and family with the gifted Bramwell Taylor who was promoted to Glory from Winnipeg on October 6, 1928. Returning to England, she had not avoided new responsibilities – first at the International Training College and later as Leader of the Women's Social Work in Great Britain and Ireland. In brief, public life did not find her wanting and in private her company was enriching.

Within three weeks of the wedding the General and his wife left London to commence a series of public and private gatherings in Kenya, Rhodesia and South Africa which occupied them until they reached Cape Town in mid-October. But such is the pressure on anyone who holds the office of international leader of The Salvation Army, that less than a week before the official announcement of his marriage the General could have been seen hurrying from the Sunday morning meeting at the Salle Centralle in Paris to the Gare St. Lazare to greet Major and Mrs Hausdorff who were returning from French Guiana in charge of a group of repatriated convicts from the penal settlement.

By this time the end of this merciful work of resettlement was in sight. The official existence of the *Bagne* had ended in 1938, but the outbreak of the Second World War had halted any orderly return of the prisoners to metropolitan France. Brigadier Charles Péan made his first visit to Cayenne by slow boat in 1928. By virtue of a priority warrant on a transatlantic Clipper he made his last flight in 1945 when it was planned that the *bagnards* should begin to leave for home in July 1946, in three stages. European prisoners would travel by monthly mailboat in parties of fifty, which operation would be completed within twelve months. The Arabs would sail directly to

North Africa calling at Casablanca, Oran, Algiers and Bone
as might be necessary. Men released individually would travel
as and when possible. The whole operation would be a joint
venture between the French government, The Salvation Army
with its headquarters in Paris and Brigadier Péan as the
principal liaison officer, and the *Comité de Patronage des libérés*
in Cayenne. The actual work of repatriation lasted on into the
fifties and was not without its difficulties for the simple reason
that no man was without his individual problems. How could
it be otherwise when so many of them had spent so much of
their life in the *Bagne*? But in the end the unwearying patience
of the Army officers assigned to this redemptive work, together
with the generous practical assistance volunteered from both
sides of the Atlantic – enough to equip a small army from top
to toe was one description of this – meant that the *libérés* arrived
home clothed and in their right mind. As Brigadier Péan wrote
in concluding his *The Conquest of Devil's Island*: 'The *Bagne* has
lasted a century. Now it is but a story . . . A chapter in social
redemption has been completed. A Christian task has been
accomplished by the power of Christ.'

The work in metropolitan France was also progressing under
the vigorous leadership of Colonel and Mrs W. Wycliffe Booth.
Mrs Booth was a daughter of the honoured house of Peyron.
To General Bramwell Booth's second son France was a second
motherland. One of the most striking property developments
in the immediate post-war days was the acquisition of the
notorious Paris brothel at 106 Boulevard de la Chapelle. By
the law of April 13, 1946, all licensed houses in the French
capital were to be closed, nor could they be relet for any other
purpose without the consent of the authorities. Some former
owners sought to reopen their premises as 'massage establishments' or 'physical culture centres'. The owner of number 106
was most unwilling to allow his lucrative property to pass into
the hands of the Army and attempted to let his rooms as
'accommodation for students'. Convinced that this was merely
a subterfuge the territorial commander called his people to
prayer and simultaneously appealed to the Minister of the
Interior. Faith and works conquered all. The reconstruction
provided a public hall for 200 people, a headquarters for the
Paris-Nord division, and living quarters for the officers serving
in that area. It was not until some years later that social

changes in the immediate neighbourhood brought this promising venture to a much regretted end.

Before 1947 was out the headquarters of the British Territory had also been moved – this time from the suburb of Norbury where it had been battling with inadequate accommodation since the destruction of 101 Queen Victoria Street in the spring of 1941 – to the heart of Westminster. Early in 1948 a public enquiry was opened at the Guildhall into the plans of the Corporation of London for the rebuilding of the city. Many interests – financial and commercial – were involved and therefore claimed their due right to be heard, so that it was not until the third day that the Army's counsel, Mr Derek Walker-Smith, MP, was called upon to state the case for a return to the Army's historic site.

One of the principal features of this reconstruction of the city was the opening up of a vista from St. Paul's Cathedral to the river which would traverse the blitzed site of International Headquarters. However, when Mr Walker-Smith had concluded his case Sir Walter Monckton, KC (representing the City of London), Professor W. G. Holford (one of the joint consultants engaged by the City corporation) and the Inspector of the Ministry of Town and Country Planning (who was conducting the enquiry) made it clear that they desired that International Headquarters should be rebuilt as nearly as possible on its former site. Old Father Thames was to roll on for more than another 5,000 days before that dream came true on November 13, 1963, but Salvationists endured this waiting as those for whom there had been prepared a city.

Summer 1948 also saw a gradual reduction in the number of food parcels sent from the less war-torn parts of the world to Europe – Britain included. Many a family had been moved to say grace-before-meat at the sound of the postman's knock. There is no knowing how many friendships began in this way nor how many were cemented. But if food no longer arrived so plentifully by the door, music stole in by the window. Conscription had not made it easy for Salvation Army bands to maintain their customary standards of musicianship, but now they were given the freedom of the air on a Sunday morning to direct hearts and minds to things lovely and of good report. This proved so welcome an experiment that before Christmas 1948 a further series of Sunday morning broadcasts were announced under the title of 'With flag unfurled'. And lest any listeners in a still sorely troubled world should suppose that the Army was content to make pleasant sounds and sweet noises, Salvationists in Sweden shared with their countrymen a cabled appeal to President Truman, Generalissimo Stalin and Prime Minister Attlee that 'a conference be convened to disperse the present crisis of mistrust . . . We appeal in the spirit of Christianity and in the name of humanity.' The message was signed by (among others) Commissioner Axel E. Beckman (the territorial commander of the Army in Sweden) and his principal executive officer, Colonel Axel Lydahl.

Precisely what should be the Army's rank structure was a small matter compared with what the Army should do and say – nevertheless this was now given attention as well. One rank, that of Adjutant, was dropped, but two new grades of Lieutenant – first and second – were introduced, and also another grade of Captain and Major, signified by the prefix 'Senior'. The other higher ranks remained unaltered, the Army continued its basic work uninterrupted, and General and Mrs Orsborn gave thought to their forthcoming Indian campaign.

There was every reason for the General to leave as soon as possible for the sub-continent of India, to stay there as long as possible, and to see as much of the work as possible. Towards the end of 1946 he had sent a goodwill mission to conduct a fact-finding tour of the five territories which made up the Army's administrative pattern, but the last General to visit the country was General Evangeline Booth in 1936. India was the Army's oldest missionary field. Viewed geographically India was the Army's largest missionary field, with over 5,000 centres of work and upwards of 3,000 officers, national and expatriate. India represented the Army's costliest investment in missionary personnel and money. Nowhere were the services provided more diversified – ranging from village corps to general hospitals and from agricultural settlements to boarding schools. But India and Ceylon were no longer a political unity. The rule of the British Raj had been replaced by three self-governing communities. The Bay of Bengal was no longer a British preserve. One of the nearest amenity centres to the fighting in Burma had been the Army's Red Shield centre at Ramkophalong.

At the same time the tide of Indian nationalism was not to

be contained. Neither the man, Mahatma Gandhi, nor his message, were to be denied. Fearing the overwhelming numerical superiority of the Hindu community, Mahommed Ali Jinnah had commenced to campaign for a separate Muslim state. The break-up of the unitary framework which had lasted since the days of Warren Hastings could no longer be discounted – not even by so apolitical a body as The Salvation Army – not when the last of the Viceroys, Earl Mountbatten, had invited Lieut.-Commissioner Herbert S. Hodgson, the senior Salvation Army officer in Delhi, to his office to tell him that the country was to be given its independence and divided into two separate nations, with Ceylon becoming autonomous as well. The Salvation Army would have to adjust its own domestic arrangements accordingly. But the work in India could no longer be directed from Lahore, nor what fell within the boundaries of Pakistan from Delhi.[2] It is possibly true to say that of all the adjustments made necessary by partition none was carried out so smoothly as the creation of a new Northern India Territory under Lieut.-Colonel Ivar Palmer with headquarters in Delhi, a new territory for Pakistan under Lieut.-Colonel Arthur T. Hughes with headquarters in Lahore, and the transfer of Lieut.-Commissioner Herbert S. Hodgson to the Western India Territory with headquarters in Bombay. Yet with deep concern and not without foreboding in their hearts, General and Mrs Orsborn set sail from Tilbury on November 25, 1948, and were travelling continuously until March of the following year.

Their concern was more than justified. The jubilation arising from the newly acquired independence was sadly diminished by the ensuing bloodshed between Muslim and Hindu. As the MacRobert Hospital was within twenty miles of the new frontier and on the only rail and road route from India to Kashmir, casualties began to pour in. Commented one eye-witness:

Some were carried from neighbouring posts and villages by Christian friends. Others came in military lorries or commandeered buses. A few stragglers crawled in wearily from the fields – a mutilated old man, a lost child, a girl clad only in the blood-stained shirt of her brother.

Everyone had to help. The staff often worked for twenty-four hours without a break and without any complaint. There is a memorable picture of Adjutant Rahmah Masih, a powerfully built Punjabi, clad in a rubber theatre apron, climbing on to the roof of a bus to sort the living from the dead and carrying them tenderly to the wards. Many had been wounded days before reaching hospital, and the stench of their unattended bodies was such that the nurses wore masks continually.

For several weeks uncertainty and fear paralysed the district. Refugees huddled in the station under military guard. Sporadic sniping resulted in periodic casualties. Gross overcrowding of trains and lorries resulted in all too frequent accidents. One fearful night rifle fire broke out and figures crumpled in the sugar cane fields a stone's throw away . . . Operating theatres and labour wards were equally busy during those nightmare weeks. Babies were born on the railway station, on the tops of trains and in lorries . . . but the needs thrown up by the emergency were wonderfully met.

A British officer, travelling down the main road in a 30 cwt truck, saw sacks of looted grain lying by the roadside, loaded them up and left them at the hospital . . . Another, commanding a Gurkha regiment in the hills, sent a donation of a thousand rupees just when money was running low. Clothing was also a problem. Most refugees arrived naked or covered in rags. Hospital sheets and blankets were sacrificed for these. Rough garments were quickly run up from remnants of cloth sent over from the neighbouring mills.

Even when communal bitterness was at its height there were acts of great kindness . . . A Muslim boy badly lacerated came into the hospital from a walking convoy. He was put into a private ward to be near a guard and warned not to try to look out of the room. Imagine the surprise of the nurses who later found this Muslim lad on the lap of a Sikh soldier who was feeding him.[3]

'Our visit to India', wrote General Orsborn in his autobiography *The House of my Pilgrimage*, 'coming so soon after the realisation of independence, and less than a year after Gandhi's death, brought us to a land in travail.' The last four words described as accurately as any brief phrase could the state of the sub-continent. In that situation, however, Salvationists remained true to their faith. No follower of the Army flag lifted his hand against a neighbour and, not surprisingly, few hands were lifted against him. As one experienced missionary officer said: 'Now that we are on our own the Indian people feel more

than ever that we belong to them.' Even the most prejudiced
could no longer equate Christianity with imperialism. It was
not unusual for an Army home to be marked by an Army flag
or by a cross made of twigs, displayed somewhere near the
door. It so happened on one occasion that a crowd which had
got out of hand was halted by such a symbol. 'We must not
hurt the people here,' declared the leader, 'they are our friends.'

While there were aspects of the Army's social concerns
which had reached the end of their useful life, there were others
which continued to develop. The work among the so-called
criminal tribes was an instance of the former; hospitals and
schools of the latter. The Army's involvement in the first named
dated from 1908. Forty years later only the Stuartpuram
settlement remained, but those living there were 'free citizens
of a free India'. The very success of this particular activity had
led to its extinction.

But with hospital services wider still and wider were their
bounds to be set. At Nagercoil where the Catherine Booth
hospital stood as the prototype of Salvation Army medical
centres throughout the world, the Maharajah of Travencore
opened a new school of nursing on one day and the General
dedicated the Golden Jubilee memorial building on the next.
At a subsequent press conference there were anxious questions
as to whether independence would mean any lessening of
the Army's involvement with the country's basic needs, and
whether there would be any diminution in the number of
those who 'like our own Dr Noble' (to quote one newspaper
representative) would continue to devote their skills to the
healing of the sick. It was not difficult to sense the unease
which prompted such enquiries. The Army's works of love
and mercy had flourished under the British Raj. Would they
survive a change of authority? By way of reassurance it could
only be repeated that the lordship of Christian believers belonged to Jesus Christ and none other – not to any party or
national leader of whatever race or colour. Before the General
had left Delhi the Prime Minister, Pandit Nehru, had declared
that 'anyone is welcome who will work sincerely for the benefit
of the people'.

Pakistan displayed an equally friendly face. At the height of
the troubles the relief centres under the Army's direction
were welcomed by Hindu and Muslim alike. Said government

officials: 'We cannot do without you. You have saved us from worse disasters.' Indeed it was at Shantinagar in 1948 that the thirty-year-old agricultural settlement accomplished one of its primary aims when proprietary rights to their plots of ground were handed over to the colonists who had fulfilled the required conditions.

In areas more remote from the upheaval caused by partition the Army's committal to the needs of the people was more evident still. One of these welcome signs occurred on Tuesday, January 8, 1949, when the Lady Colville nurses' training school was opened at the Ahmednagar hospital where Major (Dr) Daniel Andersen was the Chief Medical Officer, with his wife, Mrs Major (Dr) Andersen, his principal assistant. The school – save the mark! – had hitherto been located in a basement under one of the hospital wards. Part of the contemporary account of this event read:

> A high-ranking British medical authority who had once stumbled down the dark steps had commented: 'This is a rum hole!' – and the name had stuck. But a more encouraging visitor was the wife of the Governor, Lord Colville, who congratulated us on our teaching programmes and was actively concerned about the accommodation . . . Soon we were invited to apply to the government for a grant of fifty per cent of the total cost and for building permits as well. This was agreed and, with the help of India's first woman architect, we designed what we felt was a building worthy of its purpose.
>
> Then came independence. Would the new Indian government honour the pledge of the British Raj? They would, provided that the enrolment of nurses from all communities was encouraged and that the non-Christian would not be under any obligation to attend Christian services. This was gladly agreed . . . where the training given is recognised in Great Britain and allows the girls to undertake appointments and to do post-graduate work in England and elsewhere.[4]

This same visit of General Orsborn offered yet another testimony of the Army's continued dedication to the needs of India when Mrs Orsborn opened a new nurses' home, accommodating forty, at the Emery Hospital. Her father, General Edward J. Higgins, had opened a new wing when he visited the hospital in 1933, and her grandfather, Commissioner Edward Higgins, laid the foundation stone in 1903

when he was Resident Secretary for India. If that was an
example of commitment from past records the General showed
himself equally concerned about the future when he declared
that the missionary-to-be must meet the hunger for learning,
the longing for light, and the demand for social and medical
services. 'And if we are no longer able to send large numbers
of reinforcements,' he added, 'we must at least ensure that
those whom we do send are of the highest suitability.'[5]

4 PERSECUTED WITHOUT CAUSE

The year 1950 was one of mixed fortunes for The Salvation Army. The new decade began with a Macedonian cry from the Republic of Haiti, one of the two Caribbean countries into which the island of Hispaniola is divided. For some eight years a married evangelist had faithfully laboured to establish a mission, boasting a leaky mud and wattle hall in one of the less favoured districts of Port au Prince. A friend described this dedicated couple as the Salvation Army of Haiti – whereupon the missioner cabled the National Headquarters in New York on May 22, 1949: '*Désir s'affilier avec vous. Avons 350 membres. Réponse urgente. Carrie Guillaume.*'[1] The National Commander, Commissioner Ernest Pugmire, thereupon communicated with Colonel William P. Sansom, the territorial leader for the work in Central America and the West Indies. He in turn advised International Headquarters of the request and sent Brigadier Oliver Dadd, an experienced West Indian officer, to make an on-the-spot report.

Soon the doctrines and discipline were being studied in Haiti, and it was not long before Evangelist Guillaume wrote to say that his people 'were united in accepting with joy the laws' followed by the Army. In view of such a response Colonel and Mrs Sansom planned to visit Port au Prince on February 2, 1950, in order to raise the Army flag and enrol his new soldiers. Meanwhile the articles of war were printed in French, sundry choruses were practised in Creole (the popular language variant) and various Army badges and symbols made their appearance. The meeting hall was filled to overflowing for the gathering which followed, but when an untimely tropical thunderstorm drove the congregation to huddle more closely together under the imperfect protection of the leaky roof the missioner, distracted by this unexpected catastrophe, fell to prayer that the wrath of the elements might be abated. In due course his plea was answered – and on the Sunday afternoon in brilliant sunshine on a stretch of open ground near the Champ de Mars the Haitian flag was raised, the national anthem was sung, and the congregation joined in with

> *Du Christ la bannière se déploie au vent*
> *Pour la sainte guerre, soldats, en avant!*[2]

Next evening in the Methodist schoolroom some 200 comrades of the Port au Prince corps were handed a duplicate of the articles of war which they had signed and given a cartridge envelope for their weekly free-will offering, symbol of their obligation to the movement which they had now joined.

There was still more – much, much more to be done. The newly enrolled soldiers had to learn the difference between a loose affiliation with a local mission and the discipline practised by a world movement. The newly appointed Envoy and Mrs Guillaume, with another promising Haitian couple, were sent to Kingston, Jamaica, for a crash course in officer training. The hand-picked Captain and Mrs Jacques Egger arrived from Switzerland to take charge of this new venture. No better choice could have been made – even though the newcomers found the appointment a test of their natural gifts as well as their spiritual graces. Life was noisy and confused by contrast with the calm and order of Switzerland. Time was no man's master. A congregation might be complete by the time a meeting had ended; rarely when it began. The hall at Port au Prince was 'a miserable hut' in one of the poorest parts of the town but, to their credit, it must be said that these latest recruits could sing. Some of them found the Army too soldierly for their liking, but many were eager to learn how to be good soldiers of Jesus Christ. What counted most of all was that their new commander was no fly-by-night; he remained in that appointment for nineteen years and demonstrated that wisdom was justified of her children. At the time of writing there are more than forty officers, mostly indigenous, at work in Haiti, nineteen corps and fourteen outposts are in operation, and twenty schools provide primary education.

The news from Haiti coincided with the meeting of true minds in London. Dr Toyohiko Kagawa paid a visit to the International (William Booth Memorial) Training College, addressed the staff and cadets, and shared fellowship with General and Mrs Orsborn before their departure on one of their most taxing campaigns – travelling via the United States to visit New Zealand, Australia, Indonesia, Singapore and so home again. This great circular route enabled the General and his wife to share in the seventieth anniversary celebrations of the commencement of the work of the Army in the United States. Many were the comparisons evoked by the passage of the years. One report of a pioneer meeting in New York stated that it consisted of 'prostitutes, station house tramps, dudes with eye glasses and canes, pensioners with faded hair and stove-pipe hats . . . the floors covered with tobacco juice, the stench unbearable'. It was an unbelievably far cry to the crowded centennial memorial temple where thanks were rendered to God for the blessings of the past and hopes expressed for an even brighter future. An audience of similar size and quality said amen in Chicago to the praises offered on the previous evening in New York – as did three further congregations on the following Sunday in Los Angeles, not to mention another in Seattle on the Tuesday and yet another in Vancouver on the Wednesday.

The next port of call was Auckland – familiar ground to the General who was Chief Secretary in New Zealand from 1933 to 1936. Here was to be found an expression of Salvation Army life which must have reminded him of his own homeland where commendation of the beneficent social results of the Army's programme is linked with a personal reluctance publicly to avow the religious faith which motivates that work. Nevertheless with the opportunity to give their undivided attention to the proclamation of the gospel brought about by the end of hostilities, Salvationists in the Dominion were applying themselves afresh to the need for effective open-air evangelism, to the sale of their literature in places of public resort, to their work with children and young people and, for those bewildered by sorrow or bemused by some personal character failure, to be ready to offer spiritual guidance. The net result was that in the fifties the Army in New Zealand slowly but steadily enlarged its borders. Salvationists were encouraged by the realisation that their labour in the Lord was not in vain.

The Commonwealth of Australia followed on with a six-week programme of meetings divided among the state capitals, the most outstanding of which was the Anzac Day service on Tuesday, April 25, in the Domain, Sydney. This drew an estimated attendance of 60,000 for, as with New Zealand, both world wars were very much in the consciousness of the people, with the second coming much closer to them geographically than the first. This particular occasion was singled out by General Orsborn in his reminiscences *The House of my Pilgrimage*.

> This was by far my largest and most interesting audience. Before me stood a silent host of servicemen and women. They had marched to this assembly through crowded streets . . . The hush that fell upon this huge parade as I began to speak was almost disconcerting. I was heard in complete silence. Australia seemed greatly to esteem the contribution of The Salvation Army to this great day of remembrance. I felt especially honoured and inspired to have a part in it. Long after the event I received a transcription of my address – in Braille. It was with the compliments and thanks of a veteran of the First World War. He said that this was the address that he had been waiting to hear ever since he was blinded at Gallipoli.

But in a continent like Australia where history has been required to triumph over geography, the Army's place in these state events has been made possible only by its daily participation in the lives of her scattered population. This is a variant of the ongoing problem of the effective communication of the Christian gospel. Two attempts to grapple with this difficulty may be quoted.

In 1948 the Australia Southern Territory acquired a Percival Gull monoplane and appointed Captain Victor Pedersen, with Darwin as his base, to cover the Northern Territory – an area more than ten times the size of England. (Let no one think that maps are being held upside down. Salvation Army-wise, the Southern Territory includes the Northern Territory!) This meant that he took off from war-time airstrips which happened still to be in use, carrying a folding bicycle which enabled him to ride from the strip to the cattle station to be visited – plus a projector and suitable films, a cornet, a concertina and a quantity of song books. Sometimes his meetings were held in a station homestead, sometimes in an adjacent hangar. His regular calling points included the leprosarium, and his meetings were often attended by folk from the nearest aboriginal settlement.

Slightly earlier than this the Australia Eastern Territory had dedicated four field units to the service of the outback, and the following extracts are taken from the log books of Captains Florence Whittaker and Ruth Smith who ran the No. 1 unit.

Sunday. Cobar; dust storm blowing; intense heat. Conducted Sunday school lesson with 25 children. In the afternoon travelled to Wrightville. Conditions terrible; could hardly see to drive. However, 22 children turned up, though had to shout to explain Bible story with flannelgraph. Led public meeting in Methodist church at night.

Monday. Contacted Far West travelling sister whose base is at Cobar. Discussed cases on which we are working together. Visited daughter of ex-Salvationist who lives some miles out. Sing-song in the evening.

Tuesday. Left for Louth. Hot day; travelling anything but pleasant. Visited every home in little town. As too hot to hold meeting in the little church, hotel keeper offered use of his lounge and verandah, and afterward provided supper. Arrival of Unit always an event in this isolated community.

Wednesday. Visited school and gave religious instruction lesson. Fifteen children present. Arranged for box of dolls to be sent to this school for distribution at Christmas. Visited bush nursing sister. Arrived Bourke late in the evening.

Thursday. With temperature soaring tackled job of cleaning ourselves, our clothes and our truck. Later left for North Bourke to conduct cottage meeting.

Friday. Drove out some miles to visit a family of fettlers (rail track repairers) who live in tents along the railway line. Enrolled five children for Bible correspondence course. Drove to aboriginal reserve. Again appalled by conditions under which these people live. While conducting meetings by river bank police arrived to break up a drunken brawl.

And so on, and so on, as week succeeded week. Full marks to both territories for trying! Meanwhile the General and his party flew on to Jakarta, pausing to stop at Darwin where they were greeted by Captain and Mrs Pedersen and their group of resident Salvationists.

Indonesia awaited – and a small but significant clue to the

Army's position was that the Year Book for 1950 no longer referred to the Netherlands East Indies but simply to Indonesia. Remembering that the Netherlands had not formally agreed to a transfer of power to a national government until December 27, 1949, this was a very prompt acceptance of the realities of life. In the immediate past the fortunes of the expatriate missionaries had risen or fallen according to the vicissitudes of the war. When Germany invaded Holland the Dutch authorities interned the German officers serving in the territory. When the Japanese took over the German officers were freed and the Dutch interned. By the same token no Swedish missionaries were detained but Danish and Norwegian were. What is of importance is that no separatist Salvation Army was ever set up. One national officer sought and gained recognition for an Indonesian Salvation Army – but local support was minimal and the movement died with him. So the General was cordially received at the presidential palace and Dr Sukarno spoke of the kindness shown him when, as an Indonesian patriot, he had suffered imprisonment. But among those who showed him kindness was a Salvationist prison visitor who brought him sweetmeats, cakes and reading material. This had included a life of William Booth – and so the President knew about the Army before ever he came to office. Bread cast upon the waters indeed!

But the same issue of *The War Cry* which reported the General's welcome home in the legendary Clapton Congress Hall carried a message from London newspaper correspondents in Vienna that, under a decree issued by the central executive, the Czech government had ordered that The Salvation Army be formally dissolved 'on security grounds'.

This was not the first European country where the Army had been suppressed by government decree. In the uneasy peace which had followed the First World War the Army flag had been unfurled in Latvia and Estonia as well as in Hungary and Yugoslavia. The Russian occupation of Latvia put an end to the work there in 1940, though there was a short flicker of life when the German forces briefly gained the upper hand in 1941 – but the end came two years later. The suppression of the Army in Estonia put paid to the work in the two Baltic republics. The year 1950 marked the beginning of the end in

Hungary and the little that was left of the Army's work in that land was attached to Czechoslovakia.

By this time, however, the courageous Captain Mary Lichtenberger, who was now fighting a lone hand in her native Yugoslavia, had set up three centres of work in her country with home leagues, torchbearer groups and a guitar band, even though direct contact with International Headquarters was now impossible. As the war drew to its close and the German forces retreated, the captain was arrested, as were all who bore a German name or were suspected of German connections. After nineteen days she was set free for lack of firm evidence against her. But suspicion lingered, and an innocent attempt to secure food from abroad led to her rearrest.

Trial and a sentence of forced labour were the inevitable result. Mercifully the forced labour was waived though the sentence stood, so that when the captain was released she had to take in sewing or do knitting or teach English to anyone who wanted to learn it in order to keep herself alive. At long last, at her third application, she was allowed to leave the country in that late summer of 1951. As Salvationists in Canada had made her their special concern she was given an appointment in that country from which she was promoted to Glory in 1972.[3]

For the work in Czechoslovakia there were higher hopes, and seemingly firmer ground for those hopes as well. The Army had survived the political changes brought about by the rise of Hitler – though not without loss. On the Day of National Liberation there were but eight corps left in the command. Uniform could not be worn; open-air work was forbidden; collections could not be taken; the *Prapor Spasy*[4] could not be published. But 'Welcome to Freed Czechoslovakia' was the message in large letters which greeted Brigadier Thomas Dennis, the representative of International Headquarters, as he appeared on the platform of the Army hall in Prague to lead the first Congress to be held in the country since 1939. What was more, as reported in the international *War Cry* for March 16, 1950, an open-air meeting was held on Congress Sunday in front of the famous statue of John Huss, and was followed by a march – complete with band and flag – back to the hall. To crown all the brigadier was received, as the General's representative, by the President, Dr Eduard Benes.

All went well for another year for the next Congress was led by the Chief of the Staff and Mrs Commissioner John J. Allan, with the Deputy Lord Mayor of Prague representing the authorities at the Sunday afternoon rally. For a moment it seemed as if the pioneer days of 1919 had returned – those days when the Army was legally recognised as a movement for 'building up materially and morally the physical and spiritual standards of the people' and had been empowered to 'maintain social institutions' to further such ends. But a new regime meant new attitudes. The spring of 1948 saw the men's social home and the girls' home taken into government control, with the officers left to care for their charges but with state-appointed officials controlling the administration. On September 22, 1949, Major Josef Korbel, the officer in charge of the work of the Army in Brno, the capital of Moravia, was arrested. More than ten years passed before he was released and reunited with his family. The English-born territorial leaders, Lieut.-Colonel and Mrs Herbert Climpson, were expelled, though none could have been more devoted to the well-being of the Czech people than they.

It was 'my bitter lot' – said General Orsborn – to sign a statement which appeared in the international *War Cry* for July 18, 1950, that the Army in Czechoslovakia had been disbanded by government decree. At the lowest consideration this was to take a sledge hammer to crack a nut. The total officer strength in the country at this date numbered thirty, with thirteen employees in addition. Was the government's position so shaky that so tiny a minority group could accomplish its overthrow or challenge its authority? The General's protest read:

I deny that any Salvation Army officer in Czechoslovakia has been engaged in any action which the government of that country could accurately describe as subversive.

The Salvationist is the servant of all, and he is willing to work and witness for Christ in any land whatever the political colour of the government. His preaching is simple and uncontroversial. His testimony is to the saving grace of God which he has personally experienced, and his service is expressed by an eager hand outstretched to any in need. How can such activities be deemed subversive – unless the very gospel be regarded as such?

Brave words these – but powerless to effect any change in

the Czech government's attitude towards a movement whose world headquarters was situated in the heart of the principal city of one of the Western world's capitalist states. And powerless as well to halt the crossing of the 38th parallel by North Korean troops on Monday, June 25, of the same year. This was to prove yet another challenge to Lieut.-Commissioner and Mrs Herbert Lord, for when he was earlier in charge of the Malaya Command he had been interned in Changi after the fall of Singapore, while Mrs Lord was evacuated to Australia with other women officers. They were reunited when hostilities ended in the Pacific and, following homeland furlough, had returned in 1947 as territorial leaders to Korea.

Totally dedicated as was the remnant of Korean Salvationists who survived the Second World War, a remnant is what they were. All missionary personnel had been evacuated; all subsidies of money and material had ceased; every effort had been made by the occupying power to suppress all expressions of the Christian faith. The wearing of Salvation Army uniform had been forbidden. Salvation Army halls had been sold, or leased for commercial purposes, or vandalised. The headquarters in Seoul was rented out room by room. At the first Thursday evening's devotional gathering after arriving back in Seoul, Lieut.-Commissioner Lord and his wife were the only two people in Salvation Army uniform. The following week there were seven. Literally, fragment by fragment, the work had to be pieced together – greatly aided by the generosity of the USA Central Territory which supplied sufficient material for a new Army uniform for every officer and a new Army cap. The future had begun to look brighter than even Salvationists had dared to hope – when within two years this new blow fell.

With the arrest and detention of Lieut.-Commissioner Lord, the chief secretary, Colonel Whang, took charge and a temporary headquarters was established in Pusan. The girls in the Army's care were moved to Taegu, the boys to the island of Che Ju. The commissioner had hoped to remain in the country in order to aid the relief work which inevitably follows in the wake of war – but this was not to be. Together with consular representatives and a group of Western missionaries he was marched off to Pyung Yong, the capital of North Korea and thence to sundry border camps where they suffered three winters together. It was April 9, 1953, when seven of their number, including the commissioner, crossed into China bound for their homeland. This was the Lord's doing and marvellous in their eyes.

Not all were thus delivered – notably Senior-Major Noh Yong Soo, the commanding officer of the Chin Ju corps. Yong Soo was born in 1897, the son of Confucianist parents. He was converted to Christianity in 1915 when attending a Salvation Army meeting and in 1919 entered the officers' training college in Seoul. As a corps officer he faithfully cared for his people and, under God, was able to add to their number – though the spread of the Second World War to the Pacific area put a temporary end to all such advances. By 1940 all expatriate officers had left the country and all contact with Salvationists in other parts of the world was forbidden. No Salvationist sign or symbol might be displayed and many officers had to take up some part-time occupation to keep body and soul together.

But when peace came the life of the Army blossomed afresh and in 1949 the major was appointed to reopen the Chin Ju corps. His spirit may be judged by the fact that his first action was to hold an open-air meeting. All too soon, however, the faith of the comrades was tested afresh as North Korean forces crossed the 38th parallel, captured Seoul and overran Chin Ju. Many of the terrified inhabitants fled to the south or took refuge in the hills, though the major gathered with his people in the Army hall even when the churches had closed their doors. What he had to say was a challenge to his soldiers. As a man could die only once it was better to die for a cause – the cause of Christ, for example – than to succumb to disease or starvation. To those who wished to seek refuge elsewhere he gave his blessing and, even when the town went up in flames, he stayed as near as he could for as long as he could despite being warned of the risks he ran.

Eventually the occupying troops staged a house-to-house search and, having captured the major, subjected him to three days' questioning. Their final ploy was to persuade his wife and daughter to urge him to renounce his faith – but he refused. 'For thirty years I have preached the cross of Christ,' he answered. 'I cannot run away and I cannot lie.' He committed his loved ones to God's care and, with two young students and the mother-in-law of a South Korean soldier, was taken to the place of execution known locally as 'Death valley'. He comforted his fellow victims as best he could and, when it was his turn to face the firing squad, held aloft his Bible and called out: 'By believing you can have life.' He was shot as he did so.

Being dead he yet speaketh. The present Salvation Army citadel in Chin Ju was erected in his memory.

The universal character of the kingdom of God received fresh expression as work had progressed in the comparatively untroubled United Kingdom on the preparation of 34 Sydenham Hill, London SE26, as the International Staff College. In the past there had been several versions of this project – the first known as a Staff Training Lodge in Clapton (north-east London) from 1905 to 1914. Closed by the outbreak of the First World War, this was reopened in 1921 but later fell victim to the depression years. No. 34 – 'The Cedars' – was purchased in 1944 when emergency accommodation was needed for children bombed out of 'The Haven' in a nearby south London district. This plan did not materialise, however, and on October 10, 1950, the property was opened to provide the Army with 'officers, mature in mind and spirit, for the tasks to which they may be appointed'. Overseas territories contributed generously to the adaptations and additions needed to transform this Victorian mansion into a residential college. But perhaps the principal alteration was the subsequent change of name to 'The International College for Officers' – the ICO for short – thus indicating a specific enlargement of purpose and intake.

Twenty-four officers from fifteen territories attended the first session and, if so much space has been given to the opening of a single building, it is because this multi-racial, multi-lingual mix expresses in a practical and visible form the internationalism of The Salvation Army and the determination of the movement to keep it that way.

5   THESE ALL OBTAINED A
GOOD REPORT

Without any doubt the greatest demonstration in 1950 of the unity of the world-wide Salvation Army was the International Salvationist Youth Congress which ran from August 10 to 23. This was the brain child of General Orsborn, aided and abetted by Commissioners John J. Allan (the Chief of the Staff) and Wm. R. Dalziel (the British Commissioner), with Colonel Edgar Grinsted (International Youth Secretary) and Lieut.-Colonel Kaare Westergaard (National Youth Secretary) as the principal executive officers. There was no doubt as to the success of the venture. Upwards of 1,200 delegates attended from all five continents, united to proclaim that 'Christ is the way for youth today.' This was the congress slogan, coined by Mary Harley of Hamilton Citadel (Canada) and selected from numerous other submissions.

The British Isles had already seen several Army events of this order – in 1886, 1894, 1904 and 1914, but this congress was unique in several respects. One important difference was that on this occasion every accredited delegate was under thirty years of age. This fact caught the imagination of press and public alike – so much so that the composer of 'The Light of the World', played by the International Staff Band in the final congress meeting, was described as 'the young John Dean Goffin'. Perhaps youth was more a matter of spirit than of years though Bramwell Tillsley of Kitchener (Ontario), as yet still in his teens, actually was the youngest member of the Canadian delegation. Raymond Holdstock, of Croydon Citadel, was more of the average age for he had just completed his national service and entered the International Training College as a cadet as soon as the congress was over.

There were many young people like him. Some had already accepted officership as their vocation – such as (at the time of writing) the present International Secretary of Europe, the wife of the territorial commander for the Eastern India Territory, the territorial commanders for Germany, Switzerland and the USA Southern, the present Chief Secretary for Norway and the Field Secretary for the Netherlands. Other delegates influenced by the congress to a like dedication were Miriam Vinti (Rome), Damon Rader (Philadelphia), Olive Bottle (Sittingbourne), Peter Hofman (Cleveland Citadel), Paul Marti (St. Gallen), Audrey Grottick (Govan Citadel), Geoffrey Perry (Welling), Anna Trainer (Dundee Citadel) and Lyndon Taylor (Penge). More than one testimony had as its refrain: 'I know now what the Lord wants me to do.' With an even greater number still deeds have spoken louder than words as they have continued to play a valuable part in Salvation Army life in all five continents. The congress was a genuine mix of peoples and realms of every tongue.

Of even greater consequence was the fact that – again at this level – these youthful delegates were heard as well as seen. Of course there had always been a place for personal testimony on all Army occasions both great and small. But at this congress there was the cut and thrust of personal discussion. The final point in the official statement of the fourfold purpose of the congress was: 'To provide opportunity for the voice of youth to be heard.' And heard it was – for four of the congress weekdays were devoted to the discussion of the main overall theme – 'The faith of a Salvationist' which, in turn, was broken down into its component parts.

For example, the final discussion day centred on a basic element in the teaching of Jesus – faith in God alone. Under this heading the study groups were asked to discuss what were described as two modern idolatries – the worship of force and the worship of chance. On the former theme *The War Cry* reported the General as saying:

> The Salvationist believes that the abolition of war is both desirable and possible. But the dream palace of peace cannot be built by fine desires and lofty ideals. It has to be built of stronger material than these . . . When the kingdom of God is brought in men shall make war no more. Let us hasten the coming of that kingdom . . . Christianity presents not a creed which men must try to follow but a Saviour whom men must accept.

The worship of chance was felt to transgress the principle of human brotherhood, for any gain that might accrue to one man could only be at the expense of his neighbour. One person's gain must inevitably be another's loss. This violation of the golden rule, whether the actual sum involved be large or small, is not acceptable to the Salvationist. He cannot at one and the same time condemn the immense amounts which change hands as a result of the highly organised wagering connected with commercialised sport and yet tolerate what might be called 'the church bazaar' type of gambling. General Orsborn made the Army's position crystal clear when he declared that 'we shall not raise money by raffles or lotteries, nor will we accept money which has been secured in such a manner.'

The final vindication of the congress was to be found in its findings – the fruit of the free discussion practised in its study groups. These were announced in one of the final sessions and printed in full in the international *War Cry*, as well as in the current Year Book. They gave the lie to the fears of the few who doubted whether a generation who had been given a freedom of expression denied to their fathers would – or even could – pledge themselves as unequivocally to the title deeds of their faith. Such apprehensions were proved to be groundless. While on the one hand the old rigorism was on its way out, there was an unqualified dedication to the Lord of all good life and a quickening of desire both to know and to do His good will. Any thought of discarding the substance of the historic faith of the Salvationist found no serious support whatever. Any form of humanism was dismissed as a futile attempt to tread the Christian pathway without the necessary help of Christ Himself. Jesus was – and would ever remain – man's only Saviour.

But Christian witness is a comparatively easy option in the Western world contrasted with the hazards posed by the Far East. The warning of Jesus that in this life His followers would meet with trouble was never proved more true than in China. The Army was there in fulfilment of a pledge made in 1912 by General Bramwell Booth to his dying father, the Founder. The first Salvationists arrived in Peiping when the First World War was still raging. The Republic of China was only five years old at the time but hope was in the air. The obvious

physical as well as spiritual need which cried aloud in the
towns and villages made the Army's presence all the more
opportune and by the thirties there were ninety corps in North
China, with some 3,000 soldiers on the rolls and a further
1,800 pledged recruits awaiting further instruction. But the
scene changed with the advance of the Japanese forces in
that area and the subsequent attack on Pearl Harbour. Any
Salvationist holding a passport from a country deemed hostile
to the occupying power was required to wear an arm band
bearing the initial of that country. From early 1943 to late
1945 officers from the United States and from British Commonwealth countries were interned and, by the time they were
released, hundreds of Salvationists had been lost without trace.
However, when on September 21, 1945, the Army flag was
once more bravely unfurled on the roof garden of the territorial
headquarters in Peiping, it seemed as if the worst might
possibly be over.

The worst was yet to come – even though many of the
Chinese officers had displayed, and continued to display, a
devotion beyond the call of duty. One of them reported that
he had maintained his corps by running a small trade in
brooms and dustpans and had even organised his own self-
denial appeal. Another said that though bitter fighting had
raged in his district he had been able to care for eighty refugees
who, together with his own family, safely survived in the shelter
of the Salvation Army hall. The two children's homes in
Peiping kept their doors open throughout all the fighting and
expatriate officers, awaiting homeland furlough after release
from internment, joined the UNRRA in relief work in Peiping,
Tientsin and Shanghai. Links were restored with Salvationists
even in Mukden. Though a national training college had not
been opened until 1918,[1] eight Chinese officers were now
admitted to the long service order, and the arrival of the first
overseas officer reinforcements at the territorial centre raised
the temperature of the faithful. There must be solid ground
for hope if fresh expatriate officers were coming their way.

But the terror of civil war began to take the place of the
horror of a foreign invasion. The area under the control of the
People's Army grew with frightening speed. The headquarters
of the China South Command was moved to Hong Kong, and
while this gave the Army a central hall and a suite of offices

in Kowloon – an advantage not known before – any assured contact with the mainland was lost. Similarly the headquarters for China North was moved to Shanghai, though Brigadier and Mrs Charles Sowton remained in Peiping to guard the Army's interests there.

However, early in 1949 the capital itself was invested by the People's Army, and the area surrounding the Army head-quarters became the centre of the fighting. By the month of February Peiping was occupied, Shanghai fell a little later, and by October the Communist central government was estab-lished. Again there was a brief respite – but it was not long before open-air meetings were first restricted and then forbid-den as dangerous to traffic. Christian worship and preaching were limited to buildings specifically licensed for that purpose, and 'freedom of religious belief' was matched by an equal 'freedom to oppose religion'.

The carefully orchestrated attack upon the Christian faith continued with a 'Christian manifesto' signed by a group of religious and social leaders at the 'invitation' of the govern-ment. On the ground that past Christian activity had been a tool in the hands of Western imperialists, believers were asked to sign this declaration as a token of their loyalty to their country and the People's Government, and lists of such signa-tories were published. The technique of self-criticism – by this time a familiar political procedure – made its appearance in Christian circles as well. Church members testified against their ministers, members against one another, even ministers against their colleagues – a dismaying spectacle to many in their congregations.

By the middle of 1951 laws had been passed forbidding any foreigner to hold any executive post in any Christian organisation, and no connection was permitted with any Chris-tian body overseas. By the end of the year all responsibility for the work of the Army in China was transferred to a small council of Chinese officers, and expatriate officers were served with an expulsion order. The end aim of the government was one national church which should be 'self-governing, self-supporting and self-propagating'. This meant no control from outside China, no reinforcements from outside China, no subsidies of money or materials from outside China. A statement which appeared in the international *War Cry* for

August 23, 1952, accepted these unwelcome conditions but, in reality, there was no option. Part of this final message read:

> The compulsory departure of our missionaries . . . and the severance of our Chinese Salvationists from our international body is a distressing climax to thirty-five years of zealous and devoted service.
>
> The General has felt himself unable to agree to the transfer of the spiritual trust and the material assets of the Army to an executive council of Chinese officers working under the separatist legislation of their government. Nevertheless an instrument of transfer was enforced without the General's specific authority.
>
> Everything possible has been done to ensure the well-being of those who now take the responsibility of leadership and direction. Before the severance funds were deposited to maintain the work as operating in 1951, and to meet every Chinese officer's salary for one year, as well as to cover the maintenance of the children's home in Peiping for the same period . . .

The record of the thousands of displaced Chinese people for whom the Army had cared in refugee camps, the distribution of food to the hungry and dispossessed regardless of their political affiliation, the provision of night shelters for the infirm and aged, the care of unwanted children reduced to beggary, was not allowed to stay the forced departure of their benefactors. What was virtually the remnant of these thirty-five years – thirty corps, three institutions and eighty officers – was lost to human view, though not to the eye of Him who declared that the least of His children was of imperishable value in his sight.[2]

Fighting the good fight on such a world-wide front, The Salvation Army was bound to suffer some reverses as well as make progress, though such setbacks as occurred could rarely be laid at the door of the rank and file. It was often the untried recruit who proved the most loyal to his new-found faith. This was what happened in the early fifties when some African Salvationists were as sorely tested as their comrades in China, for the Mau Mau uprising posed a savage challenge to Christian work and witness in Kenya. In many instances the simple-hearted believer found himself caught in the crossfire between colonial authority and tribal loyalty – suspected on the one hand because of his race and colour and hated on the other because of his religious faith.

The official announcement had been that 'in areas affected by the Mau Mau, Salvation Army work had been seriously impeded', and it was to discover how seriously that Commissioner Ernest Bigwood, the territorial commander for East Africa, personally visited the most troubled districts. At the beginning of what the government called 'the emergency', the meeting attendances at Saba Saba – one of the oldest corps in the Kikuyu area – fell away completely. The place had assumed the look of a deserted village. But appearances proved deceptive and, on this particular occasion, the Army building was full to overflowing – and this heartening experience was repeated at Maragua. At Fort Hall, however, a notorious danger spot, only a handful of comrades gathered to greet their territorial leader. There was the same disappointing response at Katuto and at Mikimbi. But the African lieutenant and his wife at Fort Hall, though with only two years' service as officers to their credit, were determined to stand their ground. When disturbances became so serious that it seemed as if they would have to be moved elsewhere, the lieutenant said: 'Please let me stay with my people. My wife and I have no fear for we are in God's hands.'

At Kiamuruga the outlook was brighter. A sturdy group of uniformed Salvationists was waiting to greet the commissioner, even though their officer had recently been waylaid by one of the many gangs roving the remoter parts of the countryside in an attempt to terrorise the inhabitants into taking their own rebellious oath. Happily the officer had recovered from his ordeal and was present to share in the meeting. But at Manyatta the Army's head teacher had been murdered and at Kagaari the handful of local officers were understandably anxious about their future for at Kieni, the next port of call, all that was left of the corps hall and school were two piles of rubble. In addition to this wanton destruction the married officers and the head teacher had been roughed up and robbed as well. Nevertheless more than fifty Salvationists – at least a dozen in Army uniform – had gathered to welcome their leader. An even greater surprise was awaiting at Kagumo where the situation was considered so dangerous that the local authorities insisted on providing an armed escort. A daylight attack had been made upon the forest road within the previous week. But, as the visitors turned into the clean and well-ordered Army compound, some seventy comrades were waiting for the meeting to begin, including a group who had walked twenty miles through the bush in order to share the midday fellowship.

The spirit of Salvationists in that area was expressed by the officer who wrote: 'All around are the Mau Mau. My comrades have been warned that they will be killed if they attend the meetings. But I will not let these evil people, though they are my own kinsmen, influence me to take their degrading oath. Rather will I continue to sing: "I'll stand for Christ alone".'[3]

Almost as if to serve as a reminder that the odds have often been weighted against the soldiers of Christ, the second volume of *The History of The Salvation Army* by Colonel Robert Sandall was published by Thomas Nelson & Sons towards the end of 1950, and a first review appeared in *The War Cry* for February 3, 1951.

This covered the years from 1878 to 1886 – a period of major expansion. The number of corps and of officers rose from fifty-four and ninety-eight respectively in 1878 to 528 and 1,340 in 1886. This was also the age of 'the skeleton army' when, of the Salvationists assaulted in mob violence in Great Britain, 251 were women and twenty-three were under fifteen years of age. It was also a time of very limited material resources. When in 1881 the Army's headquarters was transferred from 272 Whitechapel Road to 101 Queen Victoria Street, only a greengrocer's cart and a handcart (so rickety that one of the wheels came off during the operation) were required to make the two journeys necessary to move the entire stock of furniture and fittings from one address to the other! But this was also the decade when the Army spread to Australia, Canada, France, India, the United States, South Africa, Sri Lanka, Sweden and Switzerland. There could be a moral in this somewhere. Perhaps it is as old as Tertullian's line about 'the blood of the martyrs' and 'the seed of the church'.

Two further world events can be linked at this point – one of which was the first international Scout camp to be held under Salvation Army auspices at Lunteren in Holland in the autumn of 1952. This was attended by scouts from both sides of the Atlantic – as many as 165 from the British Isles alone

– and graced by a visit from Queen Juliana of The Netherlands. The parallel Life-Saving Guard camp took place in August 1954, by the Oslo fjord, and enjoyed the presence of HRH Princess Astrid of Norway. Again there were representatives from Belgium, Finland, The Netherlands, Norway, the United Kingdom and the United States. 'Concordia' was the name of this camp – and the name expressed its nature.

Between these two international events there occurred a change in the Army's international leadership – in particular in the office of the Chief of the Staff. The Year Book for 1954 referred in retrospect to 'the heavy administrative and public duties' carried out since September 1946, which 'had affected the health of Commissioner and Mrs John J. Allan'. But a change of appointment did not mean any lessening of their desire to serve for, on the forty-seventh anniversary of his commissioning as an officer, the Chief of the Staff concluded his service in that appointment only to assume his new responsibility as the General's special delegate, travelling the world and reporting to him on any matter affecting the ongoing work of the Army. This arrangement continued until the retirement of Commissioner and Mrs Allan from active service on March 29, 1957. Meanwhile Commissioner Edgar Dibden, who had served as the principal custodian of the Army's finances since the beginning of 1942, became the Chief of the Staff on July 17, 1953, and Mrs Commissioner Dibden brought with her a long experience of the Army's social services, particularly in the field of nursing.

Any reference to Salvation Army leaders at this time must include a recognition of the severe loss suffered by the passing of Commissioner Ernest Pugmire, National Commander for the United States, on June 24, 1953. The honoured bearer of an honoured name, the commissioner became an officer in Canada in 1907, and was one of the few survivors of the Canadian delegation to the 1914 international congress in London when the 'Empress of Ireland' sank in the Gulf of St. Lawrence. His missionary service began in 1918 in north China and then took him to Japan where he eventually became the chief secretary, returning home to take a similar appointment in Canada West. Subsequent service brought him to the leadership of the USA Central, the Southern and (in 1942) the Eastern Territories. In 1944 he assumed responsibility for the further post of National Commander, but from 1947 devoted himself solely to the duties of the latter office.

General Orsborn received the news of Commissioner Pugmire's promotion to Glory at Heathrow airport where, with Mrs Orsborn, he was about to emplane for Stockholm to conduct the annual Swedish congress. His only option was to fly to Stockholm, conduct the opening gathering there, leave the rest of the congress in the capable hands of Mrs Orsborn, and then fly across to New York to share in the tributes paid to one whom he described as 'a good man, a sincere disciple of Jesus Christ, a wise and balanced counsellor, and a trusted leader of the first order . . . whose life was invested in other men's lives – an investment which would continue to yield returns for many years to come'.

6 THE HEAT OF THE DAY

It cannot be denied that many Salvation Army officers and soldiers were taken by surprise when they read the banner headline on page three of the international *War Cry* for January 9, 1954: 'The General to retire in June next'. This was followed by the required legal formula addressed to the Chief of the Staff, Commissioner Edgar Dibden, which ran: 'Pursuant to section four of The Salvation Army Act 1931 I hereby give you notice of my intention to retire from the office of General of The Salvation Army on the thirtieth day of June nineteen hundred and fifty four.'

The Army as a whole was unaccustomed to any officer taking early retirement save for manifest ill health duly supported by the appropriate medical certificate. Many of the older school had understood John Lawley's line: 'I'm fighting my passage of Heaven' in the most literal sense. Retirement allowances were unknown when they had enlisted. 'Nor shall we lay our armour down', they had sung, 'till we exchange it for a crown.' At the age of eighty-three the Founder had spoken on the platform of the Royal Albert Hall of going into dry dock for repairs. General Bramwell was unwilling to be relieved of the burden of office at seventy-three. General Higgins insisted on retiring at seventy because he had made a pledge to that effect to the High Council when elected. General Evangeline had passed her sixty-ninth birthday when elected to that office, and not until General Carpenter was seventy-four did the repercussions of the Second World War allow him to retire. Even then the territorial commander for Japan was not able to be present at the 1946 High Council.

In his autobiography *The House of my Pilgrimage* General Orsborn described how he made up his mind to retire.[1]

Travail and travel . . . are never separated in the life of a General. He can never be a tourist. He carries the burden of office wherever

he goes . . . To live up to this he must be fit. I was not prepared
to compromise on this. Our constitution does not provide for a
General to take a lesser position. The Act of 1931 provided for a
legal notice of retirement in statutory form. I consulted our lawyer
and followed his instructions . . . The press . . . found only a tired
man, surrendering his office for the sake of the cause he loved.

It could well be that the General was hardly doing himself
justice. As what follows will show his calendar was not notice-
ably curtailed since his flight of 'frightening hazards and tedious
delays' in the spring of 1952. On the contrary, from January 1951
to September 1952 Mrs General Orsborn had, in an emergency,
taken over the leadership of the women's social work in Great
Britain and Ireland with its headquarters at 280 Mare Street,
Hackney. From its inception in 1884 this post had been a full-
time responsibility with a staff of 700 officers charged with the
supervision of twenty-eight homes for senior citizens accommodating almost a thousand guests. Added to that was the oversight of three approved schools for girls, plus five probation
homes and hostels and another nine training homes and hostels
for girls, together with one training home and three hostels for
mothers with children. Added to this were the 3,760 births registered in the current year at the hospitals, homes and district
nursing centres in Great Britain and Ireland, together with the
almost 44,000 attendances at ante-natal, post-natal and child
welfare clinics in the same geographical area.

Over and above all this Mrs Orsborn led the sixtieth anniversary celebrations of the women's social services in Norway
and Denmark, shared in the Repentance Day meetings in
Berlin, and participated in sundry other public events in the
USA and the United Kingdom. To say that this was more
than one man's work would be no compliment to Mrs Orsborn
– but the phrase might possibly be understood.

The General was no less occupied. Matters musical as well
as ecclesiastical claimed his attention. In praise of the first
named the centenary of the birth of Richard Slater, 'father of
Salvation Army music', was celebrated on June 7, 1954. This
aspect of Salvation Army activity had been anticipated by the
Diamond Jubilee celebrations of the International Staff Band
in the autumn of 1951, which had included the first brass band
programme ever to be presented in the Royal Festival Hall in

London. Of equal significance was the fact that, in the late spring of 1953, the eighty-year-old Dr Vaughan Williams, OM, was introduced to the world of Salvation Army music through presiding over a festival given by the International Staff Band in Dorking. 'Never have I heard a band with so fine a style – a real classical style', said the veteran composer, adding that 'to be true to the function of Salvation Army bands, that of making people better, only the best music should be played – music that grips the soul.' On reflection this could be accepted as a justifiable gloss on William Booth's own words: 'Soul saving music is the music for me.' The upshot was that Vaughan Williams wrote his first original composition for a brass band which he entitled 'Prelude to three Welsh hymn tunes' – and later presented to the Army. 'Ever since I heard you at Dorking', he said, 'I have wanted to write something for you.'

But matters ecclesiastical meant even more to General Orsborn – especially when these affected the Army. The second Assembly of the World Council of Churches was due to meet at Evanston, Illinois, in August 1954. This was after the date of his retirement, but the names of the Salvation Army delegates had to be submitted without further delay. So Commissioner Gordon Simpson (International Headquarters) was appointed chairman – with Mrs General Orsborn, Mrs Commissioner McMillan (USA, National Office), Commissioner Claude Bates (USA Central Territory), Colonel Yasowo Segawa (Japan) and Colonel Joseph Dahya (India West) completing the delegation. To make sure that the officer corps throughout the world understood his mind on the matter the General wrote at length in the March–April 1954 issue of *The Officer*, explaining that the Army representation would share in the group discussions on evangelism, social questions, international affairs and the place of the laity. He went on to deal frankly with the achievements as well as the shortcomings of 'this noble experiment' (as he called it) but testified also to 'the many good things we could do together'.

We are friendly with all whom Christ has named as His own, and for that primary reason we do not refuse fellowship with the World Council. We are also in the Council that we may lend the experience and the testimony of the Army to those aims and

purposes which are especially dear to the Salvationist. We find
that members of the Council are pleased with our contribution
. . . We can make common cause with the Council on big social
issues, where our principles and purposes are clearly harmonious
with them.

But the weeks slipped by, and the busier General and Mrs
Orsborn became the more quickly time flew until on March
6, 1954, the Chief of the Staff dispatched the legal notices
summoning the forty-eight members to attend the opening of
the High Council at Sunbury Court on April 29 at two p.m.
The list of those so summoned follows below in alphabetical
order. Thirteen nationalities were represented; sixteen had
served on the 1946 High Council; because of changes in its
constitution one of their number – Commissioner William A.
Ebbs – had served on the first in 1929 as well. Two members
were absent through illness. Commissioner Tobias Ögrim
was admitted into a London hospital in preparation for an
operation which did not take place, however, until May 7, and
Lieut.-Commissioner Samuel Manuel was too ill to travel.
He was promoted to Glory on June 8.

Lieut.-Commissioner Ragnar ÅHLBERG	Territorial Commander, Finland.
Commissioner Janet ALLAN	Territorial Commander, Western India.
Commissioner John J. ALLAN	The General's special delegate, IHQ.
Commissioner Ranulph ASTBURY	Managing Director, The Salvation Army Assurance Society.
Commissioner Claude BATES	Territorial Commander, USA Central.
Lieut.-Commissioner John BEAVEN	Auditor General, IHQ.
Lieut.-Commissioner Henri BECQUET	Territorial Commander, Belgian Congo.
Commissioner Ernest BIGWOOD	Territorial Commander, East Africa.
Commissioner John BLADIN	International Travelling Commissioner.
Lieut.-Commissioner Wycliffe BOOTH	Territorial Commander, Norway.

Colonel Maurice CACHELIN	Territorial Commander, Brazil.
Lieut.-Commissioner William CLAY	Chancellor of the Exchequer, IHQ.
Lieut.-Commissioner Frederick COUTTS	Principal, International Training College.
Commissioner Owen CULSHAW	Governor, Men's Social Work.
Commissioner Wm. R. DALZIEL	Territorial Commander, Canada.
Commissioner Emma DAVIES	Leader, Women's Social Work, Great Britain and Ireland
Commissioner Edgar DIBDEN	The Chief of the Staff.
Commissioner Wm. J. DRAY	Territorial Commander, USA Southern.
Lieut.-Commissioner Norman DUGGINS	Territorial Commander, Switzerland.
Commissioner Charles DURMAN	Territorial Commander, Southern Australia.
Commissioner W. Alex EBBS	Secretary for Public Relations, IHQ.
Lieut.-Commissioner Holland FRENCH	Territorial Commander, USA Western.
Lieut.-Commissioner Edgar GRINSTED	Territorial Commander, Scotland and Ireland.
Lieut.-Commissioner Francis HAM	Territorial Commander, South America East.
Lieut.-Commissioner Fred HAMMOND	Principal, International Staff College.
Lieut.-Commissioner Robert HOGGARD	Territorial Commander, New Zealand.
Colonel Theodore HOLBROOK	Territorial Commander, Rhodesia.
Lieut.-Commissioner Arthur HUGHES	Territorial Commander, Indonesia.
Colonel Richard JACOBSEN	Territorial Commander, South America West.
Commissioner Joshua JAMES	Territorial Commander, Eastern Australia.
Commissioner Wilfred KITCHING	British Commissioner.
Commissioner Herbert LORD	Territorial Commander, South Africa.

Commissioner Donald McMILLAN	National Commander, USA.
Lieut.-Commissioner Samuel MANUEL	Territorial Commander, Southern India.
Commissioner Norman MARSHALL	Territorial Commander, USA Eastern.
Lieut.-Commissioner Herbert MITCHELL	Finance Secretary, IHQ.
Commissioner Archibald MOFFATT	International Secretary, IHQ.
Commissioner Hugh MUIR	Secretary for Trade.
Commissioner Tobias ÖGRIM	Territorial Commander, Sweden.
Commissioner Irene PEYRON	Territorial Commander, France.
Colonel Alfred SALHUS	Territorial Commander, West Africa.
Lieut.-Commissioner George SANDELLS	Territorial Commander, Central America and West Indies.
Commissioner Gordon SIMPSON	International Secretary, IHQ.
Commissioner Joseph SMITH	International Secretary, IHQ.
Commissioner Emanuel SUNDIN	Territorial Commander, Denmark.
Commissioner Ejner THYKJAER	Territorial Commander, The Netherlands.
Commissioner Masuzo UYEMURA	Territorial Commander, Japan.
Colonel Reginald WOODS	Territorial Commander, Germany.

When the High Council had assembled, officers were nominated and elected for the conduct of its own business. These were:

President	Commissioner Wm. R. Dalziel
Vice Presidents	Commissioner Emma Davies
	Commissioner Ejner Thykjaer
Recorder	Commissioner Owen Culshaw
Assistant Recorder	Lieut.-Commissioner Herbert Mitchell

Membership of the appropriate committees was agreed;

tellers were appointed; the business of the Council proceeded without interruption; in due course nominations were proposed and it was agreed that only the figures for the final ballot for the office of General should be made public. The first list of nominations consisted (in alphabetical order) of:

Commissioner John J. Allan
Lieut.-Commissioner Wycliffe Booth
Commissioner Edgar Dibden
Commissioner Wilfred Kitching
Commissioner Herbert Lord
Commissioner Norman Marshall
General Albert Orsborn

The President reported that, in harmony with rule 43 of the Orders of Procedure, he had spoken to General Orsborn who said that he did not wish to stand again for office. Commissioner John J. Allan and Commissioner Edgar Dibden asked to be allowed to withdraw, but the other four nominees went forward to the ballot. After the second ballot Lieut.-Commissioner Wycliffe Booth and Commissioner Herbert Lord withdrew, and the voting in the third and final ballot was

Commissioner Wilfred Kitching   32
Commissioner Norman Marshall   14

whereupon the President declared that Commissioner Wilfred Kitching had obtained the absolute two-thirds majority required and the High Council was *ipso facto* dissolved.

The fifth High Council showed itself content with existing Army structures, desiring only that these should be sharpened in order to accomplish more effectively the aims which the Army was raised by God to pursue. The Christian equality of men and women in the divine order was reaffirmed, as was the importance of our missionary service and our youth work as part of our evangelical enterprise. It was hoped that, age permitting, a General would be able to serve for a minimum of seven years, and there was no doubt about the warmth of the unanimous acclaim given to the General-elect before the High Council dispersed.

Salvationists were now free to turn to the happy task of

acknowledging the worth of the service rendered to the movement by General and Mrs Orsborn. In a most literal sense they had made the world their parish. The Second World War had virtually imprisoned their immediate predecessors within the confines of the British Isles. Earlier Generals had not enjoyed the swift facilities of air travel. To cross even the Atlantic had taken an average of five days. But the sixth General and his wife had seen the development of the world's commercial air services and had not hesitated to use them. What is cause for even greater thankfulness is that the generations which knew not Albert Orsborn after the flesh will for ever know him through his songs. Song books yet to be compiled will not omit 'Yet once again, by God's abundant mercy', or 'My life must be Christ's broken bread', or 'Army flag, thy threefold glory', or 'In the secret of Thy presence'. Church hymnaries could also find some rare pickings in this treasure trove.

Poetry rather than prose was his favourite medium, but what was so rarely published had a quality of its own. Of *The Silences of Christ*, the Methodist Dr Leslie Church said:

A poignant devotional book based on the idea that the things which Jesus did not do and the words He did not speak reveal His springs of character . . With knowledge that can come only from a deep personal experience, General Orsborn leads us to the silences of that most strenuous life so that we see our Lord turning aside for 'prayer after service and prayer after preaching' . . . A little book that should be read and reread . . . It has a quiet strength which is an inspiration.

To this outgoing ministry Mrs Orsborn had made her own contribution. As the daughter of a General she knew what was expected of a General and of the wife of a General as well. General Orsborn was fortunate in his partner. Their public farewell was held in a crowded Royal Festival Hall, London, on Thursday, June 10, 1954. Among the many messages received was one from President Eisenhower which said:

I am sure that The Salvation Army's progress during the past eight years is a source of great gratification to you. Under your leadership your great organisation has made notable strides in its efforts to encourage the men and women of the world to help their less fortunate neighbours.

A message from the Archbishop of Canterbury, The Most Revd and Rt. Hon. Geoffrey F. Fisher, said:

You will be sad to let him retire, but this demonstration of your loyalty to him will bring him great encouragement, and I am happy to add my own tribute to all those which will surround him on this great event.

Wrote the Earl of Crawford and Balcarres, GBE:

The retirement of General Orsborn will bring with it much regret to all who have seen his work and admire it, but regret will be mingled with much gratitude for his great services to the spiritual and social welfare of those whose interests he has had at heart.

Nothing could have been more fitting – from Mrs Orsborn's point of view at least – than that the last public engagement of the General and herself should have been the garden party held in the grounds of the International (William Booth Memorial) Training College to mark the seventieth anniversary of the Women's Social Work in Great Britain and Ireland, at which the principal guest was the Home Secretary, Sir David Maxwell Fyfe, GCVO, QC. Upwards of two thousand people enjoyed the variety of items provided for their pleasure and applauded his unqualified praise of the dedicated service of the 500 women officers serving in the 113 homes and hostels in Great Britain and Ireland for which the Women's Social Work was responsible. 'We have seen', said the Home Secretary, 'the joining of the hands of the Home Office and The Salvation Army without in any way blunting the Army's spiritual purpose and inspiration.'
The War Cry reported that Sir David addressed

a warm tribute to Mrs General Orsborn who manifested the enterprise and imagination which brought the 'Mayflower' home, the first of its kind, into being for the training of mothers convicted of child neglect.

Speaking of the high percentage of successes in Salvation Army approved schools . . . the Home Secretary commented on the progressive outlook of the officers concerned. Identifying himself with their aims he declared: 'We are not living in the past. We are addressing ourselves to the new world, but we are proud to hold fast to the great eternal truths which are as valuable today as they ever were' – which statement evoked as many 'Amen's' as 'Hear, hear's!'.

It was significant that as one General was completing his course on a Saturday afternoon, his successor was making his bow on the evening's main television programme. The good fight does not stop because there is a change in leadership.

In their retirement General and Mrs Orsborn lived in Bournemouth and were good soldiers at the very active Boscombe corps, from which the General was promoted to Glory on February 4, 1967. In her advancing years Mrs Orsborn lives near her only son in Victoria, British Columbia.

PART TWO

THE SEVENTH GENERAL: WILFRED KITCHING

(July 1, 1954–November 22, 1963)

1 MY TRUST FROM MY YOUTH

The seventh General of The Salvation Army, Wilfred Kitching, bore a name as familiar to his fellow Salvationists as that of his predecessor. His father, Commissioner Theodore Kitching, though of Quaker stock and the son of a member of the Society of Friends who had been a master at Ackworth, joined The Salvation Army as a lad and early attracted the attention of Bramwell Booth. After pioneering service in France and Switzerland the still youthful Theodore was brought on to Bramwell's own staff at the Queen Victoria Street head-quarters where he served until his promotion to Glory in 1930. Nevertheless, as his four officer children could testify, their parents never lost the habit of thee-ing and thou-ing one another. At the same time their own family was Salvationist born and Salvationist bred.

Within a few weeks of his birth on August 22, 1893 Wilfred was dedicated to God under the flag at the Wood Green corps by the Army's first commissioner – George Scott Railton, and thereafter the whole of his life was governed by the principles embodied in 'the yellow, the red and the blue'. When as a small boy he was given lessons on the piano his teacher was presented with a copy of *The Home Pianoforte Tutor* – a Salvation Army production – as the textbook to be employed. After the set exercises had been mastered there followed a selection of hymn tunes and Salvation Army songs. Nor was this pattern abandoned, for these were followed by a bound volume of *The Musical Salvationist* for 1904.[1]

Nowhere was the stamp of the Army more indelibly im-printed than on his music. After his conversion at the age of nine in a children's meeting at New Barnet where his mother was the young people's sergeant-major (i.e. Sunday school superintendent), the boy learnt to play a brass instrument. It was on the young people's band at New Barnet that he tried his prentice hand as teacher and conductor. All the music ever published over his name was for Salvation Army use. His course was firmly set. It was almost inevitable that *The War Cry* should include in its welcome report of the 1913 training session a sentence to the effect that 'Cadet Wilfred Kitching was seen at intervals behind the scenes enjoying washing up the crocks.' His wife, Kathleen, whom he married in 1929, became an officer in 1916 and, having been reared in the Penge corps of that decade, could also be described as having been 'cradled in salvationism'.

The new leaders found a favouring wind prevailing, though it might not have been easy to attribute this to any one particular cause. It could be appreciated if people who had not counted their lives dear in the cause of their own independence were sensitive about the continuing presence of expatriate nationals in their midst, especially in the significant fields of education and medicine. Countries whose cultural heritage was not historically Christian could hardly be expected to agree that the foreign missionary should be free to preach his gospel when and where he willed, however praiseworthy his personal intentions. But this reluctance faded as indigenous leadership was given a more decisive place, and as what had always been true was increasingly seen to be beyond contradiction. No overseas officer in the uniform of *Raksha Sainyam* or *Koo Sei Kun* or *Basolda Na Kobikisa*[2] was lining his own pocket while pretending to aid his less fortunate neighbour. As this basic fact was recognised the uniform of The Salvation Army continued to be welcome whether the regime was labelled colonial or post-colonial.

For example, in the year of this international change the Salvation Army hospital at Chikankata was being enlarged by developments which more than tripled the in-patient accommodation and added an X-ray unit with ancillary offices and equipment to match – half the cost being met by the generosity of the Beit Trust and half by the government. The opening in January 1955, with Senior-Captain (Dr) Sidney Gauntlett as Chief Medical Officer, was marked by the presence of the Governor, Sir Arthur Benson, who knew from previous experience how limited had been the medical facilities available in the Zambezi valley. The chief beneficiaries were of course the African people living in that area.

While this development was reaching completion the Chilean Senator Exequiel Gonzalez Madariaga was no less happy to preside at the opening of a women's home and day nursery in Santiago. Again those who would benefit most of all would be the neediest families in the city.

On October 28, 1954, a commemorative tablet was unveiled to mark the completion of a two-storey unit in the grounds of the Catherine Booth hospital in Travancore, South India, to house some eighty cancer patients, erected through the generosity of American Salvationists and friends. Responding to the welcome of the chief medical officer, Colonel (Dr) William D. Noble, the Indian Minister of Health, the Hon. Rajkumari Amrit Kaur, said: 'I welcome with a sincere heart all voluntary endeavour. You are people who give and want nothing in return.'

While these advances were being made in three separate continents, the successor to the sixth General was being publicly installed on Thursday, July 1, 1954, in a Westminster Central Hall crowded to capacity with Salvationists and well-wishers. No high-level administrative change was accomplished with less commotion and more general goodwill. The Revd Benson Perkins, Moderator of the Free Church Federal Council, wrote:

Had it been possible I would have been present at this great service of recognition . . . We are constantly mindful of the unique role of The Salvation Army throughout the world and its great ministry under the blessing of God to the cause of international unity, nor can we forget its direct service in calling on men and women of all races to accept the salvation which is in Christ Jesus.

Wrote the Bishop of Chichester, The Rt. Revd G. K. A. Bell:

My own contacts with The Salvation Army in my own diocese, and in the wider field of the World Council of Churches have been of the friendliest, and I am happy to think that, under General Kitching's leadership, these links in the chain of Christian unity will steadily be strengthened.

If this principal change was effected so smoothly, so were those which arose therefrom. Commissioner Joshua James

returned to London from the Australia Eastern Territory to
follow General Kitching as the British Commissioner. Commissioner Edgar Grinsted moved from Glasgow to fill the
vacancy in Sydney, and Lieut.-Commissioner Robert Hare-
wood was promoted to that rank to assume the leadership of
the Scotland and Ireland Territory. His place was taken by
Colonel William Davidson who had been training principal in
the Eastern Territory of the United States.

But there were other projects which were moving of their
own momentum – for instance, the Youth Charter which the
General, when British Commissioner, had set on its way
around the United Kingdom to mark 1954 as Youth Year.
Canada and South Africa had already devoted 1953 to this
end; East Africa, Finland, The Netherlands, South America
West and the USA Southern shared the British timing – which
can be used as an illustration of the general plan of campaign.

The Charter was launched on January 1, 1954, from the
Regent Hall at Oxford Circus, London, and then proceeded
along the south coast as far as Plymouth. After turning north
to Bristol and then crossing the Severn to Cardiff and Swansea,
the Charter traversed the Midlands before setting a course for
Scotland via Manchester, Liverpool, Preston and Carlisle.
Piped with due ceremony across the Border, the Charter took
the short route from Stranraer to Larne to reach Belfast. A
call on HMS *Anson* lying in the Clyde brought the Charter to
Glasgow and thence to the northernmost point of its travels at
Thurso. The way south was by the east coast route so that
when the historic Clapton Congress Hall was reached the
Charter had travelled 5,600 miles and more than 200 youth
rallies had hailed its offer of:

A FAITH – in the fatherhood of God creating a bond between all
men that knows no distinction.

A CAUSE – in fighting the evils that destroy mankind and so
forwarding the kingdom of God among men.

A LEADER – who is Christ, the only Saviour of mankind, who calls
us to accept even the demands of sacrifice in His
service.

On each occasion the challenge had been: 'Let this charter

for youth be yours and, by your dedication, let it become the charter for others.'

Before the General had been in office for six months a very different project was to bid for the support of the Salvation Army public – the appearance of *The Soldier's Armoury*. Thirty years later it is still going strong. The Founder had always desired that Salvationists should be 'a Bible loving, Bible reading people' and to this end had published *The Soldier's Guide* with 'the four gospels harmonised, the historical books condensed, and the portions of prophecy referring to particular nations omitted.' This provided consecutive scripture readings for each morning and evening, together with a daily bracket of Bible verses under the Bunyanesque title of 'Leaves from the tree of life for plucking in the dinner hour.' Later came The Sword and Shield Brigade with its annual Bible reading plan accompanied by a daily comment in *The Young Soldier* and an annual membership in Great Britain alone of over 30,000. Severe paper rationing during the Second World War put an end to this most commendable scheme, but in due course it provided the then Literary Secretary, Colonel Catherine Baird, with the opportunity for this new beginning – *The Soldier's Armoury*, a book of daily Bible readings with comments, appearing twice a year, running to approximately 150 pages, and selling at the almost unbelievable price of 1s. 4d. (old currency).

Now is as good a time as any to pay tribute to the several compilers who, over the years, entered into one another's labours. To write for heart and mind is as difficult a task as to love the Lord with heart and mind. On the one hand lies the bog of mushy religious jargon in which a writer can slowly but surely sink from sight. On the other lies the stony path of an arid intellectualism where mortal spirits tire and faint. Over the years the authors of the *Armoury* strayed neither to the right hand nor the left. Their work continues to inform and to bless, while its Salvationist flavour makes it a first choice for those who share its name.

Two further books of international interest can be mentioned at this point – the first by Raoul Gout and entitled *William Booth et le monde ouvrier*[3] (Editions Altis, Paris) was published in June 1955. Pastor Gout, a distinguished minister of the Reformed Church in France, displayed a personal interest in l'Armée du Salut by writing a trilogy planned to cover the Army's witness in France and Switzerland from the arrival of the Maréchale in Paris in 1881 to the promotion to Glory of Blanche Peyron in 1933. *William Booth et le monde ouvrier* provided the initial English background for the other two and was deservedly awarded the imprimatur of the National Centre of Scientific Research in Paris, for the author had a passion for original documentation. He believed that his sources should be pure and undefiled and manifold. The bibliography in this particular volume occupies fifteen pages of small print. One reviewer, versed in both French and English religious literature, commented on the apposite character of the dictum of Alexander Vinet quoted by Pastor Gout, that 'nothing is great, nothing is strong, save that which begins with humble folk.' So while the author gave pride of place to William and Catherine, he did not forget the part played by the multitude of 'little people' who helped to make the Army. Unfortunately the author was unable to complete *Les Temps Héroïques* (Army beginnings in France and Switzerland) which would have rounded off the trilogy, but in *Une Victorieuse* provided an unforgettable biography of the unforgettable Mrs Commissioner Peyron.

Equally well documented was volume three of *The History of The Salvation Army* by Colonel Robert Sandall, published by Thomas Nelson & Sons towards the end of the same year. This covered the world-wide range of the Army's social services from the initial efforts of Major James Barker to establish a rehabilitation service for ex-prisoners in Melbourne (Australia) in 1883, via the Criminal Law Amendment Act in Britain in 1885, and the publication of *In Darkest England and the Way Out* in 1890. This led to the spread of a variety of social services in every continent, culminating in the ending of French Guyana (popularly known as 'Devil's Island') as a penal settlement.[4] Variations of this kind of humane Christian action on behalf of the last, the least and the lost still continue without ceasing.

It could well be said that the Army retires its officers but continues its work, for while the General and his wife were preparing for their first transatlantic campaign, Commissioner John S. Bladin was concluding his active service as an officer which began in Australia in 1903. Commissioner William R.

Dalziel was also about to end his officership by relinquishing the territorial leadership of Canada and Bermuda. His place was taken by Commissioner W. Wycliffe Booth.

October 1954, also marked the twentieth anniversary of the commencement of the work in the Belgian Congo. With a credit of £100 at the Banque du Congo Belge, a former fish store boasting twenty hastily constructed backless benches capable of seating a congregation of 100, and a quarters rented for five years at the nominal figure of one franc a year, Adjutant and Mrs Henri L. Becquet 'opened fire' in Leopoldville (now Kinshasa).[5] Five years later there were thirteen corps and thirty-two outposts. Twenty years later the work north and south of the Congo – that is, in the Belgian Congo (now Zaire) and in French Equatorial Africa (now the Democratic Republic of the Congo) – could muster 25,000 soldiers, recruits and adherents. There were 7,000 boys and girls on the Army's day school rolls as well for, at this point in the history of both colonies, the education of children was under the direction of accredited Christian missions. As was rightly observed, by this time 'the work had stood the test of opposition and outlived the attraction of novelty.'

The remaining weeks of 1954 were given by General and Mrs Kitching to their intensive coast-to-coast campaign in North America which covered 32,000 miles and included eighty public meetings – not to mention a host of conferences and numerous conversations which served to introduce them to transatlantic ways in general and Salvation Army activities in particular.

This was a most timely visit. General Orsborn had confessed that though he had seen many individual drunkards set free from the chains of alcoholism by the power of God, 'never until I visited the USA had I seen this problem *en masse*, involving hundreds of human derelicts'.[6] The same could have been said by his successor as well. The social problems of no two countries are ever exactly the same – which is one reason why the Army's international leader has either to go see for himself, or else to send some responsible officer to see for him and then report back. Allied to this is the fact that the national reaction to such problems changes – sometimes visibly, sometimes imperceptibly – from decade to decade. Further, as no nation is completely homogenous, various community groups will have various ways of expressing even their common approval – let alone their disapproval.

The United States happens to provide a convenient first-hand illustration of this. *Guys and Dolls* had taken Broadway by storm. In a very different manner but with equal effect Damon Runyon and Sergeant Sarah Brown had captured New York in the fifties as George Bernard Shaw and *Major Barbara* captured London in 1905. What is of interest is that the musical and the play are still running. Were their subject matter dead their performance would no longer go marching on. But the final echoes of the applause in the Forty-Sixth Street theatre had hardly died away when President Dwight D. Eisenhower proclaimed November 28 to December 4, 1954, as the first national Salvation Army week. Source of jest or admiration, the Army could not be ignored.

This the new General recognised. He himself was neither unduly elated by praise nor cast down by ridicule. He had learned to treat those two impostors just the same since his boyhood when he had attended the Friern Barnet grammar school in his Salvation Army uniform. What concerned him was that friend and critic alike should be aware of the true order of Salvationist priorities. 'I found', he said to a *War Cry* interviewer on his return to London, 'a tendency here and there to think in terms of "soap, soup and salvation", and I did all I could to put that wording in the correct order with "salvation" in the first place.'

Apart from one campaign in West Africa, French Equatorial Africa and the Belgian Congo, the General spent the greater part of the following year in keeping these priorities in the right order at home and in Europe. For their public warfare he gave Salvationists in Europe a challenging slogan: 'One new face in every hall each week.' Behind the scenes consideration given to the long-delayed rebuilding of International Headquarters led to the appointment of Messrs. H. and H. M. Lidbetter as architects. This expert team of father and son had been responsible for a number of public buildings, including the Friends' meeting house in Euston Road, London, for which they were awarded the Bronze Medal of the Royal Institute of British Architects.

The year 1955 saw one other significant event – the centenary of the marriage of William Booth and Catherine Mumford on June 16, 1855, in the Stockwell Green Congregational Church, South London. This was marked by a commemorative issue of *The War Cry* as well as a meeting of thanksgiving led by the General in the church itself. Both events served to emphasise the lifelong character of Christian marriage – so ideally exemplified by the devotion of William and Catherine to one another and their joint dedication to the will of the Lord for their lives. In a symbolic acceptance of the principles of Christian marriage some fifty uniformed Salvationist couples occupied the Stockwell Green gallery, and the General announced that he had autographed 200 copies of the Founder's *Religion for Every Day* to be distributed among couples married under the Army tricolour. So the flag continued to be held high.

2 IN JOURNEYINGS OFTEN

For the Salvationist historian 1956 falls into three well-defined parts. From the end of January to the end of May General and Mrs Kitching were engaged in one of their lengthiest overseas campaigns. Ocean-going liners being still the vogue, they crossed both the Atlantic and the Pacific to reach New Zealand and Australia, and returned via Colombo and Suez. During this period the centenary of the birth of General Bramwell Booth was celebrated in Wellington (NZ) on Thursday, March 8, and by Salvationists at the international centre and else-where as well. From July 19 to August 1 the eyes of the Army world were turned to London where the first international corps cadet congress was held. On the last day of August of that same year two Salvation Army officers arrived in Port Moresby, Papua New Guinea, and cabled their territorial headquarters in Sydney that they had 'established a bridge-head'. This, said a fellow officer who was to spend the next eleven years pioneering on the island, was a claim 'based more on faith than fact . . . They had no house to live in, no hall to work from, no converts to follow them, and no clear blueprint of the direction they must take'.[1] But however inauspicious the beginning, the results were to prove encouragingly worthwhile.

The year had hardly begun when the Army suffered a loss which, if not to be reckoned in numbers, was of interna-tional consequence, for the influence of Bandmaster George Marshall, OF[2] who was promoted to Glory from his Tyneside home on January 14, 1956, had long been felt wherever the sound of an Army band was to be heard. As a lad George Marshall went from school to the mine and never knew the privilege of a formal education culminating in an academic degree, but music was in his heart and in his head. If, when working at the coal face, a line of melody occurred to him, he would chalk the notes on any piece of wood that lay handy or on the back of any miner's shovel that was lying around. His first vocal arrangement appeared in *The Musical Salvationist* for January 1912, and a few months later his first march, 'The Citadel' (Band Journal no. 655) was published. A heavy fall of coal threatened to bring this life of promise to an untimely end. The London specialist, summoned to examine the double fracture of the spine with other concurrent injuries, pronounced recovery impossible. The young miner might last a week or a month; it would be tempting providence to give him a year. But George Marshall lived for nearly thirty-eight years more, producing from his bed and his bath chair – his only means of locomotion – instrumental and vocal music which still demands to be played and sung. Wrote General Kitching in a personal tribute: 'While time lasts the name of Marshall will be associated with this period in our history because of his link with our music.'

It was fitting that on this campaign the General should enter Canada via the United States, for a new study of the work of the Army south of the forty-ninth parallel had just been written by the American author, Herbert A. Wisbey, and published by the Macmillan Company. Because the book comes from an independent source, noted one reviewer, it is not 'overprotective'. This was all to the good. As Cromwell told Lely to 'remark all the roughnesses, pimples, warts and everything as you see me,' so Wisbey did not gloss over the differences associated with the names of Thomas Moore (1884) and Ballington Booth (1896), but described their strengths and their weaknesses with sympathy and impartiality. Both these aspects of both these leaders have long been recognised and accepted. The official Year Book for 1957 – a quarter of a century ago now – had little quarrel with the Wisbey story.

Once in New York, where he was welcomed by the National Commander, Commissioner Donald McMillan, the General's main public engagement was the dedication of the seventeen-storey Ten Eyck-Troughton residence as a home for 330 business women – the latest link in the ever-lengthening chain of metropolitan services. Later that same week the General arrived in Toronto to declare open the new territorial head-quarters erected on the site of the former seventy-year-old Army property. The fourteen floors of the new building included the Bramwell Booth temple (seating 1,200) which the territorial commander, Commissioner W. Wycliffe Booth, announced was to be known by that name. The occasion was graced by the presence of the Governor General, the Rt. Hon. Vincent Massey, PC, CH, and it is noteworthy that the Minister for External Affairs, the Hon. Lester Pearson, should make the point that when on a recent visit to Calcutta he expressed a wish to meet all the Canadians resident in that city, half of those presented to him were officers of The Salvation Army. No limited horizons for them!

An unscheduled stop in Chicago to greet the women's social services superintendents gathered in council, was followed by a brief break in San Francisco. Here a whistle-stop meeting with the cadets of the USA Western Territory, followed by a public gathering, prefaced the 2,000-mile voyage on the *Orsova* to Honolulu. The liner docked in the early morning of Tuesday, February 21. A day's engagements followed, including the opening of a new home for girls, and by midnight the strains of 'Aloha' were rising from the quayside as the General and his wife bade farewell to the 400 Salvationists and friends with whom they had spent a crowded day.

Sailing into the Waitemata Harbour, Auckland, with the sunrise as a background, the *Orsova* was greeted by the flagship of the Royal Akanara yacht club, the Army colours at the masthead and Commissioner and Mrs Robert Hoggard, territorial leaders for New Zealand, on deck. There was no mistaking the warmth with which the General and his wife were greeted as they began their campaign in the Dominion. One representative officer was so carried away by the occasion that he concluded his speech of welcome with the white man's handshake and the Maori nose rub. Fortunately his address was limited to the General.

On the Saturday morning at Christchurch in the South Island where the welcome was equally unrestrained, the General made mention of his father's visit to the city thirty-six years previously. This was when, along with Commissioners Lamb and Lawley, he had accompanied General Bramwell Booth on his first visit to New Zealand. Members of a Salvationist family who were present on that occasion also shared in this. Nor was this the only reference to the Army's second General, for the following Thursday in Wellington included a remembrance of the centenary of his birthday in 1856. Even before leaving London the General had arranged that a simultaneous service of thanksgiving, led by the Chief of the Staff, should be held in the Regent Hall to which he had sent his own message of appreciation of the unique part played by the Founder's eldest son in the Army's development. The final Sunday's meetings were held in the Wellington Town Hall, after which the return journey to the international airport in Auckland was made by road so that the visitors could greet Salvationists on the way and also inspect the Epsom Lodge men's social service centre in course of erection. A further month of meetings in Australia lay ahead.

Sentries at the gates of Government House in Canberra saluted as General and Mrs Kitching were welcomed to the Australian federal capital by the Governor General, Field Marshal Sir William Slim, GCB, and Lady Slim. In the evening meeting which followed, the Prime Minister, Sir Robert Menzies, drew on his boyhood memories of the open-air witness of Salvationists on the streets of Ballarat to testify to the radiant optimism which had sustained the movement through fair weather and foul. Next day saw the Army leaders welcomed home to Melbourne by Commissioner Charles Durman, for memories were still fresh of the General's term of office as chief secretary in the Southern Territory from 1946 to 1948. 'Tonight', said Mrs Kitching, 'we are not among strangers; we have come home to friends.' As in previous years most of the public congress meetings were held in the exhibition building, but even that was taxed to capacity to hold the record attendances.

The following Sunday was Easter Day and was spent in Perth – though it is not to be supposed that from one weekend to the next was a time of idleness and ease. At each of the five congress centres two full weekdays were spent in council with officers who numbered – both active and retired – close on 2,000 in all. Nor are administrative problems ever far away and, should there be an unexpected unoccupied moment, there is usually some service club with a vacancy in its speakers' list. But such secular claims were not in the General's thoughts as he mounted the stage of His Majesty's Theatre with the salutation 'The Lord is risen', to which the congregation replied 'The Lord is risen indeed.' But the West Australian Salvationists were not satisfied – not even with a whole Sunday's meetings, for when the General threw out an invitation for all who would like to give their testimony to meet in the Perth Fortress the following morning at ten-thirty, more than ninety comrades responded. The meeting lasted seventy minutes; thirty-five testimonies were given; and a further Bible message from the General was heard with appreciation.

An overnight Viscount flight from Perth brought the visitors to a six o'clock welcome as the Thebarton band marched across the tarmac and sunrise broke over Mount Lofty. 'A most delightful experience', commented the General, alert as ever. As was the reception later that same morning hosted by the Lord Mayor of Adelaide in the Queen Adelaide room. As was the opening of the Linden Park senior citizens' residence, dedicated to the memory of the Australian pioneers John Gore and Edward Saunders, both of whose families were represented by Salvationist descendants on this occasion. And as was each of the weekend's meetings held in the Adelaide Congress Hall, the Pirie Street Methodist church and the Adelaide Town Hall respectively. John Gore had commented in his day that religion in Adelaide 'was so starchified'. It was undoubtedly less so after the 1956 congress.

Two more ports of call remained to be visited – Brisbane and Sydney, both in the Eastern Territory where Commissioner and Mrs Edgar Grinsted were in charge. Some onlooker might suppose that a succession of meetings, week after week, might be the most boring way of passing the time. But not so! No two meetings are alike. Each has its own unique nature – and this does not depend upon place or people, though these are contributory factors. But even in the same building and with congregations which outwardly appear very much alike, the end result can be very different – especially when a verdict is being asked of heart as well as mind.

Brisbane was different; the unforgiving tropical sunshine saw to that. The early Queensland Salvationists had known its power in their pioneering days. Their first meeting place was an iron-roofed shed which went by the nickname of 'Nebuchadnezzar's furnace'. With studied moderation *The War Cry* wrote of the congress weekend that 'overpowering heat made all activity an effort'. Nevertheless the outdoor and indoor programmes went ahead as planned, and 120 new soldiers were enrolled under the flag during the Sunday evening meeting in the city hall. Upwards of 200 seekers knelt at the mercy seat during the weekend.

Sydney – the last of the state capitals to be visited – is the largest city in the Commonwealth. Through its cosmopolitan streets flows the life of many nations, a life in which the Army shares. In a witty speech of welcome the Field Secretary, Lieut.-Colonel Hubert Scotney, described the territory as one 'containing just under a million square miles, nearly five million people and seventy million sheep, and whose most northerly corps were more remote from the territorial centre than was New Zealand from Botany Bay.' For the annual congress in such a territory a special building was required, so the manufacturers hall in the Sydney showground was hired, 5,000 seats were installed and an outsize platform was erected. 'This venture of faith was abundantly justified' reported *The War Cry* – nowhere more than in the glory which crowned the mercy seat. There was an unexpected bonus to follow. The return sailing of the liner *Neptunia* was delayed, so the international visitors were able to pay an unscheduled visit to the Arncliffe girls' home on the following Saturday and to the men's principal rehabilitation centre on the Sunday. The General's list of engagements was planned to continue without interruption on his return home. The long expected International Corps Cadet Congress was due to commence on Thursday, July 19, but to his great disappointment he had to enter hospital. He did not return to his office until the beginning of October, nor did he resume his public engagements until Thursday, October 18, when he led a day's devotional meetings in the Westminster Central Hall.

But the congress proceeded as planned. Delegates from the more distant points of the compass – New Zealand, Chile, Japan – were already on their way. Whether coming by plane or catching a bus each of the thousand corps cadets who were scheduled to be present knew what their thirteen-day programme contained. 'Saved, happy and free' was then a familiar phrase often on the lips of a lad or girl unexpectedly called upon to give his testimony. Each could be applied to the spirit of the delegates for each had made a profession of faith in Jesus as Saviour and Lord. Each was immensely 'chuffed' – to put it mildly – to be sharing in the congress. Each, lads and girls alike, was in full uniform – bonnet and all for the girls. This was accepted as a visible – and enviable – sign of the liberty to be found in the service of Christ. All that now remained was for the Chief of the Staff, Commissioner Edgar Dibden, to deputise for the General, which he did from start to finish.

By now the corps cadet movement was sixty years old. On April 25, 1896, *The War Cry* devoted the whole of its front page to the inauguration of a junior cadet brigade which would be composed of young people, the minimum age being twelve, 'who purposed to become officers as soon as age, health, experience and ability should render them eligible'. They would study the Bible, Christian doctrine and the principles and practices of The Salvation Army. William Booth reviewed a hundred of them at the Army exhibition which was held in the Royal Agricultural Hall in Islington during the following August. At the beginning of 1898, however, their title was changed to corps cadet, and Whitsuntide saw Bramwell Booth, then Chief of the Staff, leading the first camp for 250 of these bright spirits at Hadleigh. By 1956 there were more than 30,000 such young people, inspired by the fact that their present General and his wife, like their previous General and his wife, had each been a corps cadet.

At the welcome meeting the congress slogan was announced – 'For Christ and duty', coined by Corps Cadet Elaine Holman of Royal Oak, USA Central Territory, and selected from a multitude of submissions. Around the phrase Captain Brindley Boon wrote the congress song and, at the General's suggestion, Senior-Major Charles Skinner composed a march entitled 'The Corps Cadet' which was played by the International Staff Band. This embodied a song which had been a source of inspiration to the General when he himself was a corps cadet, and the refrain of which ran:

> Hear ye the battle cry! 'Forward' the call,
> See, see the faltering ones, backward they fall.
> Surely my Captain may depend on me
> Though but an armour bearer I may be.

For the first weekend the delegates to the congress campaigned at more than thirty different corps in London and the home counties. Three full weekdays were devoted to the development of the corps cadet's mind, heart and service respectively. Then there were rewards for work which the delegates had undertaken before coming to London. Quite a number had prepared a paper on 'The internationalism of The Salvation Army seen through the eyes of a corps cadet'. In the under-sixteen section the prize winners were (1st) Pamela Inwood, Sydney Congress Hall, Australia Eastern Territory; (2nd) Anna Dimitropulus, USA Eastern; (3rd) Bathal Devaiah, Madras and Telegu, India. In the over-sixteens the order was (1st) Helen Mackintosh, Tulsa Citadel, USA Southern; (2nd) Inez Martin, South America East; and (3rd) Adelheid Strub, Basle 1, Switzerland.

Saturday afternoon saw an act of witness in London's West End. Section after section marched past the saluting base in Park Lane where Mrs General Kitching stood with the Chief of the Staff and Mrs Commissioner Dibden. There was an inevitable clash of ideas between what the customary voices at Speaker's Corner had to say and the message which this army of young Salvationists, differing in race, language and colour, had to declare. With one heart and voice they said, and sang: 'Take Jesus to all the world, He'll put things right.'

Finally the second Sunday was spent in the company of young people from the British Territory who crowded the Royal Albert Hall for three meetings and then shared in the Sunday half-hour which was broadcast nationwide by the BBC. It might have been thought that any gathering subsequent to this would have been an anticlimax. Not at all! A Monday spent in outdoor fellowship at Sunbury Court but confirmed the ties of the previous week, and the farewell in the Clapton Congress Hall on the Tuesday allowed the delegates to express their thanks to God for the blessings of the congress. This had been planned, declared the Chief of the Staff, to benefit the individual corps cadet and to benefit the Army. Both aims had been achieved. Throughout the proceedings *The War Cry* had underscored the fact that this was the *first* international corps cadet congress. A new generation of corps cadets eagerly awaits the second.

Reference has already been made to the fact that on August 31 two Salvation Army officers arrived in Port Moresby to pioneer the work in Papua New Guinea. This was the culmination of a time of lengthy and sometimes hesitant consultation which dated back to before the outbreak of the Second World War. The veteran Australian leader, Commissioner James Hay, had long felt that the Army flag should be unfurled in what was then called British New Guinea. To this end Lieut.-Commissioner Wm. R. Dalziel (then territorial commander for the Australia Eastern Territory) personally visited Papua New Guinea and submitted a report to International Headquarters in August 1938. Two major difficulties stood in the way. One was the cost – and a proposal by Lieut.-Commissioner Dalziel that this should be shared was not acceptable to International Headquarters. The other was 'the spheres of influence' agreement. For some time Papua New Guinea had been one of the most heavily missionised countries in the world. Many of the Christian creeds spread all over the globe were here concentrated in a single area. The principal missions had divided the island between them and respected their self-imposed boundaries – though this was not true of the Roman Catholic church, the Seventh Day Adventists and Jehovah's Witnesses. However, with the Second World War in the offing the need for an immediate decision on this knotty point did not arise.

It was left to Commissioner Edgar Grinsted, who had been appointed to the Australia Eastern Territory in 1954, to revive interest in this possible development – which he did by sending Lieut.-Colonel Hubert Scotney and Senior-Captain George Carpenter on a detailed tour of enquiry. A report was submitted in November 1955, the tone of which was optimistic in spirit though guarded in detail. For a beginning a 'functional' approach was suggested – such as the opening of 'a reformatory (for indigenous delinquents) near Port Moresby and a tuberculosis hospital at Wewak . . . Following the establishments of these projects it was thought that welfare and spiritual work among the large number of detribalised natives in Port Moresby might be commenced.'

In the event this order was reversed. Second Lieutenant Ian Cutmore joined Senior-Major Keith Baker after an interval of ten weeks, and Mrs Baker arrived in the new year. The first Army meeting was held on Sunday, October 21, 1956, and the first convert was a teenage schoolboy who had left his coastal village to search for education in Port Moresby. Open-air work was begun in February 1957, and the first meeting for

Europeans was held in the following month – as was the initial meeting for the indigenous population living in Kaugere.

In the middle of May Commissioner Grinsted and Colonel Albert Simmonds (the territory's financial secretary) flew to Port Moresby to make an on-the-spot assessment of the current situation – but by mid-September the commissioner was back in London, having been recalled to take over the post of British Commissioner. He and his wife were succeeded by Commissioner and Mrs Frederick Coutts who arrived in Sydney at the beginning of September. However, the work in Papua New Guinea continued to grow. A home league (women's meeting) was begun in June. The first Army hall to be built was opened in Boroko in October, and as the months went by it became increasingly clear that the Army's march in this new field would be with steady pace. However if steady, certainly sure.

Firm guidelines were laid down to preserve good relationships with the existing missions. No mission-trained convert was to be pressurised into becoming a Salvationist, and any Papuan with a mission upbringing who professed conversion in an Army meeting was to attend the weekly instructional classes for three months before being considered for recruitship. If deemed satisfactory during this initial probation then, after a further three months' instruction, he could be considered for enrolment as a soldier. Where a bona fide mission member expressed a wish to become a Salvationist he was to remain on trial for the above two periods, meanwhile acquainting his family and (in writing) his pastor of his desire. Adherence to these procedures would obviate any charge of sheep stealing. Converts who came from, say, the labour line of men from the interior and who possibly had no knowledge whatever of the Bible or the Christian faith, might well need twelve months' instruction before acceptance as recruits.

At the end of August 1959 the place of Senior-Major Baker was taken by Major Albert Smith, MBE. By this time the native hostel and welfare centre at Koki was in operation, then the only institution of its kind on the island. The initial cost of £A41,000 was met by the administration. In addition to the regular programme of Sunday meetings, there had also been commenced senior and junior home leagues, a bi-weekly medical clinic, adult education classes on two evenings each week, as well as a primary school. A similar centre was on the drawing board for Lae. The mobile medical centre established at Kainantu on the high ground overlooking the Ramu river, and staffed by two qualified officer-nurses, was already serving up to thirty villages in the immediate neighbourhood and had undertaken the care of New Guinea infants in the malnutrition ward of the local hospital. The work was rooting itself in the spiritual and physical needs of the local situation.

3 THE GLORY OF THE LATTER HOUSE

This may be the point at which to recall the dictum that, next to 10 Downing Street, 101 Queen Victoria Street is one of the best-known addresses in London. Fair enough – for The Salvation Army and Queen Victoria Street have been associated since 1881. The movement's first offices were at 'The Eastern Star' – a one-time public house situated at 188 Whitechapel Road. This very down-to-earth setting was occupied from 1867 to 1870, after which a move was made to the People's Market at 272 Whitechapel Road.

One day in the summer of 1881 William Booth and his eldest son, Bramwell, were making their way from Blackfriars along the recently developed Queen Victoria Street when they espied a 'to let' notice on the opposite side of the road. At this point the principal historical authorities differ. 'Our new headquarters!' said the Founder – according to Colonel Edward Joy to whom Bramwell told the story. 'Our next headquarters!' exclaimed Bramwell according to Robert Sandall on page 207 of Volume II of the official Army history. Probably both minds were possessed with but a single thought as the two men crossed the road to catch a hurried glimpse of the see-through room which formed the principal accommodation of the vacant billiard saloon. To the Founder this was the promised land which he had been seeking and, after returning to Whitechapel Road for prayer with the staff, he made full speed for the office of one of his principal benefactors, Thomas Denny, who was persuaded to meet the cost of the first year's tenancy.

In due course International Headquarters outgrew '101' and swallowed up 97, 99, 103, 105, 107, 109 and 111. The consequent cluster of Salvation Army departments – including the national headquarters and what was then known as the fire insurance corporation on the northern side of Queen Victoria Street – brought the principal offices of the now world-encircling movement into one reasonably compact area – that is, until the fateful night of May 10/11, 1941, which saw the total collapse of the buildings on one side of the street and the destruction of the larger part of the property on the other.[1]

The initial enquiry into the rebuilding of the City of London was held in the Guildhall by order of the Minister of Town and Country Planning, and the Army's objection to the declaratory order seeking compulsory powers to acquire the movement's freehold sites in Queen Victoria Street was heard on February 5, 1948. The areas in question were nos. 101 to 109 inclusive, and the proposal most seriously in conflict with the Army's interest in these sites was described as 'the proposed paved pedestrian way' from St. Paul's to the river walk which cut across the traditional site of headquarters.

To spare the reader legal technicalities it is enough to say that agreement in broad principle seemed to be reached with encouraging speed. Mr Derek Walker Smith, the Army's solicitor, commended the past record and the present service of his clients to the Enquiry. He added that they would not wish to oppose the construction of any amenity – i.e. 'the proposed paved pedestrian way' – which the City might wish to sponsor, and general goodwill visibly overflowed when Professor Graham Holford, one of the assessors, murmured the phrase 'equivalent accommodation'.

Even with all this consideration haste was made but slowly. As General Kitching observed in his reminiscences, 'there were more than twelve different councils associated with the City of London and then the London County Council [which] had to sanction various proposals ... There were periods when even the authorities themselves were undecided about certain plans which they had in mind for the area in the city where we hoped to have our building.'[2]

This was no virgin soil in which it was desired to plant afresh the flag of The Salvation Army. At street level historical plaques testified to the conflicting claims of antiquity. To dig beneath the surface was to uncover the past as, in this instance, the former graveyard of the ancient church of St. Peter whose human remains dated back to the Great Fire of London and whose removal required both the assent of Parliament and the

consent of the Bishop of London. To look to the heavens above
was to learn that the skyline was in the care of the surveyor to
St. Paul's Cathedral. And was not St. Benet's, the work of
Christopher Wren himself, less than a stone's throw away?
The guidance of attendant angels – in the plural – was needed
at every step.

But a ball-by-ball description of the consequent negotiations
would only be wearisome. Sufficient to say that, in April 1955,
Messrs. H. and H. M. Lidbetter, FRIBA, were appointed
architects to the work of rebuilding. The bill for the temporary
diversion of Lambeth Hill, estimated to total some £38,000,
would be borne by the Army. The cost – in excess of £13,000
– of transferring some eighty coffins of relics from St. Peter's
churchyard to Manor Park Cemetery, E.7, was also met by
the Army. One major adjustment still needed attention. The
earliest plans for reconstruction provided for two separate
buildings – one on the right hand and the other on the left –
of the proposed St. Paul's Vista, each with its own entrance
on opposite sides, albeit as near to Queen Victoria Street as
possible. But, as General Kitching has disclosed in *A Goodly
Heritage*, the spectacle of a house visibly divided within itself
did not carry his judgment. Happily, his judgment carried the
day. Thanks to the agreement of the other parties, plus 'an
equity of exchange' of £87,000 paid by the Army to the City
of London, the final site was moved sufficiently to allow the
new headquarters to be built as a single unit east of the Vista,
leaving an uninterrupted view from the Thames to the dome
of St. Paul's.

Such progress enabled General Kitching to conduct an
open-air meeting of dedication during the evening of May 1,
1961 – the day on which the actual building operations were
scheduled to begin. Almost a year later, at eleven o'clock in
the morning of Saturday, April 28, 1962, the Lord Mayor of
London, Sir Frederick Hoare, and the General shared in the
stone-laying ceremony for the new '101'. Behind the stone laid
by the Lord Mayor was later deposited a canister containing
a tape of the day's proceedings, a portion of Roman piling
discovered during the excavation work, a copy of the report of
the Clerk of Works for week ending July 28, 1962, together
with a copy of the agent's report to the contractor dated August
2, 1962.

Behind the stone laid by the General was placed another canister containing a copy of his address delivered on this occasion, together with copies of the current issue of *The War Cry*, *The Young Soldier*, *The Musician*, *All the World*, *The Deliverer*, *Vanguard*, *The Salvation Army Year Book* for 1962, *The Song Book of The Salvation Army*, a copy of the current balance sheet and statements of account for the social services in the United Kingdom, as well as the ninety-fifth balance sheet and statements of account of the Army's central funds. The shape of things to come was now growing plainer, though the actual opening of the new building did not take place until ten days before the General's retirement from active service.

Meanwhile, by one of those uncovenanted mercies of the calendar, 1957 also marked the fiftieth anniversary of the Home League.

Sporadic efforts had been made to hold women's meetings at various stations during the early days of the Christian Mission. Later, during the winter of 1902/3, Major and Mrs Harvey Banks had attempted to form a women's auxiliary at their corps at Fenelon Falls in Ontario, Canada. A similar kind of gathering had been commenced in 1904 by Mrs Lieut.-Colonel Jolliffe at East Finchley in North London. But no comprehensive plan to meet women's needs in the world-wide Army had been made until Mrs Bramwell Booth unburdened her heart on the matter to the Founder early in 1907. 'I see wonderful possibilities,' he replied. 'Go ahead, my child; you have my blessing.'

Mrs Booth needed no second bidding. What she had in mind was not simply a weekday gospel meeting at an hour convenient for housewives, but a comprehensive programme which, while giving pride of place to the Christian faith, would provide education in family living, fellowship for the aged and lonely, and an opportunity of serving the needy. She formally launched the new enterprise at Cambridge Heath (East London) on Monday afternoon, January 28, and Mrs Colonel Higgins formed the first local branch of the Home League at Leytonstone, her home corps. Only sixteen women, mostly elderly, attended the initial meeting, but within four years the membership had reached 400, while similar branches had been inaugurated at such widely separated points in the country as St. Peter Port (Guernsey) and Irvine (Strathclyde). It was not long before the Home League was at work in Australia (1911), Canada (1914), United States and Norway (1915), New Zealand (1916) – until by the jubilee in 1957 the world membership was 277,000.

The congress motto provided by Mrs Edith Coxhead (then of Chelmsford, now of Hadleigh) was: 'Christ in the home in every land.' A fifteen-day conference at Sunbury Court was presided over by Mrs General Kitching and was attended by delegates from twenty-one territories. The sessions were addressed on matters of religious and social concern by various authorities ranging from the internationally known Hugh Redwood to the future President of the Royal College of Midwives, Colonel Ruth Foxton.

The high point of the congress was the Jubilee Rally on Thursday, June 6, in the Royal Albert Hall, graced by the presence of Her Majesty Queen Elizabeth, the Queen Mother. The greetings of selected delegates in national costume were climaxed by the presentation of a silver model of the home league emblem, the house upon the Bible, by Mrs Brigadier Evangeline Cooper who said: 'We believe that the home built upon Bible truths is a happy home, where children may become good citizens and parents receive wisdom for their tasks. Here is the symbol of our faith which we would ask Your Majesty to accept.'

The same evening the Royal Albert Hall was again crowded to capacity when the General presented the manifesto which had been signed by delegates representing the five continents – Mrs Lieut.-Colonel Sanjivi (Asia), Mrs Lieut.-Colonel Grace (America), Mrs Brigadier Labinjo (Africa), Brigadier Annie Stevens (Australia), Brigadier Mrs Mawby (Europe) and Mrs General Kitching as world president. *The War Cry* for June 22, 1957, reported that the statement concluded:

Above all, knowing that unless the individual heart is changed no part of society can be cleansed, we are determined by the grace of God to exercise every power . . . to preach 'Christ in the home in every land'.

The sincerity of this declaration was to be seen in the very practical form of caring expressed in what continues to be called the 'Helping Hands' programme. The idea dates back to the two World Wars when members of women's organisations did such knitting as they could when they could and where they could for members of the forces. The stories, gay and grave, to which this practice gave rise are legion but, when hostilities were over, the National Home League Secretary for the British Territory, then Lieut.-Colonel Olive Booth, felt that it would be an unnecessary loss to allow such a head of steam to be wasted. Remembering that her father, General Bramwell, had spoken of 'the Army of the helping hand', she suggested that such activities should be continued under that name.

The seed fell on good ground. For example, Mrs General Kitching appealed for an international 'Mother and Baby' chest – and over 5,000 articles were received at International Headquarters for the benefit of the needy in the Third World. At other times a personal link would release a flow of generosity. Home leagues in Scotland sent a gift of dental equipment to a Scottish missionary serving in the Lushai Hills (a remote corner of north-eastern India). Australian women bought a horse for an Australian woman officer in need of transport suited to one of the more trackless parts of Haiti. Home leaguers in the United States provided 3,000 song books for women's meetings in Pakistan, and a similar quantity for Army work in southern India. An organ was sent to West Africa; money to Chile to help provide a refrigerator and washing machine; hospital linen and bandages were dispatched to Rhodesia. Women in Manchester sent a variety of items valued at £100 to the institute for the blind at Thika in Kenya. A Scottish division provided a cottage tent for evangelical work in Zululand and another home league in the United States bought six boats for similar work on the waterways of south India. An address by a hospital doctor on homeland furlough led to the equipping of a tuberculosis ward in the hospital of Chikankata, and twenty-four giant packages of transfers, each containing 100 designs, were sent to women's groups in the Central Celebes. 'Helping Hands' continue to help to this day – and there is no sign of them growing weary in well doing.

On June 10, 1957, within three days of the conclusion of the Home League Jubilee Congress, Mrs General Bramwell Booth was promoted to Glory. In one sense the congress was a fitting swan song to her life's work for, as mentioned earlier in this chapter, she was its principal begetter.

Next to William and Catherine Booth and the elder members of their family, Florence Eleanor Soper knew more about the basic aims of the Army, and the opposition which these provoked, than most. Some time in 1880 she heard Mrs Catherine Booth speak at one of her West End meetings and, in the quiet of her own room, later committed her young life to Christ. Having become a commissioned officer while still a teenager she faced the ridicule of the Paris boulevards in the company of her future sister-in-law, the *Maréchale*. What could have been harder to take was the avowed hostility of her parents to any thought of her marrying Bramwell Booth. Nevertheless Captain Soper had a will of her own, and the wedding took place in the Clapton Congress Hall on Thursday, October 12, 1882, and the bride was given away by her father.

With that happy improvisation which was so often a feature of early-day salvationism the young bride was sent to help at the newly opened Hanbury Street shelter for women. 'See what she can do in her spare time', said her father-in-law to his eldest son. In the event she did so well that she was given the rank of commissioner in 1888 and remained in charge of the women's social services in the United Kingdom until her husband became the General in 1912.

'Motherhood and family life were among her chief concerns', said *The Times* obituary on June 11, 1957. 'The home league was her idea . . . Firm in her opinions, she was receptive to new ideas. She worked enthusiastically for women's emancipation though she was not altogether complacent afterward about its fruits . . . Her two sons and five daughters all grew up to service in The Salvation Army.'

Before marriage, before Bramwell had even met his wife-to-be, he had prayed: 'O Lord, give me the companion who will best help me to do Thy will and Thy work.' His beloved F.E.B. was God's answer to his prayer and, though widowed for so many years, she always remained faithful to that early conviction which led her to become a Salvationist. It was profoundly symbolic that, even as her coffin was being carried at her funeral along one aisle out of the Clapton Congress

Hall, a seeker should be moving purposefully toward the mercy seat along the other. In death, as in life, her dedication was being honoured by its continuing fulfilment.

4 FRUIT THAT REMAINS

Salvation Army officers will sometimes describe themselves as expendable – that is to say, what they do is more important than who they are. This is one reason why it is possible to make such changes in stationing as the demands of the work may require. The causes of some of these changes cannot always be anticipated, nor are they at all times deliberately planned. Promotions to Glory provide one illustration of this. The passage of time is another. Early-day officers regarded themselves as pledged to fight and die in the ranks of the Army. Most often the spirit was entirely willing. That was beyond question. It was the flesh that was weak – and consequently replacements there had to be. At other times differences of judgment required to be taken into account, and one of the several variations on this theme led to the retirement of Commissioner and Mrs Edgar Dibden at the end of September 1957, with the consequent appointment of Commissioner William Dray as the Chief of the Staff who, with Mrs Commissioner Dray was publicly welcomed to International Headquarters during the afternoon session of the 'Day with God' which was held at the Westminster Central Hall on Tuesday, October 8.

Coincidental were the appointments of Commissioner Edgar Grinsted, with Mrs Grinsted, to the leadership of the British Territory; of Commissioner Holland French, with Mrs French, to that of the USA Eastern; and of Commissioner Frederick Coutts, with Mrs Coutts, to that of Australia Eastern. Lieut.-Commissioner Samuel Hepburn, with Mrs Hepburn, took charge of the USA Western Territory, Lieut.-Commissioner William Davidson, with Mrs Davidson, of the USA Southern, Lieut.-Commissioner Ragnar Åhlberg, of The Netherlands, Lieut.-Commissioner Kaare Westergaard, with Mrs Westergaard, was appointed Principal of the International

(William Booth Memorial) Training College, and Lieut.-Commissioner Reginald Woods, with Mrs Woods, was posted to International Headquarters as Literary Secretary to the General. In this same year Commissioner and Mrs William Grottick were appointed to take charge of the Army's work in South Africa, Lieut.-Commissioner Gwen Taylor in Pakistan, Colonel and Mrs William Leed in Scotland and Ireland, Colonel and Mrs Erik Wickberg in Germany, Colonel and Mrs Aage Rønager in Finland, Colonel and Mrs Frederick Harvey in Korea, Colonel and Mrs Carl Richards in Rhodesia, Lieut.-Colonel and Mrs Gilbert Abadie in Brazil and Lieut.-Colonel and Mrs John Stobart in Sri Lanka.

Yet despite these unavoidable administrative changes the work of the Army in its amazing variety continued without intermission in each of the world's four corners. For example, on March 27, 1957, at the Howard Institute in what was then Southern Rhodesia, the Prime Minister – the Hon. R. S. Garfield Todd, MP – opened the new teacher training section in the presence of the territorial commander, Colonel Victor Thompson, and the principal, Brigadier Philip Rive, BA. The Prime Minister referred in the warmest terms to the generous gift of £10,000 from the Beit Trustees, and to another of £3,000 from the Central Territory of the United States.

> But [he continued] I also thank the people who have come from other countries and brought their own personal services to Southern Rhodesia. I am quite sure that those Africans who have been through mission schools – and that is practically 100 per cent of those who have received education – will not be forgetful of the service given by the men and women who, as far as money is concerned, could have done much better for themselves. But they have had other rewards in happiness for the service which they have given to the African people and to their Lord and Saviour, Jesus Christ.

Such remarks were most timely because among those present on this occasion were Brigadier Doris Dolman, the first officer-teacher to be appointed to Rhodesia in 1931, and who was followed by Major Margretta Nelson (later Mrs Brigadier Rive) in 1932.

Later in that same year away to the north, at the school for the blind in Kenya, Brigadier and Mrs Edward Osborne were saying goodbye as Mr W. J. Wadley, Director of Education in the Kenya government, was present to acknowledge the dedicated service of the Principal and his wife. The Director recalled that when he first visited the school in 1941 it was 'a rather small and dismal sort of place with about fifteen pupils of all ages'. Now, as 1957 came to an end, there were 150 pupils, boys and girls, of normal school age, the whole establishment running on academic lines and incorporated into the colony's educational system. A number of the principal business firms in Kenya were now accepting boys from Thika into their regular employment, and the remarkable fact was that not a single failure had been reported. The Director considered that the government's generous grants to the school was money well spent and, while it was proposed to extend the work of training for the blind to other parts of the country, the Salvation Army school for the blind, with its highly trained staff and fine record of work, would remain the principal centre to which the government would look – particularly for the training of teachers.

If the reader is still interested in education he can put on his seven-league boots and stride northward to Dalarö on the shores of the Baltic, about an hour's bus journey from Stockholm where, as Brigadier Osborne was concluding his service at Thika, the then Captain Karin Hartman, BA, was commencing her duties as headmistress of the Army's *folkhög-skola* or people's high school.

Adult education is an established feature of community life in Scandinavia and originated in the fertile mind of N. F. S. Grundtvig, the nineteenth-century Danish churchman and author. The first *folkhögskola* was established in 1844 in a cottage at Rødding in the south of Denmark, and in 1868 three similar schools were opened in Sweden. Initially they provided tuition for young people who had already started to work but who still wanted to matriculate so that in adult life they could serve in one or other of the professions. In addition to the basic subjects in the normal curriculum the folk school paid special attention to those spiritual and cultural values which form an integral part of the Christian faith – a fact which the churches in Scandinavia were not slow to recognise.

The value of a folk high school to so basic an evangelical body as The Salvation Army began to be canvassed seriously soon after the end of the Second World War. A six months' 'folk high school' course was mooted as far back as the spring of 1949, but the proposal fell by the wayside because of the lack of suitable accommodation. However, the leaven of this new idea was slowly but surely at work for in June 1952, the territorial commander for Sweden, Commissioner Tobias Ögrim, asked the education secretary, Lieut.-Colonel Gunnar Bolander, to chair a selected group who would research the feasibility of a Salvation Army folk high school. Immediate results were not forthcoming, but in due course members of the state Board of Education expressed their willingness favourably to consider any Salvation Army proposal which was supported by suitable accommodation.

In the early spring of 1957 a dream site was discovered at Dalarö on the shores of the Baltic Sea some thirty miles south of Stockholm. By September of that year the property had been bought – grounds, library, residential facilities, interior decor enhanced by original work by Swedish artists, complete with a view of the Jungfrufjarden (the Virgin Bay), the island of Genbote, the guardian lighthouses, plus the spacious lawns and tall trees thrown in for good measure. To crown all, a generous Swedish government met seventy-five per cent of the capital cost.

As these lines are being written the Dalarö *folkhögskola* is celebrating the twenty-fifth anniversary of its opening by Count Carl Bernadotte of Wisborg, accompanied by the Countess Maria, who declared the occasion to be 'an important milestone in the history of The Salvation Army'. Commissioner Robert Hoggard, the territorial commander, expressed the hope that the school 'would give a holy vision to the young people' who studied within its walls. Lieut.-Colonel Karin Hartman, MA, who was *rektor* from 1958 to 1966, declared her faith that the school, with its free forms of teaching, would exercise a profoundly Christian influence upon those who enrolled in its classes. Courses in youth leadership training would be offered. The school would provide a link with the officer training college, and would present soldiership in The Salvation Army as a means of furthering the work of the Kingdom of God.

Lieut.-Colonel Hartman was followed as *rektor* by Sven Wickberg (eldest son of the Army's ninth General) and he was succeeded in that office in 1976 by Anders Östman – another ardent Salvationist.

Pioneering work was also being undertaken in the realm of social endeavour. The end of the Second World War had released a flood of concern about the number of mothers in the United Kingdom charged before the courts with child neglect. The figure totalled about a thousand a year – approximately half being given a custodial sentence and the other half fined. Neither procedure was of overmuch help to the unfortunate mother involved so that when 'Abbotsford' – a woman's social centre in Plymouth – was released from wartime demands, the Home Office asked The Salvation Army to undertake the work of training neglectful mothers. The new name for this home – 'Mayflower' – was a stroke of imagination, for this was to be for many a despairing mother a voyage to a new world of family accomplishment.

The causes of neglect were manifold. Some of the mothers suffered from personality limitations, accentuated by what can only be labelled as ignorance. Some had married while yet unprepared for marriage. Others had too many babies too quickly, and each pregnancy made them less able to cope with the next. But mothers at the 'Mayflower' could have their children under five with them while receiving basic training in home management and child care.

If case histories are required, case histories can be given. Mrs K. was overburdened by the demands of a large family of small children. Her hair was lank, her shoulders sagged, her feet dragged, her whole manner was apathetic. The two little boys whom she brought with her were pale and listless. But after some weeks in the 'Mayflower' she was a changed woman. Her eyes shone, her hair was her pride, there was a spring in her step and a lilt in her speech. Sitting by the nursery fire one evening, giving her new baby his last feed for the day, she said: 'I am praying for the children now, and I know that God will hear my prayer.'

Mrs A.'s house was stated to be 'in an indescribable state of filth'. Her three little children were poorly and backward. The baby of two could neither stand nor walk nor had she any teeth. For some weeks she screamed for long periods on end but, in due course, like any other child, she responded to normal happy nursery routine, cut six teeth, learned to walk and became bonny and playful. Mrs A. returned to her home and was later visited by one of the 'Mayflower' staff. The two elder children were playing in the garden; the baby was enjoying her afternoon nap. Everywhere was clean and tea was served with real pride. The mother's sense of achievement was evident.

The key to the cure could be described as caring commonsense. The period of residence was usually three months. Incidentally it was the customary length of the sentence imposed when a mother was sent to prison. More importantly it was the minimum time required for the rehabilitation of the mother which began on the day of arrival, often with the provision of a new outfit of clothing – a real morale booster to any woman long accustomed to rely on jumble sales. The mother slept with her children in a family unit and had her meals with them as well – save where some of the smaller ones might need to have them in the nursery so that they could learn to eat properly. Every effort was made to keep the family in touch with one another, and there was a family room where husband and wife could spend the weekend together. The day was planned so as to provide each mother with a workable routine which she could follow at home. Cookery instruction dealt with basic foods, economically priced. No cooking appliances or cleaning materials were used other than those normally available. Practice was given in make-do and mend. A local health visitor called weekly, held classes in baby care, and provided guidance in family planning. The first mother was welcomed in March 1948. The sixth report from the children's department said:

> The health and social behaviour of the mothers and children at 'Mayflower' continue to show a marked improvement. Not the renting of a house but the making of a home is the chief end of the curriculum. Training is simple, informal and practical, and includes teaching in child care, household management, cooking, sewing and shopping . . . If the husband is at home preparations are made for the return of his wife and children such as having the house cleaned . . . The results of this training are most encouraging.[1]

The sequel was that a second 'Mayflower' was opened in Belfast in the summer of 1957 by Lord Wakehurst, KCMG,

Governor of Northern Ireland. Here the chairperson of the council of social service, Mrs J. W. Houghton, repeated the story of pitiful human need. The courts had no option but to fine or imprison the delinquent mother. A fine often meant that the family slipped further into debt. A prison sentence did nothing to teach her how better to manage her home. As before the second 'Mayflower' took care of the mother and her children under five for a minimum period of three months, which allowed for refresher courses in child care, domestic hygiene, family budgeting, children's dressmaking and the innumerable practical details which make for happy families. No one should think that because all this takes place in a Christian context the atmosphere must therefore be incredibly stuffy. In point of fact it is delightfully happy – full of unexpected surprises for dad, and grandma, and auntie, and any of the neighbours who meet the reunited family when its members return home once more.

Another realm where the work of pioneering is never done is in the fight against the enemy of the human race known as alcoholism. In this the Army has been engaged from its earliest days and yet, because of the highly developed commercial skills which are harnessed to the sale of alcohol, there is a constant need of new approaches both in the field of prevention as well as that of cure. Every land, save those where by law the sale of liquor is forbidden, is under the shadow of this curse, but the techniques of modern medicine together with the power of the Christian gospel, have now become formidable allies in this good fight.

Sweden provides an example of this. In 1911 the island of Kurön was offered to The Salvation Army at the knockdown price of 55,000 Swedish krōner – at that time the equivalent of about £3,000 sterling. The site then boasted little other than a solitary fisherman's cottage but the chief secretary of the Army in Sweden, Colonel Karl Larsson, saw its possibilities as a centre for the treatment of alcoholics, and to this end it was dedicated by Commissioner Johan Ögrim, the then territorial commander. At the start a quarter of the patients were directed to Kurön by the courts; the other three-fourths attended voluntarily. The average length of stay was three months, though some stayed for a year. Some, knowing when they were on to a good thing, would have been willing to stay put for the rest of their lives, did the rules of the colony allow this.

What is most encouraging is that an analysis of results over a number of years shows that forty per cent of the patients who come to Kurön are cured. As the work still continues there are more recent statistics on which to draw and, in all probability, to base variations in the success or failure rate. Every man is a study in himself. To adapt Francis Thompson slightly: 'There is no expeditious road to save men by the barrel load.' To the statistical mind the percentage quoted above might indicate failure rather than success – but not to the one who, like his Master, rejoices over the one sinner who repents rather than the many who feel no need to do so.

The new world has been as concerned as the old about the blight of alcoholism. In 1906 the New Zealand government passed the Habitual Drunkards Act which gave to magistrates the authority to declare certain persons as 'habitual drunkards' and to confine them to institutions suitable for their reception. The absence of any such institutions when this act was passed was remedied when, at the request of the government, the Army opened a home for alcoholics on Pakatoa Island. As a result of further legislation a second home was opened in 1910 on Rotoroa to which men addicts were transferred while women were housed on Pakatoa.[2]

It is not possible to pass any final judgment at the moment upon the care of the alcoholic in New Zealand because this redemptive work is continuing to take on a whole new dimension. Any initial treatment of the alcoholic had been little more than elementary. Plain living, outdoor employment – preferably to do with agriculture – allied to strong religious influences, were regarded – and rightly so – as basic elements in any cure. But a happy turn of the wheel brought Commissioner Robert Hoggard, who had served in North America where he had gained a working knowledge of the developing approaches to this problem, to the leadership of the Army in the Dominion. During his term of office from 1950 to 1956, and thereafter, existing properties and equipment were upgraded. Then followed the inspired appointment – inspired so far as the treatment of the alcoholic was concerned – of Colonel (Dr) Bramwell Cook as chief secretary. As one of the founders of the national society of alcoholism, and a member of the government co-ordinating committee on the subject, it did not take him and his colleagues long to demonstrate that they were aware of the extent of this problem and how best it could be met. The nationwide 'Bridge' programme gave proof of this, and the following sentences, though not actually in print for another decade, set out the rationale of the Army's approach.

> We welcome all that scientific research has contributed to the understanding and rehabilitation of the alcoholic. Our programme needs the services of doctors, psychologists, and social workers, and welcomes the successes obtained by various approaches used by other organisations. It would, however, be denying our experience, and therefore be unscientific, if we failed to give a distinctive witness to the power of God to transform people's lives – and this includes the alcoholic.

Much the same could be said about the efforts of the Army to rehabilitate the alcoholic in the United States – save that here the problem is magnified by a population approximately seventy times that of New Zealand and affects a third of all American families.[3] In common with his comrades elsewhere the Salvationist in the United States saw the down-and-outs and the self-defeated not as those who could be passed by on the other side but as human beings whose wounds should be generously anointed with oil and wine – in modern parlance, who should be helped by every spiritual grace and medical technique available. This was the premiss on which William Booth wrote his *In Darkest England and the Way Out* – a seminal production which E. H. McKinley has described as 'the major turning-point in the development of an Army social programme in the United States'.[4]

The Army's initial 'cheap food and shelter depot' opened at the corner of Bedford and Downing Streets in New York on December 23, 1891. By the turn of the century there were more than five thousand beds available for transients in the United States. The day was to come when prohibition left them almost empty – though with that development the Army's leaders had no quarrel. In 1931 Commander Evangeline Booth publicly praised the Republican Hoover for his stand against 'the forces of organised disorder who were agitating for the repeal of the 18th amendment'. But it was not long before the Commander was commending the Democratic Convention to God in prayer, for the people of America were feeling the icy chill of the great depression which filled the Army's social service centres once more to overflowing while simultaneously cutting off the supply of dollars and dimes needed to keep their doors open. Yet again it was not very long before the Second World War provided another kind of tragic work for idle hands to do, so that few but the old and infirm were left in the Army's care. The welcome return to peace conditions enabled the officers engaged in the social services to take a long hard look at the reasons for what they did and the ends which they had in mind. The result was the revitalised 'Service to Man' programme which has ever since continued to bear fruit in its season.

No single illustration fills this time slot adequately but a page from the history of the giant harbour light complex at Cleveland, Ohio, is as helpful as any. As a captain the youthful Edward Dimond was already tirelessly experimenting to discover the most effective programme for the rehabilitation of the alcoholic. While the principles of Christian grace and truth were the bedrock of all such recovery, it was understandably assumed in Salvation Army circles that music could also play a helpful part. Yet the traditional Salvation Army brass band had been repeatedly tried but had repeatedly failed. So sights were adjusted to use such players as were available on the instruments which they themselves favoured. A harmonica trio provided a modest beginning – with percussion, string and reed being added as time went on. Music lessons were provided for learners through the kindness of the staff of a local music school. The Salvationist composer, Emil Söderström, gladly lent his skills and contributed a number of his own arrangements to the harbour light music library.

With what result? it may justifiably be asked. Of course, everyone who seeks to help the alcoholic must be dedicated to failure. Most of those who find their way inside an adult rehabilitation centre have already been written off at most previous levels as hopeless, so that the staff are not overwhelmed in a slough of despond when they have to acknowledge that on an average three out of every five entrants leave within thirty days – still drinking. These centres are not – and never have been – penal establishments. Men can come and go as they please. Of this particular period and at this place the men who do stay for a year may possibly achieve a second year of sobriety. Over the same period in the sixties this centre gained forty-eight soldiers – and yet their case histories included the story of John who was first admitted to the centre in 1961, was readmitted on nine subsequent occasions but was discharged for drinking on a further nine occasions and, when his file was about to be closed, was again on another extended drinking bout. His average stay in the centre was two months; his longest four and a half months. While in care he bore a good witness and was able to be of help to some of the other men. The truth to which his story testifies is that at no point, drunk or sober, should any man be finally written off. The Salvationist who shares the tormented struggles of the compulsive drinker learns what Julian of Norwich meant when she said: 'The Lord looks upon His servants with pity and not with blame.' This He does – no matter where the disadvantaged are to be found nor what their race, let one more real life story witness – this time from the Republic of South Africa.

The young white husband had fallen in with his young wife's suggestion that he should not take the road to Fish Hoek by way of Newlands but go by the Marine Drive. How was she to know that his desire to please her would lead to the death of their young son? A sports car rounding a bend at too high a speed caused the family jalopy to hit the rock face – hard. From that moment the boy was beyond medical help. To the distraught driver brandy was a help, or so it seemed for a time – but then it became an obsession. Friendly relatives pled his cause with his firm – but then authority stepped in. Happily mercy seasoned justice, for a compassionate magistrate sentenced the dejected man before him to twelve months at Mulders Vlei – The Salvation Army's 'certified retreat for the rehabilitation of alcoholics', an 800-acre farm some twenty-six miles out of Cape Town.

'Near to nature, near to grace' runs the old saw. Well, at any rate, nearer. Martin found himself sharing life with about eighty other men to most of whom the environment was wholly new. But work among the fruit trees or root crops, tending the cattle, sheep or poultry, helped bodies long weakened by alcohol to grow stronger. Good food, medical care, regular work and Christian grace all played their part in making new men out of what had been drunken failures. Martin was surprised that nowhere was there a lock or a bolt to prevent him absconding. He was still more surprised that he did not want to abscond. At least he had wit enough to recognise what was good for him – and after nine months he was released on license.

His could be called a success story. Not all are such. Slightly less than half the men who enter Mulders Vlei make the grade. But that less than half means happiness for more than half. A frayed marriage is mended. That counts for two. A broken family is reunited. That could count for three or four – or even five. And, as the Saviour of sinners said to His followers: this is fruit that remains. One of General Bramwell Booth's memorable aphorisms was: 'One sinner saved by grace will outlast the British Empire.' The saying may be dated but the truth is eternal.

5 BY MANY OR BY FEW

The continuing leadership of General and Mrs Kitching displayed two complementary aspects of the ongoing work of The Salvation Army. There was the long-standing capacity of the movement for concerted activity – witness the international congress shared by corps cadets from all five continents in 1956 and by the home leagues of the world in 1957. This was followed by the British congress in June 1960, which consisted of twenty days of public gatherings, street marches, music festivals, drama nights, social displays, and a field day at the Alexandra Palace thrown in for good measure. Not that this was an instance of the Army in the land of its birth going it alone. Welcome visitors to the country for fourteen days were the New York staff band (leader: Colonel William Maltby, bandmaster: Major Richard Holz), and for ten days the Huskvarna (Sweden) young people's band which headed the march past on the national youth day.

For Salvationists the undoubted crowd-puller was the bandmasters' councils festival in the Royal Albert Hall where the New York staff band joined forces with the corps bands from Kettering and Sunderland Millfield, and the International Staff Band contributed the first public presentation of Eric Ball's 'A Song of Courage'. But no less well attended was the holiness meeting in the Westminster Central Hall which marked the centenary of the birth of Samuel Logan Brengle and which, in a variety of ways and according to the stance of the speaker, spelt out the meaning of the experience which the commissioner promoted by the kind of man he was as well as by what he had to say.

Completely different again was the open-air rally at the site of the former Quaker burial ground in Vallance Park Road where, in July 1865, William Booth held his first London meetings in a nondescript tent which, by the end of August, came to the end of its useful life and cost ten shillings to be carted away. Commissioner Catherine Bramwell-Booth (R), the guest speaker, praised the choice of a sundial for the memorial to her grandfather for he was constantly reminding his hearers that, in the language of the anonymous hymn writer, 'time is earnest, passing by'. 'Behold, now is the accepted time . . . now is the day of salvation.'

The scene which followed could have been a flashback to any evening open-air meeting in the high summer of 1865. A drunken man shouted: 'There is no God.' A Salvationist who was attempting to counsel another young man had to turn disappointedly away. However, a third man, who proved to be a backslider, pushed his way to the improvised mercy seat, followed by an urchin who enquired whether he could kneel there as well, after which a uniformed lassie Salvationist stepped forward in an act of reconsecration. The Founder would have felt that these were the best of all tributes to his life's passion – better even than the presence of the casket containing the certificate granting him the freedom of the city of London fifty-five years earlier, which was given a place of honour at the reception in the Guildhall hosted by the Lord Mayor, Sir Edmund Stockdale.

What late lie-abeds said when they were roused from their Sunday morning slumbers by the twenty-five bands which provided music for the 2,500 Salvationists marching from their assembly point in Hyde Park along Kensington Gore Road to the Royal Albert Hall for a day's meetings is not recorded – but they were given ample time for reflection, for the procession took forty minutes to pass the saluting base. But the three meetings which followed gave abundant opportunity for spiritual decisions as well, of which more than two hundred seekers took advantage.

One caveat is necessary. While there were telling events which, like this one, were organised to the last button – for the biblical poem of creation makes it clear that the Lord delighteth not in chaos – from the beginning of the Army's history there have been other good works which have been the fruit of individual effort. Instances abound – though to quote a few is to leave out many, such as those of Dudley Gardiner in Calcutta, Jim Crocker at Broken Hill and Eva Dunlap at Barberton (Ohio). But here are three examples which date

from this period – Georgette Gogibus (France), Baldassare
Vinti (Italy) and Alida Bosshardt (The Netherlands).

Georgette Gogibus, a single woman French officer, was
admitted to the Order of the Founder by General Wilfred
Kitching at the congress held in Paris in November 1958.
Professionally she began as a university-trained chemist who
became acquainted with the work of the Army through offering
spare-time service at la Cité de Refuge, a multi-purpose social
service centre situated at 12 rue Cantagrel in Paris. Once
involved she felt that her personal lifestyle was being challenged by the realities of human need which confronted her.
She accepted Jesus as Saviour and Lord, turned her back on
her promising career and dedicated – perhaps abandoned
would be a better word – abandoned herself to the service of
her fellow men and women. After training she served for ten
years at la Cité de Refuge, followed by three years as a corps
officer, after which she became assistant matron at le Palais
de la Femme. Then she found her destiny on the Asile Flottant
– a floating night shelter moored on the Seine close to the Quai
d'Austerlitz.

This floating barge had been given to the Army some thirty
years previously by a woman sympathiser who herself had
suffered greatly, and so this spartan accommodation, alleviated
by loving care, gave shelter to other sufferers. The biblical
blessing – 'Peace be with you' – greeted all who sought succour,
and an average of between 150 and 200 men slept on the boat
every night. Gogibus, the only woman there, lived in a sparsely
furnished room in the bow of the barge, a simple latch the
only fastening to the door. Creature comforts might be few but
Christian care abounded. If our Lord's blessing rests upon a
cup of cold water given in His name, then surely the bed and
hot meal offered by Gogibus to her nightly guests was an
authentic Christian sacrament. Virtually all the men who
sheltered here had a story to tell. Truth is stranger than fiction
and no script writer who talked to Gogibus would ever have
been short of a plot. But she never betrayed a defenceless
destitute – nor will this page either. Identities will be hidden
behind a letter of the alphabet.

(A) I am thirty-one years of age and suffer from a congenital
dislocation. Because of my infirmity my parents spoiled me, shield-

ing me from hardship. I was taught music but no trade. Some years ago I set up house with a woman and we had a child, but afterward she left me to marry another man. Because of the child she claimed maintenance allowance from me and, unable to pay it, I have just ended a two months' prison sentence.

(B) I am a former physical education teacher and here are documents to prove this. During the war I took part in the resistance and contracted tuberculosis. My wife was paralysed at the birth of our only son. Turned thirty years of age, he now has a good job, but my daughter-in-law does not like me, and so I do not want to seek his help.

(C) I heard about the barge on the radio and so I came here. I had a good job but I am a gambler, and finally my wife said that I must choose between her and our child – and gambling. I preferred my passion but now, in Paris, I can find no work. (Gogibus commented that this man was found a job, but what he really needed was a change of heart – freedom from the slavery of gambling. She added that the Founder's idea of marrying social rehabilitation to spiritual grace proves more than ever to be the right approach. In their own way many of the men are grateful for what is done for them. They bring gifts of shop soiled cakes and faded flowers – anything that can be rescued from the nearest dustbin.)

The staff on the barge were made up of those who, under God, Gogibus had been able to help. The cook was an ex-legionnaire who used to squander his weekly wage on strong drink as soon as he received it, yet he longed to conquer this implacable desire. Another had served three separate sentences for housebreaking, but was trying to live an honest life. A third was a simple-hearted soul who was willing to tackle all the dirty jobs which had to be faced each morning after the departure of the previous night's live cargo. Gogibus had to be given another appointment because of her failing sight but her pity for the unpitied never weakened.

Baldassare Vinti was the oldest of this trio and was promoted to Glory in the summer of 1961 – but not before he had been more severely tried than most of his European officer contemporaries during the Second World War.

Vinti was a Sicilian born in Aragona where the ruins of sun-drenched temples spoke of a faith which flourished when Jewish exiles were weeping by the waters of Babylon. Below lay the Sicilian Channel; on the horizon the island of Pantel-

leria; more distant still the shores of Tunisia. Spacious though
the physical setting, local customs were too repressive for folk
dedicated to freedom of thought and action. The family left
for the city of Milan where young Vinti believed he had found
the solution to life's discontents through economic and political
reform.

One day in 1923 a solitary Salvationist offered him a copy
of *Il Grido di Guerra* – the Italian *War Cry*. It was as if a light
from heaven shone round about him. He made his way to the
Salvation Army hall and found what he was looking for –
working people spending themselves for the benefit of the poor.
Vinti enlisted in this Army with Christ as the captain of his
salvation.

But his service as a Salvation Army officer was abruptly
interrupted in 1940 when, with others of his comrades, he was
arrested in Rome by state security officials. The Army was
dissolved, its meetings forbidden, its assets confiscated. Vinti
himself was first imprisoned and then interned, after which he
and his family were sentenced to domestic exile in a small
town near the Adriatic coast. Here he had to face new risks.
In the autumn of 1943 the local partisans sought his help. His
dangers and his anxieties proportionately increased. He could
not condone the wanton brutality of the occupying forces, yet
he could not bless the angry reprisals of the partisans. Shelter
had to be found for men on the run and food provided for the
hungry. Vinti had no organisation at his back. Even his beloved
Esercito della Salvezza was proscribed. But such was his
personal stature that, when Saltara was ultimately liberated,
he was made Mayor by acclamation – an appointment which
was subsequently confirmed by the Allied Military Government.

Mayor Vinti was happy – but not content. He made the
acquaintance of a British serviceman who was going on leave
and entrusted to him a letter for General Carpenter in which
he spoke of his desire to resume his high calling as an officer
of The Salvation Army. In due course this is what happened
and, as a first step, he came back to the men's home in Rome
which he found stripped bare of its furniture and fittings. But
by the mercy of God the Army was raised from the dead and
Vinti was one of His divine agents. From 1948 until his
promotion to Glory in 1961 he served as second-in-command

of the work in Italy and a tribute to him in the international *War Cry* concluded:

> Lieut.-Colonel Vinti was a man of great intelligence and consider-able education . . . as well as wide practical experience. Few people knew the intricacies of Italian law as he did; fewer still could deal with officialdom with the same dexterity. He had studied the Italian constitution and knew what it guaranteed. He knew also that there were officials who were not prepared to implement its provisions. With these he was politely merciless, never abandoning his efforts until the Army had obtained all that the constitution gave.
>
> He was known and respected by the leaders of the various Protestant communities in Italy. Above all, he was loved by the rank and file of Salvationists. To be with him in an Italian village was to realise what affection for him, what trust in him, the soldiery had.[1]

Different in temperament, serving in a different setting, the Dutch Alida Bosshardt was her own 'man', yet animated by the same spirit as the other two.

Bosshardt was born in Utrecht of Roman Catholic parents, against whose wishes she became a Salvationist. She entered the training college in The Netherlands in 1934, worked in a children's home during the war, and was given an appointment on the territorial headquarters in 1945. While serving there she developed a deep concern for the welfare of the women and girls in the adjacent red light district and on Friday evening, October 8, 1948, in company with two other like-minded women officers, began to make her first contacts in the neighbourhood by distributing the Dutch *War Cry*. From so modest a beginning stemmed a work which was destined to become internationally known.

The story broke in the spring of 1959 when Bosshardt appeared on the programme of the Dutch television person-ality, Bert Garthoff, who ran an equivalent of the 'This is your life' feature. 'The most human and most moving programme Dutch television has ever put before its viewers', declared the socialist *Het vrije volk*. The rest of the press from the Roman Catholic *De Volksrant* to the liberal *Handelsblad* expressed their agreement. 'She is not', said the *Provinciale Zeeuwse Courant*, 'a woman in a thousand, but one in a million. It was a rich life

that was unfolded before the viewers. Yet not one life alone
but . . . in Major Bosshardt the whole Salvation Army is
honoured.'

In terms of practical support the response of the Dutch
people to the major's casual and unpremeditated reference
to the goodwill centre's urgent need for new premises in
Amsterdam was phenomenal. That evening Alida Bosshardt
became a national figure, and before long an international
one as well. In 1965, along with Mrs Lieut.-Colonel Bordas
(Belgium) and Brigadier Mary Scott (United Kingdom), she
was one of the three Salvation Army delegates to the International Abolitionist Congress in Rome, where they were
presented to Pope Paul VI. Again in 1972 she was the Salvationist delegate to the International Abolitionist Federation
conference in New Delhi.

But the world-wide fame which came to Bosshardt unsought
did not cause her to forget her first works. Here is how an
overseas correspondent described an evening in the sixties
which he spent in her company.

Darkness had fallen and the black waters of the canals were lit by
many dancing reflections as we marched briskly along a cobbled
street in old Amsterdam. Voices blended in a lilting chorus caused
the men prowling around the red light district to look up, their
attention distracted from the prostitutes who smiled invitingly
from many windows.

Those who live in the cafes, brothels and dwelling houses of the
area are accustomed to this weekly invasion by enthusiastic Dutch
Salvationists. The faces which look out from the windows fre-
quently bear the marks of inner emptiness; the faces looking in
from the darkness outside are joyless . . .

In a narrow street, lined by brightly lit cafes, a brief meeting
was begun. Major Alida Bosshardt, the officer in charge of the
two Goodwill centres in the red light district, stepped forward to
speak. In the Major, more than anywhere else, can be found the
reason why the Salvationists are not resented in this district where
3,000 registered – and almost as many unregistered – prostitutes
operate. For thirteen years this amazing woman has served and
befriended the people of old Amsterdam until they regard her as
their true, sometimes their only, friend.

Drunks who want a cup of steaming coffee and a reassuring
word, women needing refuge after a fight at home, hungry tramps,
husbands whose wives have returned to the oldest profession, a

girl in search of 'a shoulder to cry on', day after day, week after week, make their way to the Goodwill centre and ask for the woman whose compassion they have never known to fail . . .

Last year one of these girls was murdered in her small apartment. One of the pimps, acting as representative of 'the trade' asked her to conduct the funeral service which, of course, she did. Even the favourite tunes of the participating congregation were used, and hundreds joined in the service at the cemetery.[2]

A press reporter once asked Bosshardt to tell him her favourite Bible text. She reached for her New Testament and read Matthew 9:36. 'But when he saw the multitudes he was moved with compassion on them because they fainted . . . as sheep having no shepherd.' Her life and work embody in the most practical fashion the truth of the couplet of Charles Wesley:

> To hate the sin with all my heart
> But still the sinner love.

Obviously none but those possessed of a genuine vocation can hope to meet the demands of such a vocation. The further question then is: how can those who believe themselves to be so called be best prepared for such a calling?

In this matter the Army's reach has always exceeded its grasp. A hundred years ago, in 1880, when only the most elementary forms of training were being considered, the Army's leaders were being smitten on both cheeks simultaneously. Protests against putting up lads and lassies to speak who were not masters of their own tongue were mingled with the charge that the Booths were attempting to educate their officers above their proper station in life. But Mrs Booth went on writing to Bramwell about the need for training of some kind, and he replied to his mother in like vein. 'If this ship is going to ride out these storms, ought not all our strength and skill . . . to be concentrated on the organisation of the rank and file and the training of officers?' Happily for all concerned Catherine set out the main principles which should govern such training with her customary lucidity. Abridged, they read:

We begin with the heart. If the heart is not right, the service cannot be right.

We try to train the head, so as to put officers in advance in knowledge of those whom they seek to teach.

We teach them to appeal to the consciences of people . . . to stab them awake with the gospel which condemns the sin for which it offers the remedy.

We teach them to inspire hope in the most hopeless.

We try to teach them to present Jesus as the Saviour who provides liberation from the past and victory for the future.

We teach them to use their converts as a means of converting others.[3]

These aims are timeless. They will speak to 2080 as they spoke to 1880. Especially will article two save us from supposing that the training standards which passed muster in 1880 will suffice for 2080 – or even 1980.

The cumulative pressure of these truths led to the training of officers becoming one item on the crowded agenda at the commissioners' conference which the General convened in the summer of 1958. Such a conference was no new departure, for twice within the previous ten years had such gatherings been held. Face-to-face discussions of this kind had become a virtual necessity when leaders were drawn from all quarters of the globe and spaced so widely over the whole world. The cost incurred was money well spent. Nineteen of the forty-two assembled on this occasion had never met one another before at this particular level of responsibility. It was equally important that each of those present should have the opportunity of free discussion with those to whom they were responsible – in Salvation Army parlance the General, the Chief of the Staff and the international secretaries. Half an hour's conversation could prove more enlightening than reams of correspondence.

The comments of the London press indicated how the world of affairs regarded this event. In addition to giving generous space to the presence of so diverse a group of the Army's principal officers, *The Times* devoted a second leader to 'a review of their strategy' and asked 'to what extent should they (the conference members) adapt their principles to the changing moral climate in which they found themselves . . . They would do well to think hard before abandoning the old well-tried ways'.

Fair comment! If in this setting 'well-tried ways' was intended as a synonym for 'historic Christian principles' the
conference never had the least intention of forsaking them. But
if it was to be understood as a warning signal against deserting
long-established methods, the conference was equally certain
that all methods, ancient as well as modern, needed to be
weighed in the balance. The Salvation Army has never belonged to any legendary union of evangelical Luddites who
believe that the only acceptable methods of waging the holy
war are those practised in the nineteenth (or any earlier)
century. For example, the nine months' training session had
been in operation since 1904, the only major change being
the removal of the college from Linscott Road, Clapton, to
Denmark Hill, South London in 1929. The greater the need
therefore for the most thorough-going examination of the
entire programme – a task which was assigned to a separate
international commission. The outcome was that on August
16, 1960, the William Booth Memorial Training College commenced the first of its two-year sessions, with the United States
and Canada moving in step and other territories following
their example in due course.

The two years were divided into three main sections – the
first a residential term, followed by a summer (or out) term of
four to five months spent in practical field and/or social
activities, followed by a second residential term to complete
the course. The curriculum had to be expanded so as to occupy
to the utmost advantage twice the time hitherto allocated to
it. This was the least of the difficulties afflicting the programme
planners. The cynic need not quote Parkinson's law that any
given task can always be relied upon fully to monopolise the
time set apart for its completion. This is assuredly one of the
rare situations where this law works to the advantage of all
concerned. The more the Bible is studied, the more there is to
study.

The personal problems were the harder to work out. The
cadet whose training took twice as long needed twice as much
money for his personal needs, though it is fair to say that he
received an agreed allowance during the summer term and, if
married, this included the needs of his wife and children. Of
course, the word family raised further questions. What about
their accommodation? And their schooling? Nevertheless the

principles on which the extended training session was based held good, and this is now the practice throughout the Army world – with minor variations to meet local needs.

6   THE EARTH IS THE LORD'S

Strategists, both of the armchair and the more practical variety, have been known to make great play with the number of men at base required to support one man in the firing line. Willy nilly, The Salvation Army has also had to pay continual attention to what is now fashionably called its infrastructure. The most ardent band of evangelists needs the help of those who are able and willing to serve at tables. Both are essential to the ongoing work of God. Sometimes attention has to be paid even to the size, and the shape, and the positioning of those tables.

One minor administrative alteration under this heading meant that from October 1, 1959, the ranks of second and first lieutenant, of senior-captain and senior-major (all introduced in May 1948) were discontinued. Henceforth the rank structure would read: probationary lieutenant, lieutenant, captain, major, brigadier, lieutenant-colonel, colonel, lieutenant-commissioner and commissioner. These changes meant little outside the officer corps – and for them there were to be further changes still in the years to come.

An alteration of more significance was the affiliation of the Army's Life Saving Guards and Sunbeams to the Girl Guides Association on April 11, 1959. What in the Army had been known as the Life Saving Scouts were inaugurated in the summer of 1913 and their junior section – the Chums – on June 23, 1917. The possibility of affiliation with the Scout Association had been considered in 1934 but was vetoed in favour of co-operation. This proved an unsatisfactory half-way house, however, and four of the countries sharing in that conference subsequently agreed to affiliate. This left the British Territory somewhat out on a limb and in June 1948, affiliation became an accomplished fact.

This same question now faced the Life Saving Guards who

were inaugurated just over two years later than the Scouts.
Here again there were initial proposals, counter-proposals,
discussions and emendations before a memorandum of affiliation was finally agreed – all ultimately leading to the public
meeting in the Clapton Congress Hall on April 11, 1959, when
according to the report in the *Guide*, Miss Anstice Gibbs, the
Chief Commissioner, led the assembled Life Saving Guards in
their new Guide promise. Major Helen Kelman, the territorial
guard organiser, had filled the arena with upwards of 700
wearers of the red and grey, leaving space for the entry of
seven groups in their new guide and ranger uniforms – pledge
of the nearly 10,000 girls in the country whom the Chief
Commissioner was welcoming. The affiliation was not world-
wide however, and those territories which desired to retain the
name and style of the Life Saving Guards were allowed to do
so.

There were also a number of changes in leadership personnel
due to such inevitable causes as age, ill-health and promotions
to Glory. The Chief of the Staff, Commissioner William J.
Dray – who had held that office since September 29, 1957 –
retired with Mrs Commissioner Dray on January 13, 1961,
and they were succeeded by Commissioner and Mrs Norman
F. Duggins. Within two months of his appointment, however,
the commissioner was unexpectedly promoted to Glory. He
collapsed during a weekend's campaign at Paisley, Scotland,
and died on Monday morning, March 20, 1961. To fill the
vacancy the General promoted Commissioner and Mrs Erik
Wickberg to that rank and appointed the commissioner to be
Chief of the Staff as from May 8.

These changes gave rise (among others) to the appointment
of Lieut.-Commissioner and Mrs Gösta Blomberg to Germany and Colonel and Mrs Tor Wahlström to Denmark.
Later in the year Lieut.-Commissioner Frank Fairbank was
appointed Chancellor of the Exchequer at International Headquarters, Lieut.-Commissioner and Mrs William Villeneuve
to the oversight of The Salvation Army Assurance Society,
Lieut.-Commissioner and Mrs Frank Evans to the Congo,
Colonel and Mrs John Blake to Pakistan, and Colonel and
Mrs John Fewster to the Central America and West Indies
Territory.

Two encouraging developments belong to this period of the

Army's history. Organised mining commenced in Labrador City in 1959 and immigrants were at once drawn into the area – mainly from Newfoundland but even from points as far distant as South America. What awaited the newcomers were long hours, tough winters and work that would test the hardiest.

When the first married officers arrived in Labrador City there was one uniformed Salvationist to greet them and three children with whom to start their youth work. The only building which could be rented for public gatherings was available for one meeting per week. Nothing could be done about these difficulties but to face them. A trailer, 36 feet by 10 feet, became the officers' quarters and general office. In less than a year the sale of *The War Cry* rose to 500 copies per issue. To cut building costs the pioneer officer decided to use free and voluntary labour. This at times reduced his work force to single figures. A more intractable problem was the fact that his congregations were migratory. They would build up to seventy for the one weekly meeting – but then a large proportion would disappear without warning. They had returned home or had gone in search of pastures new – and the task of introducing newcomers to the Army would have to begin all over again. Nevertheless within the first year both the children's work and the home league had been established. Two faithful junior soldiers showed their mettle by undertaking the first self-denial appeal.

The second development was that on February 22, 1962, at 359 Tetuan Street in the walled city of old San Juan, the work of The Salvation Army in Puerto Rico was officially begun by Commissioner Holland French, territorial commander of the Eastern Territory of the United States. He, and those with him, were welcomed by Mayoress Dona Felisa Rincon de Gautier, the Revd Antonio Rivera Rodriquez (Secretary of the Council of Churches) and other civic and ecclesiastical personalities, including members of the armed forces headed by Colonel James Breckenridge, Chief of Staff of the Antilles Command.

To explain how so mixed a group could assemble with so single a purpose in mind, a little history is necessary. Though Puerto is to be found geographically amid a scattering of island republics in the Caribbean, it is historically 'a free associate state' of the United States. Discovered by Columbus and colonised by Spain, the island was ceded to the United States in 1892. In 1955 the then leader of the work of the Army in Central America and the West Indies, Lieut.-Commissioner George Sandells, sent Senior-Major Tobias Martinez – currently in charge of the work in Cuba – to conduct a feasibility study as to the possibility of unfurling the flag in Puerto Rico as well.

The course of such projects never did run smooth. In this instance, the commissioner farewelled though his successor, Colonel John Stannard, was equally keen on the enterprise. There were also drastic internal changes in Cuba and in mid 1959 Martinez, with his wife and family, returned to the USA Western Territory. Nevertheless he still dreamed of opening the work in Puerto Rico, though International Headquarters ruled that it would be unrealistic to link any such project in an area politically linked with the United States to the Caribbean headquarters in Kingston (Jamaica) nor would adequate financing be obtainable from that source. However, Martinez did return to San Juan charged to reassess the prospects of an opening and to advise New York accordingly.

By this time, however, his high hopes had changed virtually to unrelieved gloom – until the proprietor and headmaster of the Academica Rovira in Caparra Terrace, San Juan (capacity 300 pupils with four teachers, kindergarten through fourth grade) offered his property, complete with fittings and furniture, to the Army for $500 a month, rent to be paid annually in advance. The school could be renamed the Academica William Booth, and on weeknights and at weekends the building could be used for Army meetings.

But for Martinez this was a false dawn. The initial enrolment numbered but sixty-two, of whom only twenty-nine paid their fees in full, with Mr Rovira retaining the first month's income. This, and sundry other difficulties, prompted an SOS which the Eastern Territory answered by posting Captain and Mrs Shaffstall to take charge of the Caparra Terrace project. Thanks to the newcomers in whom compassion was joined to competence, the property was repaired and redesigned. The school grew – with more than a hundred attending. The corps grew as well – until the meetings for children had to be held in the playground.

With the Army's long-standing rule that every dime, let alone every dollar, must be accounted for, Brigadier Freda Weatherly arrived in June 1962, charged to reduce the financial field to order. At the same time Captain and Mrs Bernard Smith, accustomed to pioneering in Latin America and fluent in Spanish, were assigned to assist in the work in Tetuan Street and, with the school and corps at Caparra Terrace in working shape, Captain and Mrs Shaffstall were given the task of opening a third corps at Ponce. At the end of January 1963, Major Eldred Churchill was appointed regional commander and, with his wife, assumed responsibility for the work. Though this meant that it was now being supervised by 'continental American' officers, steps were taken to secure the future presence of officers of Puerto Rican extraction.[1]

The summoning of the Third Assembly of the World Council of Churches in New Delhi (India) from November 17 to December 6, 1961, led the General to announce the names of the Army delegation early that same year. As befitted an international movement, the party was correspondingly international – Commissioner Norman Marshall (National Commander, USA), Lieut.-Commissioner Joseph Dahya and Colonel Donald Sanjivi (India), Lieut.-Colonel Tamiko Yamamuro (Japan), Lieut.-Colonel Benjamin (Pakistan), Brigadier Jonah Munyi (East Africa) and Brigadier Jacobus Corputty (Indonesia) with Commissioner Reginald Woods as the leader of the delegation and the Salvation Army member of the central committee of the World Council. Colonel (Dr) Bramwell Cook, who was chairman of the Commission on Missions and Interchurch Aid associated with the New Zealand national council of churches, was also present – as was Sister Prema Sanjivi as a youth delegate.

Among the significant features of the Third Assembly (wrote Commissioner Woods in a full-page feature article in the international *War Cry* for December 9, 1961) was the integration of the International Missionary Council (founded in Edinburgh in 1910) with the World Assembly (founded in Amsterdam in 1948) – with a consequent simplification of administration and the avoidance of overlapping activities.

Another noteworthy fact was the increase in the World Council membership of a further twenty-three churches – among them eleven from Africa, two from South America and four orthodox churches from Europe. 'In briefing the Army's delegation on these applications', explained *The War Cry*:

the General was guided . . . by the knowledge that questions of geography or the nature of the government of any land, east or west, were totally irrelevant to questions of Christian fellowship which overlaps national boundaries . . . Thus in two days the Army's nine-strong, eighty-country, international delegation, had a part in an historic action greatly enlarging the fellowship of those who, coming out of all the world, wished to work for the spread of that kingdom which knows no geographical limits and whose history will have no end.

Summing up the Assembly proceedings *The War Cry* concluded:

The special witness of Salvationists and the Friends to the fact that all the fullness of divine grace is available to the believer without the visible elements of water, bread and wine was graciously acknowledged . . . The Army's long experience of the great gifts which women bring to the proclamation of the gospel was greatly appreciated by many who desire to see more of their number training for the ministry.

Meanwhile General and Mrs Kitching were encouraging by their personal campaigning the witness of Salvationists in the giant half-circle of Asian countries lining the eastern shores of the Pacific Ocean. Still present in the memories of many living in those lands was the cruel travail of the Second World War for, when the actual fighting ceased with the surrender of Japan on August 14, 1945, there was no organised Salvation Army activity left east of India other than in Australia and New Zealand. From Sapporo in the northernmost island of Japan to Malang in the far east of Java, 'the yellow, the red and the blue' was nowhere to be seen. Yet now, in less than a generation, the largest public halls were repeatedly filled to greet the international leaders of the once proscribed movement, and the once forbidden uniform was to be seen in the grounds of the imperial palace in Tokyo as well as in government offices in Jakarta.

This particular campaign reassured some of the most hard pressed of any group of Salvationists that they were assuredly part of the international Salvation Army. It was thirty-five

years since a General had set foot in Korea – and that was
General Bramwell Booth in 1926. No wonder that the comrades who crammed the buses taking them to the capital's
airport were delirious with delight, or that the Army's principal
hall in Seoul was filled for every meeting, or that Korea's
oldest seat of learning, the Yonsei university, conferred on
the General the honorary degree of Doctor of Laws, or that
the President of the Republic and Madam Pasun Yun headed
the line of national leaders who graced the gathering which
filled the largest Christian church in the capital – not that
General and Mrs Kitching were not greeted with equal delight
when they visited one of the twelve feeding stations which
supplied a total of 6,000 free meals daily.

Similarly crowded halls and eager congregations gathered
when Commissioner Charles Davidson presented (in
Japanese) the international visitors at Osaka – the 'Manchester' of Japan. A congregation of 2,500 – and this in a land
where only one-half per cent of the population is Christian –
packed the Mainichi hall and, more noteworthy still, there
were sixty seekers at the improvised mercy seat. Similar crowds
assembled in Tokyo where the General, accompanied by the
British ambassador, Sir Oscar Morland, was received by the
Emperor.

More than half a century previously, in 1907, William Booth
had visited Japan, paid his respects to the Emperor, held
public gatherings – but a public farewell had to be cancelled
for fear of public disorder.[2] Though in certain quarters during
the Second World War open hostility was fiercer still, the
unrestrained welcome given to the Army's leaders on this
occasion testified to the regard in which Japanese Salvationists
were held by their compatriots.

Hong Kong was the next port of call. Army work did not
begin here until 1930 and, when the Japanese took over the
city on Christmas Day, 1941, all the expatriate officers were
interned save for Major Dorothy Brazier and Major Doris
Lemmon who, with their Chinese woman assistant, Captain
Sung, were in charge of the girls' home.[3]

As the plane was five hours late on arrival not a moment
was lost in bringing examples of current Salvation Army
activity before the visitors. Twenty-six miles of scenic roadway
brought the General and his party to Kam Tin, the corps

nearest to the border with the Republic of China. This was
opened only three years previously and, tell it not in those
professional quarters where quantity surveyors and building
contractors foregather, the hall consisted of two capacious
pig-sties, transformed out of all recognition into a habitable
Army property. Unperturbed, the General ceremoniously
turned a sod for a more permanent building which would
house the activities of a corps which already boasted ninety-two
senior soldiers, seventy-seven recruits, 101 junior soldiers,
fourteen corps cadets plus an active home league.

So that practice might make perfect, the following morning
saw the General and Mrs Kitching jointly wielding pick and
shovel in a ground-breaking ceremony for a twelve-class school
building in the Mau Tau Wei Road, Kowloon, before going
on to inspect the Wanchai school where 1,610 children, attending in morning and afternoon shifts, received primary instruction. Here half the staff were committed Christians and the
headmaster was a local officer. The night youth rally in the
Queen Elizabeth stadium would have ranked as a major event
in a territory many times larger than this command. Here with
nine corps and nine institutions, staffed by twenty-nine officers,
the scale and character of the items presented by the 1,600
young people and children were phenomenal. Nor were the
attendances on the Sunday less rewarding when, in the evening, watched by a congregation of 1,000 adults, 180 new
soldiers were enrolled under the flag. An astonished and deeply
moved officer commanding was admitted by the General to
the Order of the Founder for 'many years of meritorious
missionary service' which began in 1923.

Three hours' flying time brought General and Mrs Kitching
to Manila – a 'first' for this command as well. The work began
in the Philippine capital in 1937 – only to be interrupted by
the war in December 1941. Operations were later resumed as
a division of the USA Western Territory, but the command
was not reopened until 1956. In the past no Salvation Army
occasion had ever secured a congregation of more than 250,
but in faith a modern auditorium was hired capable of holding
500 people. Only fifty seats were empty – which set a pattern
for the meetings to follow.

The links which bind the world Army together were further
illustrated when the Tondo corps, which was presented with

the home league efficiency banner by Mrs General Kitching, also received a parcel of thirty Bibles from a gift of a thousand, paid for by the home leagues of three British divisions. The runners-up, the Undeneta corps, received twenty.

Indonesia was the penultimate call in this Far Eastern campaign – and here the work of the Army dated back to the days of the Dutch colonial empire. This heightened rather than diminished the hazards of the Second World War, for within two days of the Japanese flag being lowered, the Indonesian colours were hoisted and the war of independence began. Not until the closing days of 1949 was the national government recognised by the former colonial authority. Indeed, even ten years later the road between Jakarta and Bandung – the two principal centres visited by the General – could not be guaranteed to be free from bandits.

Bandits or no bandits, the Sunday's meetings in Bandung went through without interruption as visits to the homes for mothers, boys, girls and the aged by the General and Mrs Kitching went through without let or hindrance. Because of the hazards of travel some fifty officers in the remoter parts of the territory could not be present – and to each of these the General wrote a word of encouragement. Returning to Jakarta for the final day, the Salvationist leaders were received by Dr Leimena, a committed Christian, who was serving as acting-President in the absence of Dr Sukarno. The Minister for Communications, a Protestant clergyman, was the government representative at the final rally in Jakarta which drew the largest congregation during the four-day campaign.

At this point occurred the only major delay in the whole programme. A seventeen-hour engine breakdown grounded the entire party in Jakarta and robbed the General of a whole day in Singapore. But the mishap only made this 'Gideon's army' – as the General described them – more eager to profit from this further 'first' from any of the Army's Generals. The Rt. Revd. Roland Kow Chiang, President of the Malayan Christian Council, had made a journey of some three hundred miles to share in the General's welcome, and found in an otherwise untimely tropical downpour an illustration of the showers of blessing which the Lord would pour upon His waiting people.

As an estimated half of the population of Singapore is

considered to be under twenty-five years of age, it was no
surprise that 750 of them made their way to the air-conditioned
Victoria theatre for a youth rally and that the Sunday morning
meeting held in the central corps hall – a scheduled property
whose design spoke of a past religious tradition – resounded
to the praise of the living Lord and Saviour who is eternally
the same.

Stopovers in Colombo and Bombay allowed the travellers
to greet their Army comrades in these two centres but did not
prevent the General and his party from arriving home in time
to hear of the Pageant of Industry which formed the climax of
the year of industrial evangelism in Britain. In the words of
the organising secretary, Major Denis Hunter, this was

> not a crusade to bring the people back to the churches so much
> as the church – which means us, the Army – returning in deep
> contrition to the people.
>
> Industrial evangelism was an admission of our error in that
> somewhere down the line we had parted company from John
> Fellow and his family.
>
> Industrial evangelism was a confession that 'we had followed
> too much the devices and desires of our own hearts' – that is, our
> own dearly loved and often greatly blessed ways of worship. We
> had also 'left undone the things we ought to have done' – the
> approaches which could have brought us to where John Fellow
> sweats and swears and drinks and gambles – or where he merely
> sweats.
>
> Industrial evangelism is the Salvationist seeking to atone for
> the most damaging of all his failures – that he is out of touch with
> John Fellow and his family, out of touch with his hopes and his
> fears, his doubts and his sins.

Largely unnoticed by the public and the press the place
of the Salvationist in Western society had begun to change
considerably between the two world wars – and thereafter.
Care for the under-privileged continued to be a major concern,
but there also grew up a substantial body of Salvation Army
soldiers (i.e., lay people) who took their place in the world
about them – e.g., in local government, in the trades union
movement, in the professions as well as on the shop floor, as
craftsmen as well as managers. Their experience of, and witness to, the Christian faith in daily life brought new insights

upon which the General was eager to draw for the widening and strengthening of the Army's evangelical appeal in the twentieth century. In May 1958, he called into conference some seventy representative Salvationists – and industrial evangelism was at the head of the agenda. Those present were in the front line of Christian witness. How could their faith be best reproduced in their fellows?

Such discussions were repeated more than once in the months which followed, and finally found visible expression on November 8, 1961, in a crowded Clapton Congress Hall in the presence of the Rt. Hon. John Hare, MP, Minister of Labour, when twenty-nine groups of Salvationists, in their working garb, representing light and heavy industry, mining, agriculture, technicians and tradesmen, management, the world of education, the world of medicine and including the security forces, moved up the broad centre aisle of the building to the foot of the illuminated Cross where they offered the symbols of their employment and the fruits thereof to be placed in reverent dedication around this symbol of their faith. Not just the first day of the week, but every day, is holy because the labour of the weekday is also an offering to God and a service to man. The whole earth is the Lord's and the fullness thereof!

7   THE LANDS BEYOND THE SEA

The Army's seventh General began the last but one of his world campaigns when, with Mrs Kitching, he left International Headquarters on February 14, 1962, for South America. He was to circle the globe yet once again via New York and San Francisco in order to reach New Zealand and Australia, but these territories he had visited once before – in 1956; Latin America was entirely new ground.

Although not involved in the actual material destruction caused by the Second World War, the three South American territories – East, West and Brazil – had suffered from the resulting isolation as much as any other. During that period there had been no missionary reinforcements and only an occasional international caller. The principal exception during those years of separation was the visit of General and Mrs Carpenter who, on August 28, 1942, left London secretly in a darkened plane for New York and who reached home – on the last stage of the return journey by a converted bomber – on January 6, 1943. These two ageing but indomitable leaders used this opportunity to journey as far south as Rio de Janeiro and Buenos Aires. It says much for the spirit of the South American officers and soldiers that, under God, both their evangelical and social services continued to prosper – especially when their scanty resources in men and material are kept in mind.

Before the end of 1946, that is, within six months of his election, General Orsborn flew to Brazil – calling at Paramaribo and Cayenne on the way – to be welcomed by Lieut.-Colonel and Mrs William Effer in Rio de Janeiro. From there the General journeyed on to Buenos Aires where Commissioner and Mrs Marcel Allemand had been in charge of the Argentine for eight years, and finally on to South America West – which included Bolivia, Chile and Peru – where the Swedish Colonel

and Mrs Victor Lundgren were in charge with headquarters
in Santiago and who, after more than forty-five years' service,
were shortly to retire. The General also visited Lima, capital
of Peru, the first General to do so, where he described
his task as that of cheering 'one of our fighting minorities'.
The expression is justified when it is remembered that
the officers' meeting at which he was welcomed numbered
nine.

The next visit of an international leader to South America
was in 1962 and the gap between these two dates must now
be filled in – even if but briefly. The gatherings addressed by
General Orsborn in Rio de Janeiro were the largest the Army
had yet known in the then Brazilian capital, and in 1947 the
twenty-fifth anniversary of the commencement of the work in
the Republic was also marked by encouraging congregations
both in Rio and in São Paulo. In addition a new wing in the
girls' home in the latter city was declared open by the state
governor. The place of Lieut.-Colonel and Mrs Eliasen was
then taken by Colonel and Mrs Maurice Cachelin who served
with unqualified devotion for seven years until their retirement
in 1957, during which time a new building was erected for the
use of the central corps in São Paulo.

Lieut.-Colonel and Mrs Gilbert Abadie followed on and
began to plan for the removal of the territorial centre to São
Paulo, then described as the fastest-growing city in the world.
This was described as a calculated risk which more than
proved its worth. A modern social service centre was opened
up and a central property was acquired which was used first
of all to provide temporary accommodation for the training of
cadets, and then as the territorial headquarters. The scheme
was successfully completed when, on the day prior to congress
Sunday, 1962, General Kitching declared open the new training college, described by the chairman of the Army's advisory
board in São Paulo as 'a monument of faith'.

Now to deal in turn with the other two Latin American
territories, South America East consisted of the Argentine,
Uruguay and Paraguay. Happily both Commissioner and Mrs
Allemand, and Colonel and Mrs Cachelin who succeeded
them, were equally at home in the Spanish language and in
South American ways. The colonel and his wife were married
in Chile. For reasons which are not clear after this lapse of

time, it was not deemed essential that the next three territorial leaders should be so well equipped with the language. Colonel and Mrs Francis Ham were Canadian officers who had been in charge of the Central American and West Indies Territory and who, on retirement from active service, were followed by Lieut.-Commissioner and Mrs Charles J. Duncan and then by Lieut.-Commissioner and Mrs Hubert Scotney – both of Australian origin. To say this is not to detract in the least from the value of their service. To triumph over the language handicap was in itself a testimony to their devotion to duty. Colonel Ham presided over the sixtieth anniversary of the Army's work in the Argentine, an event covered by a special issue of *El Cruzado* which drew favourable comment from *La Prensa* – an Argentine daily which then ranked with *The Times* of London or *Le Monde* of Paris.

After three and a half years in Buenos Aires the colonel (who had been promoted to the rank of lieut.-commissioner) and his wife retired and their place was taken by Lieut.-Commissioner and Mrs Duncan who had served with distinction in the Antipodes. The commissioner brought to his new appointment his skill as a Bible expositor and it was not long – despite the necessity for translation – before the weekly central holiness meeting began to show increasing attendances. Permission was once again secured to hold open-air meetings in the city plazas, and the twelve-year ban on the work of the Army in the country's prisons was lifted when the band and songsters of the central corps were allowed to present a Christmas programme in one of the city jails. The Army continued to share in the united efforts of the evangelical churches – as in the city campaign conducted by the Cuban Dr Cecilio Arrastia where some congregations reached the figure of 15,000. By contrast, when the territorial commander visited Santa Fé he dedicated a hall built on land donated by the municipality where the work was first begun by a solitary blind Salvationist.

The year 1960 saw Lieut.-Commissioner and Mrs Scotney installed as the new territorial commanders, with twenty-seven of the 150 active officers in the territory drawn from Australia, France, Great Britain, Norway, Sweden and the United States respectively. Yet this mixed company was 'one in hope, in doctrine' – as was evident from their first campaign under their new leaders – '*Cada uno gane un alma*' ('Each one win one soul').

No hour is untimely for a General to arrive and so it was not unexpected that a company of enthusiastic Salvationists would be present to greet General and Mrs Kitching as they deplaned at the Carrasco airport, Montevideo, at three o'clock in the morning on March 12, 1962. A meeting that same evening in the central Methodist church enabled the General and his wife to make their first contact with a South American congregation, and next morning a short flight brought them to Buenos Aires, the largest city south of the equator in the sub-continent. The spacious Unione e Benevolenza hall was the principal venue for the main congress gatherings and Dr Roberto Brora – 'government director of non-Catholic entities' – expressed the thanks of the people for the service of the Army to the community over the past seventy years.

Although congress Sunday was national election day the central hall in Buenos Aires was filled three times over, and the unity of Christian believers was demonstrated yet again when Bishop Barbieri, former President of the World Council of Churches, presided over the afternoon gathering. It is not often that one General has the privilege of honouring the work of another but, on this occasion, General Kitching was able formally to declare open the Parque Jorge L. Carpenter – a property within easy reach from Buenos Aires – for use as a youth camp, a conference centre and an officers' rest home. The attractive grounds included a large swimming pool and were so named after one who had been both a beloved territorial leader and a respected General as well.

The South America West Territory consists of Peru, Bolivia and Chile and, from north to south, is possibly the longest Army territory in the world, stretching as it does some 6,000 miles from Trujillo in the north of Peru to Puntas Arenas in the far south of Chile, whence food and clothing could be taken to a point in Tierra del Fuego where the remnants of an Indian tribe called the Alacalufes were living. At the other extreme, at Warizata in Bolivia in the far north, 12,000 feet above sea level, another group of Indian Salvationists secured and presented a plot of ground, promising sufficient labour to ensure the erection of a property for Salvation Army use. 'Fighting minorities' of this kind were to be found mostly at infrequent intervals, many of them sorely isolated but maintaining their unity of purpose through such dedicated leaders as the recently appointed Lieut.-Colonel and Mrs Richard Jacobsen. Without total dedication the work could not survive – but survive it did as in the opening of the new hall at Viacha (Bolivia) and the extensions to the Army farm outside Santiago to accommodate another forty boys. Changes in administrative leadership did not lessen public confidence in the value of the work accomplished. The action of the juvenile protection authorities in the Chilean capital in asking the Army to receive a further group of problem boys, placing them according to age, testified to this.

In Ororu (Bolivia) the commanding officer, who also served as the local child welfare officer, skilfully organised several 'raids' by which means he was able to ensure the safety of a number of under-age girls. Some entered our own girls' home, others changed their lifestyle as they had long wanted to do. Work of this description caused the retiring president of Chile, Señor Gonzalez Videla, to express his personal thanks to the territorial commander who, before handing over to Lieut.-Colonel and Mrs Ray Gearing, was able to see his service crowned by the opening of new halls both in Santiago and La Paz.

Though the finances of the territory were severely strained at this time because of the continuing rise in the rate of inflation, the gratitude of the community for services rendered continued to rise as well. In Santiago an advisory board was formed for the first time, and both the Chilean government as well as the municipal authorities increased their grants to our social services. Thanks to the generosity of the comrades of the USA Central Territory, a new college for the training of officers was opened in the capital as well.

Of equal, if not greater, significance was the increasing part which Salvationists began to play in the religious life of the people. In Santiago a new Christian fellowship called the 'Union of Evangelical Women' was formed, and Mrs Colonel Gearing was nominated as its first president. On Easter Sunday morning, under the auspices of the Evangelical Council of Chile, a dawn procession of 800 people, with the Army band at the head, marched to the central corps hall. When the much respected Brigadier and Mrs Magnenat retired after a combined period of seventy years' service, the Chilean government admitted them both as first-class members of the 'Bernardo O'Higgins' Order of Merit – the first married couple thus to be jointly honoured. And at long last a much-cherished dream came true – the first harbour light centre in South America was opened in the Chilean capital on July 28, 1963.

'We are very glad to welcome you,' sang the girls of the La Aurora home to General Kitching who, with his wife, was but the second General to visit Chile. But perhaps the varied work which the visitors saw on this campaign was best embodied in the service of Envoy Luis Orellana who, himself a trophy of grace, had conducted meetings in his own home for more than twenty years, and whose witness where he was so well known had led many of his friends and neighbours to Christ. Admission to the Order of the Founder was a worthy recognition of his worthy service. For Lieut.-Commissioner and Mrs Gearing the decade 1954–64 made an outstanding conclusion to their dedicated years of active officership.

General and Mrs Kitching returned to London over Eastertide, 1962, and after fulfilling a weekday engagement at the Pump Room, Bath, were present at the stone-laying of the new International Headquarters on Saturday, April 28, to which reference has already been made in Part Two, Chapter 3. Just as the Army's leaders were ever seeking to respond to the many demands of many lands, so with equal zeal individual officers were endeavouring to meet the particular needs of their individual appointment. Here are four illustrations, each taken from a different country but all from the year 1962.

The first could be entitled 'Maid of all work', and the principal character an Australian single woman officer in charge of the Army's activities at Fond des Nègres, Haiti. As travellers may possibly know, roads on the island had long left much to be desired, so that when at last the authorities took what was hopefully described as appropriate action the locals returned thanks, even though unfeeling bulldozers piled small mountains of mud against gateways and damaged garden fencing beyond swift repair. The captain prudently waited lest some over-eager workman might be seized with a sudden desire to improve upon his existing handiwork. She was already skilled enough in binding up the long and ugly scratches caused by loose strands of barbed wire, as well as in extracting savage thorns from bare feet. She had also thought that her master plan should include the fencing of the hall at Morriseau – walking time some five hours distance from base. She would have to find transport, for her faithful horse was weakened by shortage of fodder due to the prolonged drought. But she managed to secure a lift part way in a friendly truck while the half-dozen lads who were to help her fell back on shanks's pony. This meant that only an hour's daylight was left on the evening of their arrival. Early on the following Friday morning, however, work was started on the overgrown plot on which the hall stood and on the digging of the needful holes required for the 272 supporting posts. When these were securely sited they were linked by a triple row of barbed wire. The work took two full days and was not completed until dusk on the Saturday evening. Then the lads went for a bathe in the nearby river and the captain showed some film strips on her transistor projector.

After the Sunday morning meeting she made her way home on the local bus. The vehicle was so crowded on arrival that all she could do was to secure a fragile purchase against the back of one seat and lean her arms between two passengers on the equally overcrowded facing seat, keeping her head low to avoid playing an involuntary tattoo on the roof. Not exactly travelling de luxe and there were moments when she envied the boys who were walking home. However she was back at base in time for the children's meeting at which there was an attendance of 125.

The completion of a new latrine at the school at Fond des Nègres was also engaging her spare time. The framework was being built at Port au Prince, dismantled and then forwarded to her, re-erected on site – and proudly hailed as the first prefabricated latrine in Haiti. 'Cleanliness is next to godliness' is a well-known quotation from one of John Wesley's sermons. The captain practised what she preached. She knew no difference between the sacred and the secular.

No one plays more parts in his time than does the Salvation Army officer and so the second sample story can be called 'In prison and you visited me.'

The young English married officer stopped his jalopy outside a cluster of huts in the shadow of a group of foothills outside

Nairobi. Four children, the eldest carrying the youngest, stood watching him. An old man made his way inside the nearest hut where an old woman was stirring a cooking pot. The children followed without speaking. They were missing their mother, though they did not realise the full implications of the charge that she had been responsible for the death of their father. Eventually the captain unfolded an official-looking sheet of paper – though this he did not need to do for he knew the contents by heart – and addressed the old man. 'Kamau, the court has rejected your daughter's petition and the sentence must stand.' He did not add that he himself had interceded with the justice department but, as he rose to go, simply said: 'I am very sorry.'

Next day he visited the young mother of four in prison. They had met several times before though the authorities had not yet told her that the appeal against the death sentence had been refused. He talked to her about her children instead, discussing what would happen to them if anything happened to her. Their grandparents were too old to look after them properly. There was a famine in that part of the country as well. Would she agree to their entering an Army home where they would be cared for? To this she agreed, whereupon the captain went back to her home and arranged for the children to come with him. That night they were washed, given an appetising meal and medical attention, and provided with clean clothing. They soon settled down with the other boys and girls.

A few mornings later he took the children to the prison to see their mother. She had not yet been told that this would be their last meeting. Rightly or wrongly – possibly rightly – this was thought the best approach to so tragic a situation, and any tears which the baby shed on leaving her mother were dried with a sweet and a hug from the matron. The captain returned yet again to the prison for in the interval the fateful news had been broken to the mother. They sat down on the cell floor and talked together. She was not afraid, she said. She was truly sorry for what she had done and had asked God to forgive her. Words were of necessity few, but in a while the captain read Psalm 23 and the young mother began to repeat four words from verse four: 'Thou art with me.' So speaking she was led from her cell.

The third story could be headed: 'Never despair – not of anyone.'

In December 1962, 'Redheugh', Dipple Road, Kilbirnie, Scotland, was listed as an 'adolescent unit housing thirty-five young people'. *The War Cry* for December 1 of that year quoted the annual report of the principal probation officer for the county of Ayrshire that it possessed 'very good facilities for young people placed on probation with a requirement of residence by the courts, and as a unit for children in need of care and protection'. The local probation officer worked in close liaison with the Salvation Army officers in charge of the home – in this instance Captain and Mrs William Ruby.[1]

During the first ten years of its life 212 boys had passed through Redheugh. During 1961 fifteen boys had left the home – five had joined the forces; nine had returned to their parents; one had been required to appear again before the courts and was later committed to an approved school. Though details of case histories cannot be disclosed, it is an open secret that over the years a number of boys of school age had figured prominently in the prize lists of the Kilbirnie central school. In 1961 the Dux boy was again from Redheugh and was subsequently placed in suitable employment. 'If changes are to take place', ran the careful officialese of the annual report, 'the developments which have been carried out at Redheugh will be of real assistance . . . to the departmental committee on the probation service.'

The final story had better have a religious title – though not because it is unique. On the contrary, it is distressingly commonplace; too commonplace for the comfort of any sensible man. But because it has a happy ending it will be called: 'With God all things are possible.' For though this true-life tale is so mundane that its principal character could be called Joe Neighbour, and so familiar that Joe's address could have been listed in Helsinki or Tokyo or Auckland or Nurnberg, for the purpose of this page it will be found in Chicago.

As we pick up his story, Joe was without family or friends. He was desperately hungry, for regular meals were not his happy lot. A one-time successful executive in a nationally known corporation – he had been used to saying 'Go' and men went, and to say 'Come' and they came – he now elected to walk on the darker side of the road. He had no wish to be seen.

Alcohol, which had once been his pleasure, was now his tyrannical master. As he trudged through the side streets of the capital of the midwest wondering where he could sleep for the night, he saw a truck labelled 'The Salvation Army' unloading by the sidewalk. He had never met anyone from the Army before – but beggars couldn't be choosers. He would have to chance his luck.

Hesitatingly he moved through the entrance – to be stopped by a desk man who asked him his business. Joe hardly knew what to say. He had grown less and less articulate in recent days but his dejected appearance spoke louder than words. Without further ado the desk man took him to a nearby office where his obvious plight told its own story. It was the same as that of four out of every five men who came into the centre. What he most needed – and what he was given – was a shower and a shave, a change of clothing, a meal and a good sleep. These were provided without any more questions being asked. Tomorrow would take care of itself.

The morrow did – as Joe discovered, for in a clinic near to the office where his immediate needs had been so expeditiously met the night before, he was given a medical check-up. Then before he hardly knew what was happening, he was unburdening himself to a friendly kind of man who treated him as if he were an old buddy.

The early stages of Joe's cure were very down to earth. He was to serve on one of the Army's pick-up vans and he was not troubled by the discovery that Bill, his driver, had once been bothered by a drinking problem himself.

'Do you like this place?' Joe enquired cautiously.

'I do,' was the reply. 'The food is good. The work takes a chap into the fresh air. If you keep your nose clean no one bothers you. And I like the religious programme most of all.'

The religious programme! Joe had never given high marks to religious guys or to religious talk. Perhaps he should. There might be something in it. Regular hours, regular meals, regular sleep had begun to do much for Joe's ill-used body. He became linked with the Henry Milans club, named after a newspaper editor who had hit the skids but who had been remarkably changed by the power of Christ. It was a story that impressed Joe greatly – as did what the man in the next bed to his own said to him.

'I am the father of six children', he explained, 'who was thrown out of his own home because I drank too much. I came to this place a beaten man – and I stayed that way until I asked the good Lord to help me. You can see for yourself what I am now and, by the help of God, I intend to stay that way and return to my family soon.'

Joe thought long and hard about this and finally, if hesitatingly, decided to give it a go. He asked God's forgiveness for the past and God's strength for the future. Some months later he was given a sobriety pin – a recognition for the man who stayed clear of the drink for an agreed period of time. Joe is not at the centre now. It dawned on him that the good Lord who helped him master one problem could give him victory over the whole range of life's temptations. So he has been back with his family for some time, and even his firm gave him back his job. As our title said: 'With God all things are possible.'

8 STEADFAST UNTO THE END

The month of January 1963 brought the surprise announcement for readers of *The War Cry* that 'following consultation
with all commissioners on active service, the Chief of the
Staff has asked the General to continue in office for three
months beyond the date on which he would normally retire.'
This extension to November 22, 1963 – explained this official
notice – would enable members of the High Council to
attend the dedication and opening of the new International
Headquarters. There was no doubt that the involved negotiations entailed by the erection of a new building within
the historic square mile of the City of London, combined
with the adverse weather conditions which prevailed during
the winter of 1962/3, had seriously delayed the work on
site. The postponement of the date of opening was inevitable.

Nevertheless come wind, come weather, the work of the
Army had to continue and, while in office, the General
remained responsible for all international changes in leader-
ship. The serious deterioration in the health of Commissioner
Reginald Woods meant that he had to be relieved of his
post as territorial commander for Switzerland, and sadly
this gifted and respected leader was promoted to Glory from
a London hospital on March 16. Lieut.-Commissioner
Mrs Violet Stobart was appointed in his place. Lieut.-
Commissioner Catherine Jarvis succeeded Mrs Stobart in
Sri Lanka, and Lieut.-Colonel Jean Bordas became Officer
Commanding for Italy. Following the promotion to Glory
of Commissioner George Sandells on May 8, 1963, Lieut.-
Commissioner Hubert Scotney was transferred from South
America East to lead the Australia Southern Territory with
headquarters in Melbourne. Later in November of the same
year Commissioner Norman Marshall (National Commander

for the United States) and Commissioner Owen Culshaw (International Secretary for North, South and Central America, with Australia and New Zealand) retired from active service and their places were taken by Commissioner Holland French and Lieut.-Commissioner Edward Carey respectively. As a consequence Commissioner William Davidson became territorial commander for the USA Eastern Territory and Lieut.-Commissioner Paul Carlson for the Southern.

The last of the prolonged campaigns undertaken by General and Mrs Kitching occupied them from February 14 when they left Southampton for New York, until April 29 when they returned to the same port. On the outward journey they opened the impressive Parkside Evangeline residence in New York, and then conducted meetings in San Francisco on their way to New Zealand and their subsequent five-day campaigns in each of the state capitals of Queensland, New South Wales, Victoria and South Australia. This was no strange ground to the General for not only had he been Chief Secretary for the Australia Southern Territory from 1946 to 1948, but had visited the Antipodes in the early months of 1956. Of greater interest would therefore be extracts from the comments which appeared in the international *War Cry* for May 18, 1963, on his return home. Asked what were his outstanding impressions of his campaign the General said:

First of all, the fact that in every city visited there was a quick response in all the meetings where an appeal was made. Invariably before we had entered the prayer meeting proper there was a steady flow of seekers. Here was evidence surely of the influence of the Holy Spirit . . . But I also attribute this to the fact that there was an absence of unnecessary 'trimmings', making it possible to have an early start to the prayer meetings . . . By an economy of time in the contributions of music and song, and by keeping the address to about twenty minutes' duration, the way was cleared for their early commencement.

There has also been a vast increase of virile youth in our ranks. They are intelligent, many of them holding university degrees, but these and many others show a commendable appreciation of the Army's principles and purposes.

Government grants are undoubtedly helping with our social properties. I would say that our eventide homes in Australia are among the best in the world. Many corps are also showing a praiseworthy awareness of the growth of their cities and of the shift of population. New corps and new outposts are revealing an encouraging willingness to follow the people.

The final overseas event was the corps cadet congress in Canada, with the principal meetings in the Massey Hall, Toronto, after which General and Mrs Kitching returned home via New York, holding their concluding overseas farewell rally in the centennial memorial temple.

Meanwhile on Thursday, July 25, the Chief of the Staff dispatched the formal notices calling upon members of the High Council to assemble at Sunbury Court on September 19. There were forty-nine such members, one more than in 1954, and their names in alphabetical order were:

Lieut.-Commissioner Gilbert ABADIE	Territorial Commander, Brazil.
Lieut.-Commissioner Frederick ADLAM	Territorial Commander, East Africa.
Commissioner Ragnar ÅHLBERG	Territorial Commander, Sweden.
Lieut.-Commissioner George BELL	Secretary for Trade.
Lieut.-Commissioner John BLAKE	Territorial Commander, Pakistan.
Lieut.-Commissioner Gösta BLOMBERG	Territorial Commander, Germany.
Commissioner W. Wycliffe BOOTH	Territorial Commander, Canada.
Commissioner William COOPER	Governor, Men's Social Work, Great Britain and Ireland.
Commissioner Frederick COUTTS	Territorial Commander, Australia Eastern.
Commissioner Owen CULSHAW	International Secretary, North, South and Central America, West Indies, Australia and New Zealand.
Commissioner Joseph DAHYA	Territorial Commander, Southern India.
Commissioner Charles DAVIDSON	Territorial Commander, Japan.

Commissioner William DAVIDSON — Territorial Commander, USA Southern.

Colonel Victor DUFAYS — Territorial Commander, Belgium.

Lieut.-Commissioner Francis EVANS — Territorial Commander, Congo.

Commissioner Frank FAIRBANK — Chancellor of the Exchequer, IHQ.

Lieut.-Commissioner Ernest FEWSTER — Territorial Commander, Rhodesia.

Lieut.-Commissioner Lawrence FLETCHER — Territorial Commander, North-east India.

Commissioner Holland FRENCH — Territorial Commander, USA Eastern.

Lieut.-Commissioner Raymond GEARING — Territorial Commander, South America West.

Commissioner Alfred GILLIARD — Territorial Commander, New Zealand.

Commissioner Edgar GRINSTED — British Commissioner.

Commissioner William GROTTICK — Editor in Chief and Literary Secretary, IHQ.

Lieut.-Commissioner Stanley HANNAM — Territorial Commander, Western India.

Lieut.-Commissioner Frederick HARVEY — Territorial Commander, Korea.

Commissioner Samuel HEPBURN — Territorial Commander, USA Central.

Commissioner Theo HOLBROOK — International Secretary, Asia and Africa.

Lieut.-Commissioner Catherine JARVIS — Territorial Commander, Sri Lanka.

Colonel Sture LARSSON — Territorial Commander, Finland.

Colonel Arthur LONG — Territorial Commander, Madras and Andhra, India.

Commissioner Norman MARSHALL — National Commander, USA.

Lieut.-Commissioner Albert MINGAY — Territorial Commander, Scotland.

Commissioner Dorothy MUIRHEAD — Leader, Women's Social Work, Great Britain and Ireland.

Commissioner Arthur PALLANT	Secretary, Advisory Council, IHQ.
Lieut.-Commissioner William PALSTRA	Territorial Commander, The Netherlands.
Commissioner Charles PEAN	Territorial Commander, France.
Lieut.-Commissioner Carl RICHARDS	Auditor General, IHQ.
Commissioner Aage RØNAGER	International Secretary, Europe.
Lieut.-Commissioner Eustace RUSSELL	Special Service, IHQ.
Commissioner Glenn RYAN	Territorial Commander, USA Western.
Lieut.-Commissioner Hubert SCOTNEY	Territorial Commander, Australia Southern.
Lieut.-Commissioner Mrs Violet STOBART	Territorial Commander, Switzerland.
Lieut.-Commissioner William VILLENEUVE	Managing Director, Salvation Army Assurance Society.
Colonel Tor WAHLSTRÖM	Territorial Commander, Denmark.
Lieut.-Commissioner Herbert WESTCOTT	Principal, International College for Officers.
Commissioner Kaare WESTERGAARD	Territorial Commander, Norway.
Commissioner Erik WICKBERG	The Chief of the Staff.
Lieut.-Commissioner Clarence WISEMAN	Principal, International Training College.
Commissioner William WOTTON	Territorial Commander, South Africa.

The doyen of the 1963 High Council, both in age and experience, was Commissioner Norman Marshall, and his choice as President was a right and fitting honour. The youngest member was Colonel Tor Wahlström. Eight members only had attended the previous council – a smaller proportion than on earlier occasions.

The public welcome in the Westminster Central Hall on Wednesday, September 18, gave many of the visiting leaders the rare opportunity of sensing the quality of London Salvationists and friends, and provided the congregation with

an equally rare opportunity of listening to the voice of the
international Army. World voice it was – for each of the five
continents was represented by one of its national leaders.
Perhaps Lieut.-Commissioner Gösta Blomberg (Swedish-
born territorial commander for Germany) summed up the
world situation by quoting the theme of the recent Dortmund
Kirchentag – 'To live with conflict'. The congregation showed
itself well aware of the international situation with its differences between East and West, white and black, left and right,
old world and new – and with no small insight the International
Staff Band (under Lieut.-Colonel Bernard Adams) chose to
play a hitherto unpublished selection by Eric Ball entitled
'Good News' – the good news of the reconciling gospel of Jesus
Christ. This was followed by the counsel of the General to
'strengthen the things which remain' (Revelation 3:2) – a
divine word which reminded the members of the High Council
of their immediate task, and recalled the members of the
congregation to their daily Christian duty.

The following day the members of the High Council assembled at Sunbury Court. In military parlance, all were
present and correct and, under the guidance of the Chief of
the Staff, proceeded to elect their own officers. To assist the
President, Commissioner Norman Marshall, Commissioner
Owen Culshaw, Commissioner Arthur W. Pallant and Lieut.-
Commissioner Herbert Westcott were elected as Vice-
President, Recorder and Assistant Recorder respectively. Later
the appointment of Commissioner Joseph Dahya as chaplain
to the Council was carried by acclamation.

Those who view the proceedings of a High Council from
afar may question why the election of a General could not
proceed more expeditiously. Apart from the basic consideration that so important a decision should not in the least be
hurried, it has to be remembered that some members of a High
Council will not have met each other before. This is no one's
fault. For better, for worse – for better, most readers will agree
– the Army is scattered all over the globe. Even a nominee
may be known but by hearsay if he has served in only one or
two territories. For example, India is one country – but the
great majority of the officers who have spent their life in the
Punjab will not have met their comrades who have served in
Kerala, nor will the territorial leader in an independent African

state have met his opposite number in South America. The miracle of miracles is that they all share a common loyalty to the same Lord and to the same movement. The less than fifty officers (out of a world strength of approximately 25,000, active and retired) who make up a High Council must be given time to pray together, to chat together, to eat together, to agree and disagree with one another, to see life through each other's eyes – in short, to come to know every other officer on the High Council as fully as possible so that they may be assured of the integrity and capacity of the man or woman to whom, under God, they are prepared to commit the supreme leader-ship of the Army. This is what lies behind the deliberations of any High Council – in 1963 no less than at any other time.

Each High Council member can submit the name of one nominee for election to the office of General, and on this occasion these were (in alphabetical order) Commissioners Wycliffe Booth, Frederick Coutts, Edgar Grinsted, Glenn Ryan, Erik Wickberg and Lieut.-Commissioner Clarence Wiseman. Each nominee addressed the High Council and each answered the questions, both general and personal, which were addressed to him. Under the agreed rules of procedure there was no cross-examination of the nominees nor were further speeches made by them. Three withdrew in course of the voting and, on the fourth and final ballot, the President announced that Commissioner Coutts had secured the re-quired two-thirds majority. Official word of this appeared in the international *War Cry* for October 12, 1963, though the news had already been circulated by the media.

Meanwhile General and Mrs Kitching had led the Irish Congress in Belfast, and the General-elect left for Australia in order to return with his wife to London in time for the public welcome on November 28. They were succeeded in Sydney by Lieut.-Commissioner and Mrs Bramwell Cook.

The first of the five farewell meetings to General and Mrs Kitching in the United Kingdom – (the others took place in Bristol, Glasgow, Manchester and Sheffield) – was held in London on October 30, and could be summed up by his observation: 'I want to go out to the waving of flags, even as I was launched into life under the folds of an Army flag.' So three corps flags were among the many to be seen on that night in the Royal Albert Hall – from Wood Green, on which corps platform the General was dedicated; from New Barnet, at which corps he was converted and from which he farewelled for the training college; and from Penge – home corps of Mrs Kitching and where she and the General were married.

Wednesday, November 13, saw what the General described as 'a long-cherished dream' come true. Queen Elizabeth, the Queen Mother, declared open the new International Headquarters – successor to the building which the Army first occupied in Queen Victoria Street in 1881, though it was not called by that name until the first sixteen-page issue of *The War Cry* appeared on February 20, 1886. Though both buildings occupied almost the same site, none could have been more dissimilar. The old '101' had been acquired piecemeal over the years. Its offices and inner passages had been adapted and readapted. A stranger could easily have lost his way in the warren of stairways. Wags had been heard to say that only the electrical wiring held the inner structure together. Until its untimely destruction in 1941, coal fires warmed many of the offices. Grates were cleaned, fire irons dusted and scuttles refilled every working morning from October to March. Clocking on and clocking off took place under the watchful eye of Bandmaster Fred Sherwood of the Penge corps and receptionist – though the title did not come into general use until much later – on all working days at '101'. But now the Army flag flew from a functional office block whose rectangular lines were relieved by the Portland stone facings and the warm Blockley brickwork. Nevertheless, as the Queen Mother observed in her speech, the spirit of those who served in this headquarters was now, as ever, the same.

Said Her Majesty:

It was, I know, a great disappointment to the Queen that she could not be here today, but I am very pleased that it was possible for me to be with you and to bring the Queen's good wishes to all the members of The Salvation Army on this memorable occasion . . .

William Booth, the Founder of the movement, was surely a prophet in his time, for many of the social schemes from which we benefit today were brought into being as he saw the needs of the people. Not only did he take a spiritual message to thousands, but he also realised how great were their physical and material needs. His aims and endeavours have been followed by dedicated men and women of many generations, whose willingness to serve is an inspiring example to us all.

I would like particularly to welcome the international representatives who are here today, many of whom have come from countries thousands of miles across the sea. Their presence is, I feel, a symbol of the unity and strength of The Salvation Army, and a demonstration of the fact that peoples of all races can work in happy relationship . . .

This new building will now become the focal point of the administration of your far reaching organisation – an administration which involves its literature, its music, its social and youth work and, above all, the religious life of a growing body of people. I am confident that the incalculable good which The Salvation Army has done since it was founded will continue in ever increasing measure, and I pray that God's blessing may continue to rest upon your work.

Before leaving the Queen Mother made an unhurried tour around the building, engaging in conversation with a number of the officers and staff, returning to the General's office to sign the visitors' book and to bid farewell to the assembled company.

Later that same evening a meeting of thanksgiving was held in the Bramwell Booth Memorial Hall when the General expressed his gratitude to Commissioner W. Wycliffe Booth and the Canada Territory for their gift of £46,000 which defrayed the cost of building and equipping this most practical remembrance of the Army's second General. The total cost of erecting the new International Headquarters to the standards required by the city planning authorities was £1¼ million and though, as the General stated in presenting the Queen Mother, this sum had not been fully reached, he paid an unqualified tribute to the generosity of Salvationists and friends in all parts of the world.

The Army's seventh General completed his last Sunday on active service – happily there were many Sundays of 'retired' active service to follow – at the corps most closely connected with his earliest years, Wood Green and New Barnet. As might be expected he was occupied with Army affairs to the very day of his retirement when he cabled a message of sympathy to

Generals:–

Above left: ALBERT
ORSBORN 1946–1954

Above right: WILFRED
KITCHING 1954–1963

Left: FREDERICK COUTTS
1963–1969

Below left: ERIK WICKBERG
1969–1974

Below right: CLARENCE
WISEMAN 1974–1977

When the Second World War ended this was the site of the Army's international headquarters in Queen Victoria Street, London.

And this the shell of the territorial headquarters in the Dresdener Strasse, Berlin.

Twenty-two years after the destruction of '101', a new international headquarters was opened on November 13, 1963, by H.M. Queen Elizabeth, the Queen Mother.

Commissioner W. Wycliffe Booth with the Dean of Westminster, Dr. E. S. Abbott, unveiling the memorial to William Booth in the St. George's chapel, Westminster Abbey, on Founders' Day, July 2, 1965.

H.M. Queen Elizabeth II with the platform at the inaugural meeting of the centenary in the Royal Albert Hall on June 24, 1965.

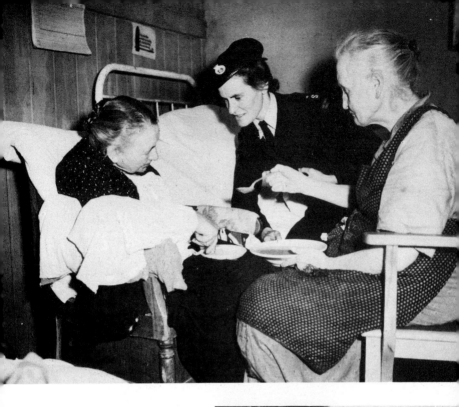

Need is no respecter of age or sex.

'I was hungry, and ye gave me meat.'

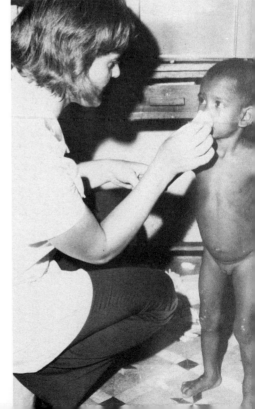

'Naked...and ye clothed me.'

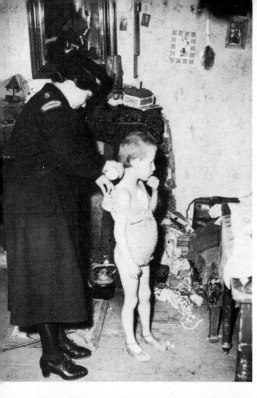

'Sick … and ye visited me.'

'Thirsty … and ye gave me drink.'

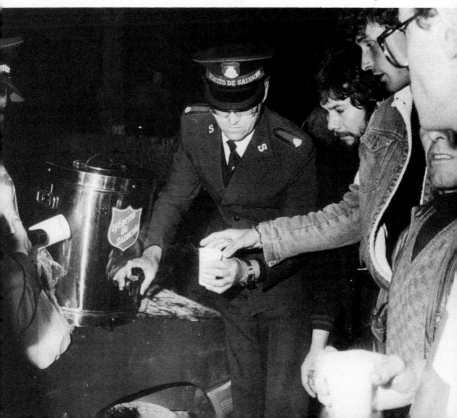

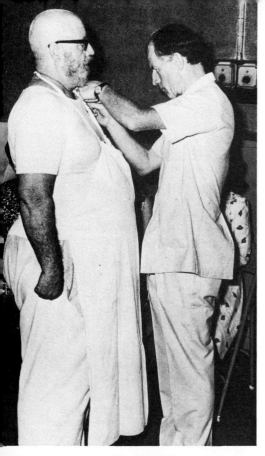

In 1973, at the Army's main food distribution centre in Calcutta, Major Dudley Gardiner received the M.B.E. from Sir Terence Garvey, the British High Commissioner, for his selfless care for the poor of that city.

ON THE MARCH IN –

Kangundo (Kenya)

Port Moresby (Papua New Guinea)

Malawi (Africa)

SINGING WE GO! 'These people will sing their way round the world', declared Dr. John Fulton of New York, a prophecy which William Booth himself quoted in 1886. Here it is happening –

Above: in a meeting in Taiwan *below:* in Kinshasa (Zaire)

on the air in Seoul (Korea)

in the 'local' round the corner.

Peaceful treatment centres for troubled alcoholics at
Rotorua Island in New Zealand.

Kuron – 'the island of hope' in Sweden.

the American people on the assassination of President Kennedy. To the last he sought – as far as in him lay – to heal the world's sorrows in the name of Him in whose presence sorrow changes into song.

PART THREE

THE EIGHTH GENERAL:
FREDERICK COUTTS

(November 23, 1963–
September 20, 1969)

1 PRAISE WAITS FOR THEE

Just before five o'clock on the afternoon of Thursday, October 1, 1963, the Army's solicitor, Mr Vincent Ranger, made his way to the conference chamber at Sunbury Court where members of the High Council were waiting and commenced to read from a statement which began:

> In the ballot taken for the election and appointment of a General of The Salvation Army as and from November 23, 1963, in succession to the present General, Commissioner Frederick Coutts has obtained an absolute two-thirds majority of the votes cast . . .

In one sense this was no break with tradition for, like his predecessors, the manner of life of the eighth General was well known. Born of officer-parents, dedicated under the flag, enrolled in his early teens as a soldier, commissioned as a bandsman as soon as he was eligible for that office, a one-time corps cadet, he had followed a well-worn path. But he had never enjoyed any close personal links with the leaders of the past for his parents, though commissioned officers in the early nineties, had been appointed mainly to provincial corps until their retirement soon after the end of the First World War.

Mrs General Bessie Coutts grew up in Warrington, an industrial town halfway between Liverpool and Manchester. There, with her parents and two brothers, she worshipped in a hall which had been a disused malt kiln – until a purpose-built citadel was erected in 1932 in Buttermarket Street – one of the main feeder roads to the town centre. While an active Salvationist – songster (choir member), company guard (Sunday school teacher), leader of the local guard (now guide) troop, as well as making her regular round of the public houses on a Saturday evening with the Army papers – she had taken a science degree with honours at the University of Manchester. After serving on the staff of what was then the John Howard secondary school in Clapton, she entered the Army training college and was commissioned as an officer in the spring of 1925, marrying the youthful Captain Frederick Coutts in November of the same year.

During the First World War the General had served as a flying officer in the RFC (later the RAF) and, after demobilisation early in 1919, entered the Clapton training college and was commissioned in May 1920. After their marriage corps appointments took the young couple from the Channel Islands to the Clydeside. They were still learning – by the time-honoured method of trial and error – how better to fulfil their calling when a change of appointment brought the adjutant (now an obsolete rank) to the literary department at International Headquarters. Here he remained for eighteen years – first preparing the Bible notes used for teaching purposes in the Army's young people's corps (or Sunday schools), then acting as editor of *The Officer* – a monthly magazine circulating among all English-speaking officers throughout the world, and finally as literary secretary to the General. In 1953 he was appointed Principal of the International Training College and, four years later, was sent as leader of the Australia Eastern Territory where he remained until his election as General in November 1963.

The one cloud in the sky was that as a result of a routine vaccination required in order to travel back to England, Mrs Coutts became paralysed from the waist downward only weeks before the planned date of departure. Medical opinion spoke hopefully of recovery and remedial treatment was begun before she left Sydney. Though still unable to walk unassisted when she arrived in London, her message to the welcome meeting – read by her youngest daughter, Elizabeth – was: 'I am eager to be with you as soon as possible.' In faith she quoted a modern translation of Isaiah 40:31: 'They that wait upon the Lord shall go marching along.' And, she added, 'if this is behind the Army flag and in front of an Army band, so much the better.'

Two events faced the new General – one to which he had already given some thought; the other entirely unexpected. The first – the worthy celebration of the Revd William Booth's initial breakthrough in the East End of London – called for instant attention. As with any international figure of note, there were many who had sought – and now were seeking more ardently than ever – to associate themselves with his otherwise unheralded beginnings. The number of those who claimed to have stood with William Booth when he stood alone on Mile End Waste was legion. Happily the legends which multiply and grow around such an occasion had already been faithfully dealt with by Robert Sandall, the veteran officer-writer who was responsible for the first three volumes of the Army's history. In sober fact there should have been little need for this, for William Booth himself had put the record straight in a letter which appeared in the August 17, 1865, issue of *Revival*.[1]

> Invited by Messrs. Stabb and Chase I have held a week's services in a large tent erected in the Quaker's burial gound, Thomas (Vallance) Street, Whitechapel. So evident was the divine approval that the services have continued until now.
> Nearly every night two meetings are held – first in the Mile End Road and afterwards in the tent. On the last two sabbaths we have conducted four services each day ... There have been but two or three meetings of the whole course at which sinners have not professed to find mercy, and sometimes thirteen or fourteen have done so in the one evening.

A centenary planning council was set up under the chairmanship of Commissioner Arthur W. Pallant, and one of the ablest administrators in Salvationist circles in Great Britain, Colonel Frederick Kiff – who for the previous three and a half years had been Chief Secretary of the British Territory – was appointed Chief Executive Secretary for the forthcoming celebrations. Corps as far apart as Miami in Florida and Boscombe in Dorset led the way in offering to sponsor an officer-delegate from a missionary country, and Canada furthered the good work by promising to provide twenty such sponsors. Other missionary territories such as Indonesia let it be known that, rather than be a charge on any Army fund, they would themselves meet the full cost of their national delegation to London. Before April was out it had been announced that, by courtesy of the Dean, the Very Reverend Dr Eric S. Abbott, a meeting of thanksgiving would be held in Westminster Abbey when a bust of the Founder and a plaque to his memory would be unveiled in the chapel of St. George.

In the midst of all these preparations there occurred an unexpected but most opportune irruption by younger Salvationists in the time-honoured field of Salvationist evangelism – though at first this was not everywhere welcomed. There had grown up a certain orthodoxy of Army method which, though unorthodox enough in its own beginnings, had hardened into 'the done thing', and any departure therefrom was challenged by some and resented by not a few. 'The Joystrings' was one such challenging departure.

The indignant protestors at this supposedly new and undesirable mode of evangelism could have forgotten that, before the century had begun until his promotion to Glory in 1944, such a well-known Army character as Brigadier Tom Plant had delighted congregations at home and abroad with music and song based on what was undoubtedly a lineal descendant of the biblical instrument of ten strings. At the international congress in 1914, and again in 1921 and 1925/6, a singing party from the West Indies had captivated their British listeners with their lilting melodies and haunting harmonies. And if the guitar was the principal stone of stumbling, it was that instrument, played by Jenny Svenson, which accompanied the singing of 'We're bound for the land of the pure and the holy' when the Army opened fire in Sweden in December 1882.

As changes in the social habits of the people of Britain thinned out the crowds who – in some instances – actually waited for the Army to begin its evening open-air meeting in the local market place or city square, so did the desire increase in the hearts of many Salvationists, young and old alike, to find some equally compelling way of bringing the gospel of our Lord and Saviour Jesus Christ, to the public notice.

Like other Army leaders before him, General Kitching had stressed the need to catch the ear of the crowd in the shopping centres and the young folk thronging the amusement arcades. At this juncture skiffle was all the rage, and the response of a group of cadets (officer-students) at the International Training College in south London was to include washboards, tea chest basses, bazookas and shakers made from cocoa tins and filled with dried peas, in their campaign equipment. A provincial reporter saw a newsworthy item in this novel way of music making and, marvellous to the one-track participants, it was but a step to the radio studio, even to the television screen, with the world of commercial entertainment in close attendance.

But the meretricious glitter of the cash prizes of that world had little attraction for the single-minded Captain Joy Webb and her small team who were officially called 'The International Training College Rhythm Group'. Mercifully that mouthful of a name soon died the death and, in fairness to their leader, it should be said that the more popular one-word title had nothing to do with the Christian name given her by her officer-parents, but everything to do with the Christian joy which, as she herself said, 'can never be explained away by the most confirmed cynic or seasoned sophisticate'.[2]

The first public appearance of the 'The Joystrings' – that is, apart from the release of their first forty-five single, a Cliff Michelmore programme and a Jimmy Young 'Saturday Special' – was at the Army hall in Lomond Grove, Camberwell. *The War Cry* for March 18, 1964, reported:

> A note on the programme stated ... ' "The Joystrings" are a group of eight salvationists composed mainly of officers and cadets from the William Booth Memorial College ... Their highest privilege is to present ... the gospel message to you tonight'.
>
> Captain Joy Webb, the leader of the group, also emphasized the mission of the music. Time will probably show that this meeting at Camberwell last Saturday night was historic, marking the first of a new kind of Army meeting – or is it a revival of an earlier kind, but in modern dress?
>
> Like all musical programmes should be, it was a salvation meeting which ended with a lined mercy seat. But this gathering had the uninhibited gaiety and the glorious informality – both as a salvation meeting and a musical programme – which the Army has seemed in danger of losing.
>
> At times the joyful noise was deafening, as was the applause ... Yet there were also times when the excitement was subdued to the hushed acceptance of a tender appeal, particularly during what became the final number, when the seekers began making their way forward.

Within the week the group received – and accepted – an invitation which provoked increased assent and dissent the world over. This was to appear as the third act in the cabaret show in the 'Blue Angel' night club. 'The Joystrings' were to be preceded by the coloured singer, Joy Marshall, and 'Hutch' with his piano – after which the compere, Noel Harrison, announced on each of the three successive nightly appearances: 'And now we are proud to present from The Salvation Army – "The Joystrings"' – and the beat of 'It's an open secret' followed without a second's hesitation.[3] As followed as well in due course the questionings of those who queried the wisdom of the whole enterprise and the abuse of those who totally disagreed with the whole endeavour. Well for 'The Joystrings' that some of their comrades at the training college had set their alarm clocks for the small hours of the morning so that they might intercede in prayer while the group played.

The children of the light should not have allowed their fears to get the better of them. Salvationists who know their own story can recall that their beloved and revered General Bramwell has described how

> . . . I once actually came into a music-hall variety show. This was at a theatre in Plymouth and I was 'Item no. 12'. The orchestra played me on to 'For he's a jolly good fellow', and I received an amazing welcome from a house packed in every corner . . . When the first thunders of the applause had died away there came from the topmost gallery into the expectant silence a thin but penetrating voice: 'Now fire a volley!' The whole house roared its response . . . I spoke that night of every man's need of true friendship – above all his need of the friendship of God.[4]

The Canadian *War Cry* reported that Dr Billy Graham expressed his regret that a Salvation Army musical group should have entered a night club. To this the 'stand-no-nonsense' Commissioner Samuel Hepburn replied that 'the Army had been going into saloons, tap rooms, pool rooms and dance halls for scores of years, playing their music and singing their songs. "The Joystrings" were following in the Founder's footsteps – with equally desirable results.'

It has long been the Lord's good pleasure to fulfil himself in many ways, and early in 1964 the Army returned thanks for a valuable ally who had been promoted to Glory – Hugh Redwood, the 'big brother' of the slum services, later known as the Goodwill Department.

His association with the Army began in Bristol at the turn of the century and, after it had ended almost as abruptly as it had begun, was renewed early in 1928 when he met a handful of women Salvation Army officers belonging to the 'Slums'.

They were endeavouring to cope with some of the immediate
results in the back streets of Westminster of the Thames floods
in the early morning of Saturday, January 7, 1928. Since that
date upwards of half a million copies of *God in the Slums* have
been sold. Its near cousins – *God in the Shadows*, *God in the
Everyday* and *God and the Listener* – with others that followed in
due course – have yielded an untold harvest of which The
Salvation Army has been but one of many beneficiaries.

But the Army's regular services were not neglected by
reason of these unusual events. The inevitable changes in
international leadership could not be avoided. Commissioner
and Mrs W. Wycliffe Booth farewelled from Canada and
joined International Headquarters as travelling commissioners. Commissioner and Mrs Edgar Grinsted became the
new Army leaders in Canada, with Commissioner and Mrs
William F. Cooper following on in Britain and Commissioner
and Mrs Herbert Westcott undertaking the oversight of the
Men's Social Services. Later in the year Commissioner and
Mrs William Grottick retired from active service, Commissioner and Mrs Alfred J. Gilliard succeeded them at International Headquarters and, in turn, Commissioner Charles
Davidson in New Zealand. The last named had made a unique
contribution to the life of the Army in the Far East, and one
of his last services to the land to which he had ministered so
devotedly was to plan relief work in the stricken city of Niigata
in mid-1964 – which had been visited by an earthquake that
recalled the even more fearsome devastation which overtook
Tokyo and Yokohama in 1925.[5]

The eve of the centenary proved to be an opportune moment
for the publication of *The History of The Salvation Army* (Volume
IV, 1886–1904) by Nelson & Sons. This was the work of
Lieut.-Commissioner Arch R. Wiggins, successor to Colonel
Robert Sandall who had been promoted to Glory. A hardback
of over 400 pages, selling at 30s., was value for anyone's money.
Put briefly, this covered a period when the overseas structures
of the Army were being formed, and when – particularly in
the British Isles – the fight for the freedom to march in
procession on the streets, and to hold religious meetings in
the open air without being charged with obstruction of the
highway, was fought – and won. This was somewhat of a war
of attrition for the last skirmish was reported as late as 1912

when the officer at Scunthorpe, Adjutant A. F. Feltwell, was sentenced to seven days' imprisonment (which he served in the third division, picking oakum) for obstruction. Nowadays it is any absence of the sight and sound of the Army on the streets, rather than its presence, which provokes comment.

While giving attention to centenary plans and himself making the initial approaches to secure the sympathetic interest of Buckingham Palace and Westminster Abbey, the General maintained a full list of meetings during the first of his six years of office. The New Year saw him in Edinburgh, Glasgow, Dundee and Aberdeen. His overseas campaigns began in mid-January with a visit to Stuttgart, the cradle of the Army in Germany and, as the year progressed, on to France, Belgium, Switzerland, The Netherlands and Sweden – in that order.

A midweek break in June gave him the opportunity of accepting the invitation of the headmaster, Mr James Drummond, DFC, MA, to revisit his old school, Leith Academy, after a lapse of more than half a century, for commemoration day, 1964. In true Scottish tradition the proceedings began with the singing of the metrical psalm and, with customary Scottish generosity, included a cheque from the pupils to be given to one of the Army's secondary schools in Africa.

In the last three months of the year campaigns were held in what were then the Belgian Congo, French Equatorial Africa, Nigeria and Ghana. On this occasion the General was joined by Brigadier Ephraim Zulu, Divisional Commander of the mid-Natal and Ixopo division in Southern Africa. 'He is with me', explained the General, 'as a witness to the place which we desire to give the African officer in the corporate life of the Army in his own continent.' A General can have no favourite territory. All are equally important to him. But it would be idle to deny his special interest in Nigeria where he dedicated his youngest grandchild, Marian, daughter of Captain and Mrs John Coutts, principal of the Army's secondary school at Akai.

Mrs Coutts was able to accompany her husband to Finland for the seventy-fifth anniversary of the Army's work in that country and, in appreciation, all the state churches – representing ninety-five per cent of the Christian community – joined in presenting to the Army a united free-will offering. Last but not least in the year's calendar, ten days later a European leaders' conference was held at Ringgenberg (Switzerland) to consider prospects and plans for the work of God in that part of the world where the Christian faith was first established. For the Army, however, this did not mark the shades of evening but the promise of a new dawn. The Army was soon to be a hundred years young.

2   BEGIN THE THANKSGIVING

The beginning of 1965 found the Army ready, lamps trimmed and loins girded, to celebrate its centenary. There had been anniversaries of some specific Army activity – e.g., the home league and the corps cadet brigade – during General Kitching's term of office, but there had been no international congress celebrations since 1914. For the centenary more than thirty major gatherings had been planned for London alone between June 24 and July 3 inclusive. Westminster Abbey, the Royal Albert Hall and the Westminster Central Hall were each to resound with songs of praise. The Clapton Congress Hall – still boasting its original spaciousness – and the Regent Hall at Oxford Circus were to be in use nightly as well. Trafalgar Square and the Crystal Palace were to testify that the Army was still the church of the open air. It even seemed as if the media were conspiring to focus attention upon what one of our liveliest Army writers had, in a telling phrase, called 'a hundred years' war'. The year had hardly begun when 'Cassandra' of the *Daily Mirror* and Lieut.-Colonel Bernard Watson were confronting one another over the top of their respective type-writers.

The War Cry for January 9 – pp. 10, selling price 3d. (old currency), weekly circulation 210,000 rising to 224,000 by the end of the year – carried a front-page article headed 'The Bond Mania'. In the 'best' tradition of his previous exploits 007 was concerned to destroy the atomic bomb which was threatening the gold reserves at Fort Knox. As was his wont he was accompanied by the inevitable bevy of glamorous girls, high-speed cars, cocktails galore and automatic weapons in abundance. 'Violence in the Bond books', commented Watson, 'reaches psychopathic proportions. There is no pity for the maimed and tortured people who go screaming through a typical Bond plot. Cruelty seems to exist for the love of cruelty.

Sadism is present as well . . . As most Bond fans are youngish
it may not be coincidence that the latest Home Office criminal
statistics for England and Wales show a nine per cent increase
in indictable offences, including robbery, murder and crimes
of violence.'

The ensuing brouhaha may have been louder and more
confused because Watson's centenary history of more than 300
pages was just off the press,[1] and had been described by the
Daily Mirror in a full-page review as 'compellingly interesting'.
But when a news agency reported that James Bond was 'under
fire' from The Salvation Army, 'Cassandra' replied in kind.
While commending Salvationists in general for their good
works, he smote Salvation Army colonels – doubtless a generic
term for the top brass – hip and thigh. But the ever-vigilant
War Cry caught 'Cassandra' misquoting. Four points to Watson
for a foul stroke! And, remembering the Irishman's enquiry as
to whether the squabble he was watching was a private fight
or a free-for-all, certain bolder spirits in the media joined in
without so much as a by your leave. Head unbowed, Watson
found himself featured in a BBC news review, quoted in
a televised programme on violence in modern society, and
interviewed on Granada TV as well.

Shock waves reverberated across the Atlantic. *Time* magazine conjured up a vision of a British Salvation Army colonel
'roaring: "Backward, Christian soldiers, heed no James Bond
movies" . . .' But these harsh altercations died away when the
James Bond association was given leave to reproduce in full
the original *War Cry* article so that they could form their own
judgment as to whether or not their idol had been defamed.

Sweeter sounds stilled the storm as the music of 'The Joystrings' continued to endear them to their viewers – particularly by their spring appearance on the steps of St. Paul's on
behalf of Third World needs. The ancient Wimborne Minster
was crowded to the doors when the group travelled down to
Dorset. With equal readiness 'The Joystrings' shared in a
Scripture Union rally at the Westminster Central Hall, and
played at a public reception at Burlington House sponsored
by the National Savings Committee, at which the Governor of
the Bank of England was the guest of honour. So great was
their nationwide popularity that, about this time, a provincial
youth group invited the General to address them, adding the

sure word of prophecy that, if he would bring 'The Joystrings' with him, a full house could be guaranteed.

During centenary year the Army could hardly keep out of the news as when, in harmony with his own last wish, the funeral of Lord Morrison of Lambeth was conducted on Thursday, March 11, 1965, by the General. The Home Office was – and still is – closely associated with a number of the Army's social services in the United Kingdom and, on one occasion at least, the one-time Home Secretary had left the House to address an Army rally in the Westminster Central Hall. The large crowd who gathered for the interment – ranging from peers of the realm to the Pearly King and Queen of Lambeth – could not be accommodated in the chapel at the Eltham crematorium but overflowed on to the grassy slopes and verges to listen to the tribute paid by the Rt. Hon. George Brown, MP, to the music of the International Staff Band, and to the comfortable words of Christian hope contained in the vocal solo of Captain Leslie Condon, FTCL, L.Mus.TCL – 'In heavenly love abiding'. All this reminded the sympathetic congregation that 'he who dies believing dies safely through Thy love.'

Whether righteousness can be too well publicised or not is a moot point, but the current interest in Army activities led to the story that a night club was to be opened in the West End where there would be music and dancing. Some readers of the Army's press expressed their fears that William Booth would be turning in his grave, but their unjustified anxieties were given their due quietus when Major Fred Brown, the commanding officer at the Regent Hall stated that, in his judgment, 'dancing in connection with Salvationist gatherings for youth was neither desirable nor necessary.' The truth behind this canard was that a group of cadets from the International Training College, supported by the tireless 'Joystrings', had been holding an informal gathering for teenagers at nine o'clock on a Saturday evening and 200 of them had come in off the streets to the Regent Hall. Other late Saturday evening meetings were to follow, and these irregular but highly praiseworthy evangelical forays were copied in centres other than London and in countries outside Europe.

To link the past still more closely with the present Major Fleur Booth, herself on the staff of the International Training

College, journeyed to Redruth to recall one of the outstanding ministries of her great-grandparents. After their break with the Methodist New Connexion, William and Catherine sought to fulfil their calling by accepting whatever opportunities might come their way and, with previous experiences in mind, turned to Cornwall. But Methodism had firmly closed her official doors. Neither husband nor wife were to be allowed the freedom of her pulpits. However, in September 1862, the Free Methodists of Redruth welcomed these two evangelical castaways into their building and the ensuing meetings were marked by large congregations and many seekers.

Wrote Catherine to her mother: 'The movement here has stirred the whole town ... The chapel was open all day yesterday, and the people in their homes could hear the cry of the penitents.' The Army Mother's biographer added that 'Mr Booth had the usual communion rails extended across the entire breadth of the chapel, beside erecting barriers to keep off the crowds of onlookers who pressed so closely to the front that it was found almost impossible to deal effectively with those who were seeking salvation.'

On the Sunday of her commemorative visit Major Fleur Booth addressed the united congregations of Wesley Chapel and Fore Street Methodist Church, with upwards of a thousand people present in the evening meeting.

Nor was this the only link with the past. A commentator so alert as Lieut.-Colonel Bernard Watson could not fail to make a feature out of the link between Mr Charles Chaplin and the south London Salvation Army hall then standing in Kennington Lane, Lambeth, SE11. When Hermione Hammond was asked why she had included this somewhat nondescript building in her All Hallows exhibition of notable London churches she replied: 'It is the place where Charlie Chaplin worshipped as a boy.'

Commented Watson:

Chaplin's father drank himself to death. The shy sensitive boy saw his mother lose her reason and have to be put away in what was then called a lunatic asylum. Charlie was sent to a grim home for destitute children. There he was once so savagely beaten that he had to have medical attention. For a while the family was in the workhouse. On another occasion the woman supposed to be looking after Charlie threw him into the street where the police found him at three o'clock in the morning huddled beside a night watchman's fire . . .

So it was that sometimes Charlie the boy went along to the 'Joy Hour' at The Salvation Army – a children's meeting where the songs were gay, the music bright, and the youngsters clapped their hands . . .

A lot of water has flowed under Lambeth Bridge since then and one day, not long ago, Charlie came back. He managed to evade the press cameras and quietly entered that same hall. The band played 'The old rugged cross'. The congregation sang: 'Can a poor sinner come to Jesus?' – and Mr Chaplin told one of the officers about his boyhood visits to the Army. These he had not forgotten.

During the centenary celebrations there were many others who showed that they had not forgotten – and it was to link as many such remembrancers as he could that the General visited southern Africa and western Canada. Both occasions showed that the centenary infection had made light of distance.

The Saturday morning march through the crowded Rissik Street – the Oxford Street of Johannesburg – witnessed yet once again to the gospel of the whosoever. An appropriate scripture passage from John 3:14–21, was read in Afrikaans, Zulu and English by individual officers whose first languages these were. Two new building sites were dedicated during the day for centenary projects. One was in the heart of the city and would carry a new territorial headquarters, the city corps hall and a young women's residence. The other was further afield where a new residential home for African girls was to be built. For the moment the tuneful voices of the Strathyre girls' choir could be heard as an earnest of things to come.

Sunday saw three multi-racial meetings in the city hall with the Mayor, Councillor Aleck Jaffe, presiding and the civic authorities, along with the mayors of fifteen Rand townships, supporting. The same sincere cordiality was shown in Durban, Port Elizabeth and East London as well as when the General moved inland to Amatikulu where he presented a fifty years' service medal to Corps Sergeant-Major Joshua Mthembu who, in replying, fitly quoted words spoken by the Army's Founder when he visited South Africa in 1908.

Moving still further up country the General, accompanied

by Mr V. Leibrandt, chief regional commissioner for Bantu affairs, was received by Prince Tshivhase, senior chief of the Ba Venda, and then presented Brigadier Mary Styles – 'Saint Mary' to all and sundry in that isolated and retarded corner of the Republic – with the Order of the Founder, a justified recognition of more than twenty years' selfless service to the people of Vendaland. Then back to Johannesburg for the weekend's African gatherings in the Mofolo community centre, and thence to the final gatherings in Cape Town where, in the concluding salvation meeting in the Gordon's Institute, black, white and coloured Salvationists joined in praise to God – with a repeatedly lined mercy seat again in evidence.

After a break of little more than a week the General left for western Canada – with stopovers in Montreal and Toronto to share in well attended Holy Week gatherings. Once more all that took place led to a clearer understanding of the meaning of the self-offering of God in Christ for us men and our salvation. Western Canada – with time and meetings divided between Calgary and Vancouver – gave the international visitor a characteristically robust welcome – with the centenary again taking pre-eminence when a peak in the Rockies was named Mount William Booth.

The last three pre-centenary engagements undertaken by the General were in Scotland – the first in Glasgow, the second in Kirkcaldy, the third in Edinburgh. These could be described as a son's token of filial respect – for in earlier years his parents had commanded five corps in these three places and he himself had served in two.

St. Mungo's Cathedral is the mother church of Scotland, and the music and song for this thanksgiving to God were supplied by the Clydebank band and the Parkhead songster brigade. Adjutant and Mrs John Coutts were stationed at the latter in 1914–16; Adjutant and Mrs Frederick Coutts at the former in 1934–5.

On the following day, Monday, May 31, in the flower bedecked Adam Smith hall in Kirkcaldy, the General was admitted as a 'guild brother, burgess and freeman of the royal burgh'. The burgesses have always jealously guarded this honour, and this was but the tenth name to be added to the roll since that of William Booth on April 16, 1906. But having received his burgess ticket, the key of the burgh, and having signed the roll, the General went on to give credit where credit was justly due and said:

> This recognition of me is not, I am quite sure, a recognition of me alone, but is an acknowledgment of the integrity of my fellow Salvationists who belong to the royal burgh.
>
> I cannot imagine your honouring me if you did not hold in equal regard your fellow citizens who are also my fellow Salvationists. You would not grace me in this high fashion if their lives were clouded by the least shadow of disgrace. And so to this indirect but highly significant tribute to the worth of my Salvation Army comrades who share in the corporate life of our burgh, I am glad to add my own.

Four days before the official programme of the centenary was due to begin the General was back in Edinburgh. Here it was not possible to walk past St. Giles – let alone enter the cathedral – without treading where both saints and sinners had jostled one another, disputed with one another and, alas, come to blows with one another in the stormy course of their ancient history. This time it was the flag that knows no national boundaries, and the music of Christ's universal gospel, which was seen and heard along the royal mile.

Despite the demands of these public occasions the unseen preparations for the international centenary were proceeding at a determined pace. Eager that so historic an occasion should yield a permanent dividend to the work of the Army in the land of its birth, in August 1964 the General had appointed Lieut.-Colonel Arnold Brown – whose creative gifts had proved their worth many times over to the Army in Canada – to head the Public Relations Department at International Headquarters.

Three major developments – among others – resulted therefrom. The first was the introduction of Salvation Army advisory boards to the United Kingdom; the second was the publication of a well-researched study of the country's current social needs; the third was the launching of a three-million-pound appeal to help meet those needs. The idea, though not the name, of advisory boards dated back to the 1890s when the Ballington Booths were in charge of the Army's work in the United States, and was revived twenty-five years later by Colonel Fletcher Agnew in Chicago. Their existence was lim-

ited to North America until the 1960s – when the centenary
opened the way for their introduction to the British Isles.
Three short paragraphs in a manual of guidance indicate their
nature and purpose.

An advisory board is composed of representative men and women
who are interested in the spiritual, moral and physical well-being
of their fellow citizens, and who –

  (i) have confidence in The Salvation Army as a vehicle for
      community service;
 (ii) believe in its programme of spiritual and character building
      and social activities for the amelioration and relief of need
      of all kinds;
(iii) are joined together for the purpose of assisting the Army
      in the carrying on of its work.[2]

For the purpose of the Army's work in the United Kingdom
and Northern Ireland, it was thought best to introduce these
boards only to the larger centres of population where two or
more aspects of the Army's activities were in operation. In
the meantime the ground work was prepared for what was
described as only the second nationwide appeal for funds for
the development of the Army's social services since William
Booth's 'Darkest England' scheme in 1890. He then asked for
£100,000 for capital projects and £30,000 for annual maintenance. He was able to raise the first figure but was denied
the second – with the result that he often had to struggle along
on a shoestring.

Tragedies of Affluence was written to provide statistical and
photographic evidence of human need in the United Kingdom
in the year 1965. Some of it was frightening; all of it was
compelling. There were 800,000 fatherless children around –
one third orphaned, the rest were children of divorced, separated or unmarried parents. Some 675,000 elderly people lacked
the elements of basic human interest and care. Ten per cent
of them lived alone. Another 400,000 could only be described
– in all charity – as social misfits – alcoholics, addicts of one
variety or another, the homeless, the ex-prisoners, the young
offenders, the forgotten army of the socially inadequate.

To care for these on a national scale demanded an expendi-
ture of at least £3 million. Speaking at a press conference to

launch this appeal, the General quoted the retort of Warren Hastings to the charge that he had appropriated the wealth of India for his own benefit:

> 'I am amazed at my own moderation.' I would gladly settle for a hundredth part of the TSR2 programme . . . As a church the Army is largely supported by its soldiers and well-wishers. As a social service we appeal to the community to help us to serve the community. As far as in us lies we are determined that the deprived child shall not have to endure a deprived future, that the aged and infirm shall not lack a friend in need, and that the social misfit shall be given a chance to make good.

The same issue of *The War Cry* that reported this press conference also carried an account of the opening of the new Redcliffe hostel for women and girls in the city of Exeter in the presence of the Mayor (Alderman P. A. Spoerer) and his lady, the Bishop of Crediton (the Rt. Revd. W. R. E. Westall), the city fathers and Commissioner Dorothy Muirhead, leader of the Women's Social Work in Great Britain and Ireland. This was the first on the list of centenary projects to be completed. Deeds were keeping pace with words – and would so continue.

3   TO GOD BE THE GLORY

Thursday, June 24, 1965, dawned sunny and bright and the weather so continued for more than a week. None welcomed this more than the eager Salvationists who were London-bound from the world's four corners and from most places in the British Isles as well. Celebrations on this scale were bound to spill over the edges, and this they were doing ten days previously when the General led a party of early arrivals in a commemorative open-air meeting alongside the memorial which marks William Booth's first appearance as a freelance missioner in the East End of London. No event could have looked more like a chance affair than this one. A small party of campaigners were looking for a campaign leader. A 36-year-old minister – formerly of the Methodist New Connexion but against whom his church had closed her doors – happened to pass by. Though he knew it not there was a divinity which was shaping his ends, and it was to recognise this truth that this meeting was being held in 1965.

Not everyone on the Whitechapel Road that Saturday afternoon was aware that he was treading where one of the prophets of the Lord had trod. There were few obvious signs of the divine presence. As might be expected in summertime the air was hot, noisy and dusty. The capital's familiar red buses were busy setting down and picking up. Stall holders and shoppers were mutually occupied with getting and spending. Private motorists were adding their personal obbligato to the raucous music of the traffic. The pavements were crowded with people most of whom were more set on reaching journey's end than willing to stop and listen. But Booth's twentieth-century successors were no less determined than he was to gain a hearing for the Christian gospel, and sounds of salvation began to compete with the confused noises of the A11. Commented the General: 'The truths of our faith demand to be proclaimed at our street corners. In seeking thus to make them known we are following not only the example of William Booth but the practice of our Lord Himself, much of whose ministry was exercised in the open air.'

Many and varied were the ways in which the towns and villages of the British Isles sought to honour the life and work of the Army's Founder. During the summer of 1965, upwards of 150 of them said it with flowers. Some were as professional as the floral display in Princes Street, Edinburgh; others as unpretentious as the garden seat erected in a London street where William Booth and his young family used to live. All testified to the sweetness and light which he had brought into shadowed human nature. Twenty of the country's cathedrals – from Aberdeen to Exeter and including Canterbury and York – remembered him in a service of thanksgiving. Civic authorities followed suit. On the eve of the principal celebrations the Lord Mayor of London, Sir James Miller, and the Lady Mayoress, received the entire body of Salvationist delegates in the 600-year-old Great Hall of London's Guildhall, bringing to mind the fact that sixty years had passed since the freedom of the city had been conferred on William Booth. Commercial interests were no less responsive. One of Oxford Street's largest departmental stores staged a ten-day exhibition which provided innumerable visitors with a fuller understanding of the scope and motivation of the Army's worldwide work.

Expectation was at its height when on Thursday, June 24 at three o'clock, with royal promptitude, Her Majesty Queen Elizabeth II entered the crowded Royal Albert Hall. The swelling waves of applause almost drowned the fanfare of the International Staff Band whose scarlet tunics formed a tight circle of brilliant colour, backed by the more sober greys and blacks of the clergy, government ministers and invited guests, together with the diplomatic representatives of the many countries where the Army was at work. Against the broader band of dark blue formed by the 500-voice centenary chorus the Queen's lime green costume glowed fresh and opalescent. At equal remove from Her Majesty was the Archbishop of Canterbury, Dr Michael Ramsay on the one side and the Archbishop of Westminster, Cardinal John Heenan, on the other. To her right the General and the Chief of the Staff stood beside the traditionally bonneted figures of Mrs General Coutts

and Mrs Commissioner Wickberg. Almost without being
aware of what was happening the congregation began to sing
in full-throated fashion the majestic lines of 'Now thank we all
our God'. Then in an intensity of stillness which matched the
volume of the song the congregation stood silent, broken only
by a murmur of amens, as the Moderator of the Free Church
Federal Council, the Revd. Peter McCall, MA, returned
thanks to God for His grace and guidance over the past
hundred years.

Before Commissioner Joseph Dahya, as a representative of
the Asian world, read from the scriptures, the centenary chorus
voiced the praise of God in the Handelian chorus: 'Worthy is
the Lamb' and then, with a five-word introduction, the Queen
was addressing the gathering. One of the memorable features
of the Centenary was that music and song and speech each
held the attention of the congregation in turn. There have been
occasions when the last named has been a poor third – the
audience listening with polite interest without being gripped
by what was being said. Not so now. Said the Queen:

> The service conducted by William Booth in a tent on a disused
> burial ground in the East End of London in July 1865, was
> the start of one of the great world-wide religious organisations,
> supported and respected everywhere it works. The secret of its
> success lay in William Booth's complete self-dedication to the will
> of God and to His service, and in passionate love for the souls of
> men and women . . .
>
> Here in the Royal Albert Hall are men and women of many
> races from nearly every country in the world gathered together
> with one accord, in one place, to celebrate the completion of one
> hundred years of work . . . In the past century The Salvation
> Army has grown from a small mission in a London side street, with
> no permanent base, into a religious and humanitarian organisation
> which encircles the world . . .
>
> Today we all thank God for what He has accomplished through
> you in the cause of man's salvation, and we pray that under His
> divine providence and blessing the great work of The Salvation
> Army may grow and prosper in the years to come.

The congregation rose to sing again – this time the verses
of General Albert Orsborn (R), himself in the meeting, which
were inspired by the international congress of 1914: 'Army
flag, thy threefold glory greets the rising of the sun' – and then

the impressive figure of the Archbishop of Canterbury was heard thanking the Queen for her presence and then reminding his hearers of the words of Jesus which were most fully exemplified in the life of William Booth – 'The Son of man is come to seek and to save that which was lost.'

Some of these [continued the Archbishop] have lost their place in society through undeserved poverty and misfortune. Others are lost in the sense of having lost touch with God and consequently are in spiritual darkness. Do we not need caring Christians in both kind of ways . . .?

You of The Salvation Army do show us how to care and inspire us to care. At the same time, putting first things first, you also show how the caring Christian has to care about man's greatest predicament and greatest need, namely, the estrangement of his soul from God, his Father and Creator . . .

It is very thrilling to look at this great concourse of Salvation Army men and women from every part of the world . . . It is wonderful to think of the variety of qualities and gifts that must be brought together in such a gathering, but there is one gift that I believe every Salvationist has in a wonderful measure – and that is the gift of joy. I have seen many odd things in my time but I do not think I have ever seen a gloomy Salvationist. The gift of joy is wonderfully yours. May it continue to be yours.

After such an address all that the International Staff Band could do to cheer the congregation still further was to play Lieut.-Colonel Skinner's 'Songs of the Salvationist' – and allow the music to speak for itself. The Home Secretary, Sir Frank Soskice, QC, MP, then paid tribute to the urgency with which William Booth addressed himself to the material needs of the people in his day, and then spoke of the need for a similar urgency in our own time.

The great modern paradox is that in a world of plenty there is still want and . . . the ever-increasing work of The Salvation Army shows that there is a real need for voluntary organisations to supplement what central and local government can provide. There are some things which they can do very much better. They can work with different emphasis and experiment in different directions . . . Because we believe that there are no unimportant people in the world we welcome, and will always welcome, the continued service which The Salvation Army can provide.

The heart of the meeting had yet to be reached and, when it was reached, it was almost by surprise. A single uniformed songster moved quietly in front of the centenary chorus and then, above an introduction which but stole over the vast congregation, was heard the unadorned fall of the opening line of General Evangeline's song: 'I bring Thee my sins and my sorrows.' It was enough. To quote one pressman present: 'A meeting that had been festooned with applause fell into silence.' The voice was the voice of Songster Mary Edge. The word was the Word of the Lord. Here was the immemorial cry of the penitent sinner to the forgiving Lord whose salvation is always nigh. In the stillness the singer resumed her seat. All that was left for the General to do was to explain how the biblical word 'salvation' had become an integral part of the name of the movement whose centenary was being cele-brated.

Here was no divergence from the historic teaching of the Christian church; no one-sided theological extravaganza born of some personal whimsy. Here was a reaffirmation in strength of the New Testament message that man is sick and needs to be made whole . . .

If a biblical word, by the same token a comprehensive word. For the salvation of which the New Testament speaks had always to do with the healing of the whole man . . .

If we ourselves, for want of a better way of speaking, refer to our evangelical work and also our social work, it is not that these are two distinct entities which could operate the one without the other. They are but two aspects of the one and the same salvation which is concerned with the total redemption of the whole man. Both rely upon the same motive. Both have the same end in mind. And as the gospel has joined them together we do not propose to put them asunder.

The final song – this time the words by Songster Will J. Brand – allowed the congregation to affirm that this was their own faith as well.

> Earthly kingdoms rise and fall,
>   Kings and nations come and go,
> Thou, O God, art over all,
>   None Thine empire shall o'erthrow.

> Of Thy grace are we enrolled
>   In the train of Thy dear Son,
> Pledged our faith undimmed to hold
>   Until victory is won.

As the centenary began so it continued. The same evening at seven o'clock saw the Clapton Congress Hall – scene of the first international congress in 1886 – filled with rejoicing Salvationists under the leadership of the British Commissioner, Commissioner William F. Cooper. At the same time in the Royal Albert Hall a similar gathering was led by the Chief of the Staff, Commissioner Erik Wickberg. The General addressed the former and concluded the latter. The one was as international as the other, for if at the Clapton Congress Hall the division of interests was between east and west, at the Royal Albert Hall it was between south and north. There the final moments spoke a language which every Salvationist could understand. A solitary spotlight fastened on Lawrence Fisher of Nottingham standing at the back of the auditorium whence he was to march behind the corps flag of the Nottingham Memorial Halls to the platform where he was to stand beside his commanding officer, Brigadier Frank Burrell, to be enrolled as a soldier of The Salvation Army by the General. The simple pledge of dedication to God, and the consequent sign of acceptance under God, symbolised the larger number of men and women, young and old, who would enrol ''neath the yellow, the red and the blue' during the Army's second century. The youthful Lawrence was not left to sing 'I'll be true, Lord, to Thee' by himself. Six thousand voices joined with him.

On the following day (Friday, June 25) the Earlscourt (Canada) band played in Lincoln's Inn Fields in the dinner hour, and in the afternoon the welcome to the 1,800 official delegates in the Westminster Central Hall was an uninhibited affair at which the universal password was 'Hallelujah'. With the larger delegations this one word was like the sound of many waters; with the twos and threes like the whisper of a breeze. But no matter, all were one in heart – and by seven in the evening the Royal Albert Hall along with the Clapton Congress Hall were once again well filled. At Clapton the Chief of the Staff was in his element leading a European rally

for, with Mrs Wickberg, he had long known the continent like
the back of his hand.

The General was piped in to the Albert Hall by Marie
Cameron of the Edinburgh Goodwill Centre – after which
anything could happen, and it did. Irish colleens, Canadian
scouts and guides, young folk from the land of song, Australian
timbrels, *afectuosos saludos* from South America, drama from
Hawick, the youth band from North Toronto and students
from the national school of music joined forces with 'The
Joystrings'. Nor should it be forgotten that, on this same
evening and on every other evening in the week, a carefully
prepared devotional meeting attracted its own congregation
in the Regent Hall.

Saturday at the Crystal Palace park and the National
Recreation Centre could well merit a chapter by itself – were
that space available. The international *War Cry* described it as
'probably the largest Salvationist gathering ever; certainly the
most international' – and estimated the attendance at 50,000.
Officially the day began at ten-thirty but much earlier than
that coaches and trains, cars and bicycles made for two had
begun to leave town centre and village rendezvous for the flag
break conducted by the Chief of the Staff. Mrs Wickberg lit
the torch to start the games – after which there was no
interruption in the varied fellowship which filled the day until
the shadows began to fall across the grassy arena which had
been covered with Salvation Army uniforms in the final act of
praise.

Sunday saw this international company divided between
the three gatherings in the Royal Albert Hall and seven
other centres to which groups of delegates were assigned,
even if the number of corps in London and the home
counties which carried out their regular Sunday programme
as if there was not a counter attraction in sight is not
here recorded. In alphabetical order the main centres
were –

Clapton Congress Hall	Commissioner Edgar Grinsted	Earlscourt band and selected delegates
Croydon Citadel	Commissioner Kaare Westergaard	Norrkoping string band and songsters

Luton Temple	Lieut.-Commissioner Sture Larsson	Cardiff Canton band
Reading Central	Commissioner William Davidson	Belfast Citadel band
Regent Hall	Commissioner Holland French	Amsterdam Staff band and selected delegates
Southend Citadel	Commissioner Hubert Scotney	Edinburgh Gorgie band
Wood Green	Commissioner William F. Palstra	Tranås band and selected delegates

The General led the televised holiness meeting at the Regent Hall on Sunday morning and then joined the Chief of the Staff – who had led the morning gathering in the Royal Albert Hall – for the afternoon and evening. Each occasion exemplified the truth that in Christ there is neither east nor west. With his customary ease the Chief used four languages in the Royal Albert Hall to invite seekers to the mercy seat. First in English, then in Swedish –

Låt oss nu bli stilla i bön. Låt oss lyssna till Herrens röst och lyda Honom, nar Han kallar till en ny överlåtelse och en ny invigning! Kom i Jesu namn för att bedja!

In German –

Lasst uns alle beten! Und wenn der Heilige Geist uns mahnt, zu kommen, dann wollen wir auch gehorsam sein und den Weg zum Altar gehen.

And in French –

En ce moment nous voulons prier. Et si l'Esprit de Dieu vous appelle, venez, approchez-vous de l'autel. Que Dieu vous bénisse.

At the Regent Hall as well many different peoples had been sharing in the one approach to the throne of grace. Lieut.-Colonel Jean Fivaz of Belgium offered prayer. Commissioner Holland French (National Commander, USA) led the congregation in the Founder's song. Mrs Ani Taureti Brown, a Maori Salvationist, read from the scriptures. Lieut.-Colonel Gulzar Masih (Pakistan) and Major Karin Hartman (Sweden) shared in personal testimony. The principal of the Army's training college in Lahore said:

My parents were Salvation Army officers and I was brought up in a Salvation Army boarding school. I was converted in a children's meeting and since that time my desire has been to fight for my Lord and Master . . . While uniform wearing is a cross to some people, to me it was my glory. As my father's red coat was too big for me, I used to put on my mother's jacket and felt myself more proud than those who stand in the presence of kings.

By birth I am a Punjabi. It is said of the Punjabi that he is a fighter by nature and, if he hasn't anyone to fight at home he must go out and find someone . . . I became an officer in 1930. The name of my training session was the 'Fighters'. I learnt the true and proper way of fighting for God . . . As William Booth said: 'While there remains one dark soul without the light of God I'll fight, I'll fight to the very end.'

Major Karin Hartman, the principal of the Army people's high school at Dalarö (Sweden) recalled her early spiritual struggles.

An Indian woman officer once came to Sweden and I had to translate her testimony. She spoke English with a strong native accent and I was not an experienced interpreter. The result was not a success . . .

Many difficulties in this world are due to wrong interpretations – as when some people get the notion that holiness and dullness are synonymous . . . Nothing could be further from the truth. For my part I knew the Christian phrases but had not yet grasped their true meaning. As the years went by I found it increasingly difficult to link what I was learning at college with the teaching of my home . . .

One of my school teachers once asked me if I was related to Ellen Hartman, a famous Swedish actress. I answered 'no' but, glancing at the class register where the profession of each pupil's parents was registered, the teacher went on: 'But Salvationists are a kind of actors too, aren't they?'

I was indignant. It dawned on me then that I believed in the reality of my parents' religious experience. There was a real purpose and a real sacrifice in their lives. Their joy and their communion with God were real . . . Today I am thankful for their interpretation of the Christian life . . . I find myself a Christian not merely because I grew up in a Christian home . . . nor because I find it easy to understand Christian doctrine. I do not. But I have met with Christ who is the interpreter of God's love (John 1:18, Knox).

Dalarö is a very free type of school and provides many opportunities for discussion and conversation. One of the girls once said to me: 'I don't know what to think about Christ yet, but I want to know more about Him.' That made me very happy.

In the Royal Albert Hall alone that day more than a hundred seekers found their deepest needs met in Jesus, and hundreds upon hundreds of Salvationists were happy on that account.

The good work went on throughout the ensuing week as daily four – and sometimes five – meetings continued to attract capacity congregations. There was a positive embarrassment of riches – that is if it is possible to have too much of a good thing. Monday saw two festivals of praise – afternoon and evening – in the Royal Albert Hall, with a third at night in the Westminster Central Hall under the leadership of General Wilfred Kitching (R), plus the programme presented earlier in the day by the Cardiff Canton band in the Victoria Embankment gardens.

On Tuesday afternoon two women's rallies were held in the Royal Albert Hall and the Westminster Central Hall respectively, with Mrs Coggan (wife of the then Archbishop of York) and Mrs General Coutts sharing in the former, and the Hon. Lady Egerton, President of the Women's Council with Mrs Commissioner Wycliffe Booth participating in the latter.

During the dinner hour on the Wednesday the Amsterdam Staff band played in Lincoln's Inn Fields. Simultaneous afternoon rallies for the over-sixties were held in the Royal Albert Hall and the Clapton Congress Hall. General Albert Orsborn (R) who led the first-named, evoked his own early-day memories to the great delight of his hearers. Commissioner Emma Davies (R) was in no less reminiscent mood at Clapton. In the evening a missionary panorama and a review of the Army's social services were presented in the same two venues.

Such was the demand for seats for 'The Century of Salvation Song' that the entire programme had to be presented both in the afternoon and again in the evening at the Royal Albert Hall. The same evening in the Clapton Congress Hall was featured a 'New World Night' in which sections from North and South America shared their gifts with a generous hand. There was – said one reporter, undoubtedly calling upon alliteration's artful aid – 'fun and faith, noise and nostalgia'. Seven territorial commanders participated in the programme, which included both a Salvation calypso from Bermuda and a group of 'rootin', tootin', shootin'' delegates from the west complete with stetsons and carrying six shooters. Happily the only shots they fired were gospel shots.

The celebrations had two more days to run but these were so important in their own right that they must be left to the next chapter.

4   WILLIAM BOOTH COMES INTO HIS OWN

It would be a fruitless exercise to discuss which of the centenary meetings was the climax of these ten days of rejoicing. The argument could be advanced that each was a climax after its own kind. Certainly the opening gathering, graced by the presence of H.M. Queen Elizabeth II with heads of church and state in attendance, set the standard for all that was to follow. On the final Friday afternoon in Westminster Abbey – Founder's day in the Salvation Army calendar – William Booth came into his own bringing the Army with him.

For one thing history was laid in fee. The Abbey had been the coronation church, as well as a burial ground, of the sovereigns of England since 1065. Poets' Corner in the south transept honoured the greatest of England's writers from Chaucer onward. The Unknown Warrior rested in his noble anonymity in the nave. If the Thames could be described as liquid history the Abbey was history shaped in stone – and here a space was being found for a pawnbroker's assistant from Nottingham.

The Salvation Army was also being given a recognised place in the religious life of the land of its birth. In past decades folk at many levels of society had tipped their hat in the direction of William Booth as an acknowledgment of his compassionate concern for the submerged tenth, but a substantial minority were still uncertain as to what place should be given to former, though now reformed, members of that tenth.

Time was when Dean Church had been approached by Bramwell Booth about the possibility of arranging a service in St. Paul's Cathedral which Salvationists could attend as a body. No Army personality would take part. Enough if one and all enjoyed the privilege of being present as members of the congregation. Names were suggested as to who might share

in the service. For example, J. B. Lightfoot, Bishop of Durham
– who had commended the Army's literature to his clergy in
a recent diocesan letter – was one. H. P. Liddon, himself a
Canon of St. Paul's, who had already attended one or two
Army gatherings, was another. But what concerned the Dean
was the possible character of the congregation. Were not most
Salvationists drawn from the working classes? Bramwell Booth
could not but agree. And would they not be wearing hobnailed
boots? Thus pressed, the Founder's eldest son could not deny
that some – perhaps a number – might be so shod. Whereupon
the Dean replied that, as St. Paul's had recently been repaved
at some expense, he could not risk any scratches to the marble.

But time's ever rolling stream has since borne away many
past misunderstandings and no one could have been more
welcoming than the Dean of Westminster, Dr Eric Abbott;
none more ready than members of the Chapter to make every
Salvationist completely at home amid the Abbey's ancient
grandeur; no one more eager to ensure that no ceremonial
error should mar the order of service than the Sacrist who
rehearsed the processional entry until the colour party moved
through the Abbey to the steps of the sanctuary as befitted the
occasion. This was no small feat when it is remembered that
none of the chosen representatives had ever undertaken such
a duty before and the group included an Australian, American,
Argentinian, Brazilian, Canadian, Chinese, Dane, Dutchman,
Finn, Frenchman, German, Ghanaian, Indian, Indonesian,
Italian, Japanese, Korean, a Maori, Sri Lankan, Swiss and a
West Indian. The flag officer was from Welling.

Others who shared in the service were drawn from sources
equally diverse. The opening flourish for trumpets, band and
organ was specially written by a contemporary British composer, Richard Arnell, and incorporated phrases from the
melody of 'O boundless salvation'. The first lesson from the
Old Testament and the second from the New were read by
the American Mrs Lieut.-Colonel Muriel Mackenzie and
the Sri Lankan Brigadier James Wickramage respectively.
Between the two readings a section of the Centenary Chorus
sang Dean Goffin's arrangement of the Founder's song, with
accompaniment by organ and brass. Prayers were followed by
Will Brand's verses which would grace any hymnary: 'Set
forth within the sacred word'. The address was given by the

General, based on the sentence testimony in 1 Corinthians
15:10 (NEB): 'By God's grace I am what I am, nor has His
grace been given to me in vain', and described William Booth
as a man of faith, hope and charity, concluding:

> His was a love, like that of his Lord, for the world. His last
> conversation with his eldest son had to do with the needs of the
> world. 'Promise me', he said, 'to do something more for the
> homeless. The homeless in every land. Not just in England but
> throughout the world.'
> And if one of his dying concerns was for the needy of the world,
> his other had to do with the unity of the world. 'I have been
> thinking of all peoples as one family,' he said – a dream toward
> which our sadly divided world is still struggling.
> Lest anyone should confuse this with a Wellsian love for man-
> kind in general which could go along with a distaste for the
> company of men as individuals, let there be recalled an occasion
> when, as often happened, William Booth had been besieged by
> reporters. He ended the press conference by saying: 'Now, gentle-
> men, as I've given you half an hour of my time, I'll take a couple
> of minutes of yours.' And with that he prayed for the assembled
> group of pressmen. A man has to care for people to take time to
> pray with them and for them. And William Booth cared. This
> was the love of God shed abroad in his heart.

Meanwhile members of the Founder's own family – officer
grandchildren, officer great-grandchildren, younger great-
great-grandchildren – were seated near the altar steps and,
with the rest of the congregation which filled the Abbey and
overflowed into the nearby parish church of St. Margaret's and
into the Abbey cloisters as well, were awaiting the unveiling of
the memorial to the Founder in the St. George's chapel.

This was a bust of the Founder in Palumbino marble by
Albert Siegenthaler, based on a clay modelling by Colonel
Mary Booth made more than sixty years earlier. During an
interval in the congregational singing of 'At the name of Jesus'
the Dean of Westminster, the General and Commissioner W.
Wycliffe Booth (the Founder's eldest active officer grandson)
moved to the chapel and engaged in a brief dialogue.

> *The Dean to the Commissioner:* Sir, I ask you to unveil this memorial
> to William Booth.
> *Having unveiled the memorial the Commissioner replied:* Mr Dean, I ask

you to take this memorial into the safe custody of the Dean and Chapter of Westminster and to dedicate it.

The Dean: We accept this memorial to William Booth and will guard and preserve it.

To the greater glory of God and in memory of His faithful soldier and servant, William Booth, we dedicate this memorial in the name of the Father and of the Son and of the Holy Ghost. Amen.

May we in our generation fight manfully under the banner of Christ against sin, the world, and the devil, and continue His faithful soldiers and servants unto our life's end. Amen.

Commissioner Dorothy Muirhead offered a prayer of thanksgiving. The offering was received as the International Staff Band played J. S. Bach's chorale: 'Wake, O wake', after which the congregation joined wholeheartedly in Charles Coller's verses: 'Salvation, shout salvation!' The Dean pronounced the blessing. The flag officer received back the Army colours from the high altar. The colour party returned to the west door. The unmistakable sound of the Abbey bells could be heard above the noise of London's traffic as the flag with the star in the centre flew from the Abbey tower.

But the day was only half done. Two evening meetings of dedication were to follow – one in the Royal Albert Hall led by the General, the other in the Westminster Central Hall led by the British Commissioner (Commissioner William F. Cooper) along with Commissioner Wycliffe Booth, Commissioner Catherine Bramwell-Booth (R) and other speakers. A captivating contribution was a song by eight of the Founder's great-great-grandchildren, and the gathering ended with the greater part of the congregation sharing in an act of dedication.

In the Royal Albert Hall the pattern of the meeting was designedly similar. Personal testimony was given by a local officer member of the Canadian parliament, the officer-matron of a home for the blind situated amid the Himalayan foothills, and the Australian leader of one of the West African territories. Making use of Isaiah 51:1, 2, the General spoke of the need to remember the rock from which our movement had been hewn, yet also ever to keep in mind that the God of the past was the living God of the present as well. The early resolve that God should have all there was of William Booth was the pattern still to be followed by Salvationists everywhere. Said *The War Cry*:

> Within minutes (of the appeal) there were queues in the three aisles leading to the mercy seat of those who were quietly awaiting their opportunity to renew their vows in public. It was a moving sight. They knelt for a few moments, signed a simple statement of dedication and then quietly returned to their place in the hall. Whole families, officer couples, innumerable overseas delegates, veterans, scouts, guides and songsters from the Centenary Chorus made their offering.

The conclusion was equally simple and equally uplifting. General Wilfred Kitching (R) prayed. The last verse of the Founder's song was sung twice. The benediction was pronounced – and the congregation streamed out of the now familiar building into the summer evening air.

The final day was no anticlimax. As the Founder had begun in the open air on Mile End Waste, so the final afternoon was given up to an outsize outdoor rally in Trafalgar Square. The eventual ten days covering two, and often three, public gatherings every day, had each been described with unfailing freshness by the Army's own team of skilled reporters – as the files will bear witness. Here then is how *The War Cry* reported the final centenary open-air meeting on page 10 of its issue for July 10, 1965.

> By lunchtime on Saturday it was obvious that the square's traditional cosmopolitan atmosphere had given way to a truer internationalism as Norwegian greeted Italian – in French, and a Swiss chatted in English to a group of rockers. The international Salvation Army, having already captured the hearts of Londoners during the centenary celebrations, had now taken possession of the heart of London.
>
> Soon after two o'clock the first contingent of delegates moved off from Horse Guards Parade, passed under the chestnut trees of St. James's Park and swept into Parliament Square. Strange but surely significant that the route of the final procession should take them past St. James's Palace, Westminster Abbey and the Houses of Parliament – the city's most ancient symbols of court, church and people.
>
> Up Whitehall the march continued, national flags fittingly

outnumbered by 'Blood and Fire' banners, national costumes setting off to advantage the preponderance of navy blue uniforms.

'William Booth' was there and 'John Lawley' – in a vintage Renault, the sort of vehicle they had often used in the first decade of the century. The various branches of Salvation Army social service were represented by decorated floats which later toured the West End streets.

As each territorial contingent reached the saluting base, faces turned to greet the General and the Chief of the Staff who were waiting to receive them.

Léopoldville (now Kinshasa) band, the Amsterdam Staff Band, together with the International Staff Band and corps bands from the four London divisions, provided music, but many of the delegates marched on their way singing.

At last the great square was full of Salvationists and beyond the barriers, even on the balconies of the National Gallery, stood hundreds of onlookers. To the limits of the square was an unbroken sea of faces and, from the plinth at the base of Nelson's monument, the Chief of the Staff led this immense congregation in a song. The International Staff Band played. 'The Joystrings' sang – and the British Commissioner could be seen singing with them! Prayer was offered by Mrs Major Willem Krommenhoek (The Netherlands); the scripture was read by Captain Chiyeko Mochi- maru (Japan); testimonies were given by Songster Leader Jonah Matswetu (Rhodesia), [now Zimbabwe] and Brigadier Arthur Pitcher (Canada). 'We could not allow the Centenary to conclude', said the General, 'without an open-air rally . . . Our presence here out of doors on a weekday contradicts the utterly wrong impression that the gospel of Jesus Christ is for one particular day of the week and then only in one particular kind of building, and witnesses that the faith we declare is for all men, at all times, and in all places.'

It was inevitable that the Founder's song, particularly the last verse, should be sung and sung again. Flags could not remain still as the waves of enthusiasm rose higher and higher. They began to be waved, full size and miniature alike, and were kept waving – as if the huge company was unwilling to break up so memorable an occasion, as indeed was true. But end there had to be – and without delay for there was yet one more gathering, this time in St. Paul's Cathedral. With the help of the orchestra of the Royal Academy of Music (by permission of Sir Thomas Armstrong) a section of the Centenary Chorus, led by Major Dean Goffin, presented George Frederick Handel's 'Messiah'. No more fitting finale to these rejoicings could have been conceived than the last prolonged 'Amen' echoing and re-echoing around the dome of the cathedral which was filled to capacity.

There is no doubt that music and song proved to be a significant help in furthering the principal aims of the centenary. No one present on Sunday morning in the Royal Albert Hall would readily forget the singing of Captain Norman Bearcroft's arrangement of Herbert Booth's 'Cleansing for me'. Here was a setting which held the ear and gripped the heart by virtue of its unforced simplicity. By contrast General Albert Orsborn (R) spoke of the singing of 'Worthy is the Lamb' in the opening meeting as 'an indelible memory'. Winifred Caney was inspired to write some verses which appeared in *The Musician* 'On hearing the International Staff Band and Organ in Westminster Abbey'. Nor were these moving moments limited to Salvationists. On the final Friday evening in the Royal Albert Hall one steward (all of whom serve in their professional capacity) was to be seen unashamedly in tears as he kept the aisles clear so that seekers could more easily join one of the queues which led to the mercy seat. The world-wide nature of the Army meant that the interest in the centenary was also world-wide, but the event had a special significance for the British Isles for there the movement took root and there it remains rooted.

There was a time when any man in Salvation Army uniform was taken to be a reformed profligate. It was thought exceptional for him to possess any different background. William Booth himself had suffered this compliment. Young women in an Army bonnet were deemed to have been rescued from the Victorian fate that was worse than death. The centenary bore witness past all denying that the Army not only embraced all races but, what was acknowledged rather more hesitantly, included all classes. Salvation Army uniforms emerging through the ancient gateways of Oxbridge on a Sunday morning just before ten o'clock was a post Second World War phenomenon – but in due time was taken as a matter of course. Personal testimony during the centenary by a war-time glider pilot, the assistant director of religious broadcasting in Sweden, a Bantu business man from Harare, a former Antarctic explorer turned Salvation Army officer, and a holder of the Duke of Edinburgh's gold award – to name but a few – made it plain that the Salvationist was no longer to be socially despised and rejected. Happily – and long may it be true to say – the Salvation soldier cares but little for these things.

The outcome was that at all levels in all five continents the centenary was greeted with good will. The Speaker in the Legislative Assembly of Alberta announced that an unnamed peak in the Rockies should henceforth be called Mount William Booth. The Hammersmith council placed a seat in Furnivall Gardens to commemorate the fact that William Booth once lived in that area. The Académie Française was accustomed to award a *Prix de Vertu* to the person or movement giving outstanding service to the Republic and, on the recommendation of Académician Marc Boegner, this was presented to The Salvation Army. The Postmaster General in the United Kingdom issued two centenary stamps, the first time a white man and a coloured man had appeared symbolically together in a British stamp design. The United States Post Office printed 184 million stamps of their Salvation Army issue. The much-visited floral clock in Princes Street, Edinburgh, displayed the centenary design – a task taking three men three weeks to set out in all its detail. And if to be near to nature is to be near to God, then this may be the right place to mention that cathedral services of thanksgiving ranged from St. Machar's in Aberdeen to St. Paul's in Melbourne, travelling – to name a few ports of call – via St. John the Divine in New York, St. George in Jerusalem and St. James in St. Helena on the way.

The single-minded Salvationist would simply say: 'Give to Jesus glory!'

5 TO THE ENDS OF THE EARTH

The ripples from the centenary rejoicings in London quickly spread far and wide. The plans of most overseas territories were already well and truly laid and were only waiting for the parent gatherings in Britain to conclude. These initial meetings and marches had not been angled to attract the media but their appeal to sight and sound could not but capture public attention. The press voiced its praise – albeit with certain qualifications. Some commentators saw the Army still wrapped in a discredited Victorian mantle – witness its uniform, its evangelical phraseology and its refusal to dissociate its social services from the overall need for the saving grace of God. As one War Office spokesman said in General Bramwell's day: 'You're so religious!' Half a century later 'Victorian' was a handy adjectival substitute when what really stuck in the throat of some observers was the movement's determined – here and there regarded as obscurantist – loyalty to the Christian lifestyle. However the *Freethinker* thought that the religious side of the Army's work had been 'under-stressed', though in the opinion of the *Catholic Herald* 'the Army was coming into its own.' But the *British Weekly* dismissed our uniform as an 'anachronism', and the *Church Times* declared that there were 'some aspects of The Salvation Army which remained unacceptable to other Christians, notably the persistent repudiation of the sacraments.' 'Repudiation' was a somewhat harsh word to employ when all that the Army had ever said was that divine grace did not require any material elements nor any human intermediary for its reception. As emphatically as the devoutest of Christian worshippers the Salvationist believes in the Real Presence without whom his belauded evangelism would be little more than a beating of the air and his own inner life be reduced to a barren desert.

It was well that the spiritual heirs and successors of William

Booth had learned from their Founder never to reply in kind to their harshest critics. So *The War Cry* drew the sting of Lord Soper's lengthy article in *The Glasgow Herald* calling 'for the disbandment of this regiment of the Army of the Lord' by reprinting it in full in its own pages. Indeed the immense amount of comment which the centenary provoked might have gone to their heads had they not most truly and firmly believed that God's work was far more important than His workmen.

More objective, and therefore more reliably encouraging, was the way in which Christian communities in widely separated places and of widely different viewpoints, joined in praise to God for His work during the century. The Methodist Conference, meeting in Plymouth, prayed that 'the Army, together with the whole church of God, might be used yet more mightily for the extension of His kingdom'. In Trinidad the Lord Bishop of the diocese, accompanied by the Governor General and Lieut.-Colonel Ernest Kenny, the Army's divisional commander, united to sing William Booth's verses 'Thou Christ of burning, cleansing flame, send the fire' to the lively Army tune of 'Tucker'. At a meeting held in the cathedral at Reykjavik the Bishop borrowed a phrase of the apostle Paul and addressed the Salvationists present as 'my beloved brethren'. In the Scillies a small group of young Salvationists, led by Major Will Brown, held a series of campaign meetings – one of which was attended by the holidaying British Prime Minister and Mrs Harold Wilson.

The first of a long list of centenary celebrations held outside Great Britain began in Oslo when the cathedral bells rang out their welcome and the Dean, Domprest Fredrik Knudsen, welcomed the General in English as well as Norwegian. Throughout the weekend the Filadelfia hall, seating 2,000 people, was crowded to excess. The first of two other noteworthy occasions was the placing of a commemorative tablet on the site of a new social service centre in course of erection for the rehabilitation of ex-prisoners. Dr Olav Gjærevoli, the Minister for Social Affairs, spoke of the Salvationist's lively faith in the possibility of human redemption. Sometimes, with the best will in the world (he added), the authorities reach the conclusion that, in a particular case, there is nothing more which they can do. But with the Army no case is hopeless.

From this consideration of basic human needs the General

proceeded to the final meeting in the City Hall which faces Oslo's picturesque harbour. The principal guest in a congregation which was dressed as elegantly as the marble hall in which they were seated was Bishop Johannes Smemo. But the youthful Corps Sergeant-Major Willy Lundgaard spoke for the Salvationists present when he declared that they had received no message from the Lord to call off the holy war. Nor, judging by their response, had the rest of the company either as they renewed their dedication to the Christian faith which, in the words of the General, 'triumphs over geography, redeems human personality and provides a goal to history'.

One day Oslo, the next day Copenhagen – where their majesties King Frederik IX and Queen Ingrid graced the opening meeting in the Odd Fellows concert hall, as did Prime Minister Jens Otto Krag and the Over President of Copenhagen, Count Carl Moltke. The waiting congregation was plainly delighted to hear that, before entering the concert hall, the King had personally decorated Commissioner Aage Rønager – a Dane by birth and the Army's International Secretary for Europe who was accompanying the General – with the knighthood of the Order of Dannebrog.

Among the memorable words spoken during the evening none were more searchingly direct than those of the Danish Primate, Bishop Willy Westergaard Madsen, who said:

In an over-intellectualised, self-satisfied, sophisticated Christendom, you in The Salvation Army have been bold enough to be God's fools, and have dared to use songs and strings to express the truth about the love of God which will not let itself be confined within the bounds of reason. There is something in this boldness which is akin to the daring of God in sending His Son into this world ... Salvationists were not to be regarded by the church as competitors but as co-workers. The market for the goods we have to sell is big enough for us both, and the Army's kind of goods often open doors where no one else can gain an entrance.

However, these centenary gatherings were not held solely to glorify the past. They proved to be occasions when current needs were currently met.

One of the centenary issues of the international *War Cry*

carried the story of an American serviceman who owned a double allegiance – an AC2 hailing from Ocala, Florida, presently serving in Taiwan, who was also a Salvationist. Second-class airman maybe, but a first-class Salvation soldier – for he had a dream of the good which might be done if the Army flag was unfurled in Taiwan. It had been once – but fell victim to the bitter changes and chances of world politics. So he wrote to the nearest Salvation Army leader of whom he knew – the officer commanding in Hong Kong. Word of this reached the General – and he asked Lieut.-Commissioner Frederick W. Harvey, then territorial commander for Korea, personally to investigate and report. In the meantime young Salvationists in Florida had heard of Leslie's dream, and the corps cadet honour clubs in the state agreed among themselves to contribute $1,000 to the project. Meanwhile the commissioner had visited Taiwan and talked with Leslie who, help or no help, had begun to hold meetings in the city of Tauchung with the knowledge and support of some of the local community leaders.

Living in retirement in England at this time were Colonel and Mrs George Lancashire. They had given a large part of their active service to the people of China, and had been praying for the mainland Salvationists who had crossed the Formosa Strait to resettle in Taiwan. These dedicated missionaries did not hesitate to respond to this situation as a call from the Lord and, in its centenary year, the Army repeated its early day history when youth showed age the way to a new field of service.

But at home there were events just as significant though they involved only the ones and the twos as against whole populations. A baby girl, little more than an hour old, was found in a parcel lying close to the statue of William Booth which stands at the front of the training college overlooking Denmark Hill station. Some young mother in distress must have left her there, counting on the strong probability that a Salvationist would be the first to discover the child. So it turned out – and at the nearby hospital the baby girl was named Sally Ann by common consent.

Close to the same time a Glasgow paper described how the corps officer stationed in a Scottish county town was in the habit of taking up his post just before seven o'clock in the morning when prisoners were due to be released. If they agreed, Captain Ronald Johnson would then take them home for breakfast before seeing them off by train. One of the captain's early morning guests later returned and said that he would like to talk – whereupon the two men walked along the road that ran by the side of the Tay. The ex-prisoner revealed that he made his living by burglary and had already collected enough keys to set up in business again. The conversation was long, slow, quiet and earnest – after which the man let the keys fall from his hand into the river. There was then further prayer to Him who is happier over one sinner who repents than ninety-nine good people who do not need so to do.

Truth is not always stranger than fiction – save when it has to do with the work of God, as one more story from the centenary year will demonstrate. Towards the end of the Second World War, Dr and Mrs J. Bennett Alexander were living in Walthamstow in north-east London – he busy with a suburban practice and she with her works of love and mercy which enrich the life of those who serve in Christ's name. An unusually frank observation by the officer in charge of the local corps brought the doctor to the Army hall where he renewed his committal to Jesus as Saviour and Lord. Change of scenery did not weaken his deepened faith so that, when practising in the Lake District some years later, the Alexanders welcomed the suggestion of a visiting Army officer that an informal meeting should be held in their lakeland home. This was to prove a turning-point in their life for, next morning at breakfast, they told their visitor of their call to full-time service with the Army.

Unknown to the three at the breakfast table the next issue of the international *War Cry* was to carry a letter from Lieut.-Colonel (Dr) William T. B. McAllister, Chief Medical Officer at the MacRobert hospital at Dhariwal in the Punjab, and headed 'The single-handed surgeon'. Chief medical officer he was, but this was a case of one chief and no braves – save the indomitable nursing and ancillary staff. Neither assistant nor replacement were in sight – save to the eye of faith – and homeland furlough was due in a matter of months.

To the Alexanders this was a Macedonian call which they could not refuse and on the evening of Monday, August 5, 1965, as the Millom band played softly outside the village hall, scores of folk from the fells gathered to pray godspeed to the uniformed Dr and Mrs Alexander who were exchanging the coolness of Cumbria for the heat of India. Before the centenary year was out they had arrived in Dhariwal.

In preparation for centenary year in the United States where celebrations were led by General and Mrs Coutts in San Francisco, Atlanta, St. Louis and New York respectively, Sallie Chesham – wife of Brigadier Howard Chesham then serving on the territorial headquarters in Chicago – had written *Born to Battle*. With a foreword by former President Dwight D. Eisenhower, this was the updated story of the work of the Army in the Republic. Over the years the Army in the United States had both received much from – and given much to – the parent body, and Sallie Chesham made a fascinating list of these debits and credits. The original debit – the very original George Scott Railton and the original seven Salvation sisters – can never be repaid. Nevertheless the Army world owes the United States for – among other items – the music camp for musically minded young holidaymakers; the annual Brengle institute for the teaching of holiness, and the advisory board for the furtherance of our social services through community advice and aid – not to mention the generous help given to succour the Third World.

In recognition of these and other contributions made over the years, the General and his wife – accompanied by the National Commander, Commissioner Holland French and Mrs Commissioner French – spent a full month campaigning from coast to coast. In one sense Salvation Army meetings follow a recognisable pattern however varied individual contributions to each particular gathering may be, and it would be unpardonably rash to pronounce any one occasion better than another. But in San Francisco one of the outstanding assemblies was the midday open-air rally when four columns of Salvationists converged on Union Square to welcome the city's mayor to the Army's meeting of witness, to share in the prayers offered by the Rt. Revd. Monsignor Murphy and Dr F. D. Haynes (President of the Californian State Baptist Convention) and to listen to the General speaking of Jesus as the world's only Saviour.

In Atlanta the congress began as it intended to go on – with an assembly of more than 2,500 in the new mammoth exhibition hall for the initial youth rally. In the well-planned St. Louis programme a congregation of more than 3,000 were moved in heart and mind by the historical pageant based on Mrs Brigadier Chesham's *Born to Battle*, and in New York the Sunday afternoon meeting of thanksgiving in the cathedral church of St. John, attended by leaders of the Protestant, Roman Catholic and Orthodox communions, together with personalities from the world of government, commerce and social service, drew an estimated congregation of 10,000.

Any judgment of a congregation of that order is never reckoned to be correct to a decimal point. But there is no doubt that during those thirty days sixty-one public meetings were held, and the unabashed friendliness of the American public to the stranger within its gates took at least one of them completely by surprise – witness, for example, the standing ovation spontaneously accorded to the General by the New York rotary club. Even more significant testimony to the Army's accepted place in the work of Christian evangelism was the fact that on Congress Sunday in Atlanta a Salvation Army officer occupied every church pulpit in the city. Equally noteworthy was the fact that in the national capital band which maintains a regular public ministry in Washington, DC, white bandswomen, black bandsmen and white bandsmen play side by side.

As for future prospects, in the same city the General shared an eight o'clock breakfast with over a hundred members of The Salvation Army students' fellowship which included a couple of doctors, graduates of Mainz (Germany) and Jefferson respectively, a Princeton graduate who had taught at the University of Barcelona, a Groton girl specialising in sociology and numerous others of that ilk. And in case anyone should deduce from this that the Army was forsaking its first love, the two folk with whom the General spent his final moments on a station platform before boarding the overnight train were the personnel manager of the local harbour light centre (himself a converted alcoholic) and the resident officer in charge (again a converted alcoholic). A tree is known by its fruits.

These references to the centenary year will conclude with what can be described as three statements of account.

On August 1, 1964, the international *War Cry* printed a list of projects in the United Kingdom which would be completed,

or at least commenced, in 1965. On December 11 of that year
The War Cry published a progress report.

For the women's social services in Sydenham a purpose-built
eventide home was ready for occupation; an enquiry and
preventive centre for women and girls in central London
was actually in service; a property to be developed as an
international hostel for overseas students had been purchased
and was being prepared for occupation; a hostel for women
and girls in the west country had been opened in Exeter earlier
in the year; an extension to the approved school for girls in
East Grinstead was in course of construction.

In the midsummer a purpose-built hostel for servicemen in
Devonport had been completed and opened. New halls for
adult and youth activities were either at tender or in course of
construction at Bangor (Northern Ireland), Borough (south
London), Dundee, Easterhouse (Glasgow), Gravesend, Har-
penden, Hartcliff (Bristol), Motherwell, Northwich, Romford,
Stowmarket and Wellingborough. New halls had been completed and opened at Cadishead, Maddiston, Nuneaton and
Stratford.

Lest it be thought that centenary year was selfishly limited
to domestic enterprises, the following is an abbreviated list of
what would now be called Third World projects proposed
during 1964/5 and, thanks to the generous response of Oxfam,
undertaken by the Army.[1]

	£'s
Feeding programmes, north and east	
Algeria	7,250
Food programme, Barbados	500
Additional programme, Barbados	1,000
Emergency relief, Brazil	1,000
Feeding programme, Guyana	700
Vehicle for above distribution	938
Water tank, Tamwe	64
Earthquake relief, Chile	1,000
Additional relief, Chile	1,000
Mobile clinic and medical relief,	
Brazzaville	1,000
Refugee relief, Brazzaville	2,000
Food relief, Ghana	600
Purchase Volkswagen, food relief, Haiti	1,285

	£'s
Repairs, old people's home, Haiti	100
Erection creche, nursery, women's home, Hong Kong	5,000
Extension costs, Behala home, Calcutta	235
Feeding programme, MacRobert hospital, Dhariwal	2,000
Grant to cost wells and hand pumps, U.P., India	1,000
Grant cost extension leprosy wards, C.B.H., India	3,000
Grant cost mobile clinic, E.B. hospital, India	1,000
Flood relief, Andhra Pradesh	1,000
Flood relief, Trivandrum	1,000
Relief, Burma refugees	1;000
Multi-purpose van, Nagercoil	929
Food relief, Jamaica	2,500
Food relief, centre for the blind and handicapped, Jamaica	600
Maintenance, blind trainees, Jamaica farm	1,000
Maintenance, trainees, Westerham, Jamaica	1,000
Food relief, Kolyana, Kenya	500
Sponsorship, Korea	126
Relief, child care centres, Mexico	5,000
Purchase and adaptation, child care centres, Mexico	2,150
Shantinagar dispensary	250
Grant, Howard hospital, Rhodesia – car	565
Irrigation plant construction, Usher, Rhodesia	6,308
Food relief, St. Helena	900
Steriliser, Eadie hospital, Vendaland	160
Air fare, medical student, UK to Chikankata	230

In addition, during the centenary year the international funds of The Salvation Army supported their evangelical, educational, medical and social work throughout the world by grants in aid as below.[2] Each of the specified areas also contributed as substantially as possible to their own upkeep. These geographical definitions have no national or political significance, but are used solely for the purpose of Salvation Army administration.

	£'s		£'s
Algeria	20,670	Kenya, Tanzania	
Brazil	12,169	and Uganda	42,400
Burma	4,172	Korea	31,283
Caribbean	61,792	Malaysia	10,073
Congo	27,609	Mexico	4,650
Equatorial Africa	32,728	Nigeria	28,948
Ghana	14,998	Pakistan	20,703
Hong Kong	21,203	Philippines	21,882
India		S. America W.	17,288
Northeast	49,511	S. America E.	23,765
Western	62,263	Southern Africa	29,290
Madras and		Sri Lanka	12,863
Andhra	39,927	Taiwan	1,157
South	68,600	Zambia and	
Indonesia	32,415	Zimbabwe	52,961
Italy	14,399		

6   A WILL TO WORK

Enough has already been written about the centenary yet, though it was a past event, it would not be banished from Salvation Army thought. 1966 was described as 'C + 1' – and this logo appeared on official paper and posters – even on the skin of a drum used by a band which rather prided itself on its technical skills. However, the plus sign testified to the fact that the Army continued to be on the move and, while January was still on the calendar, the General left for the Caribbean.

The Central America and West Indies Territory (as it was then called) was one of the most fragmented in the Army world, consisting of numerous independent island states such as (among others) Cuba, Barbados, Haiti, Jamaica and Trinidad, the narrow isthmus linking the two halves of the American continent (Panama, Nicaragua, Costa Rica and Honduras) and including Guyana and Surinam on the southern side of the equator. Since then some administrative adjustments have been made – and there may be more to follow. But the use of four basic languages – Dutch, English, French and Spanish – and of ten different currencies, have not been able to fragment the unity of Salvationist fellowship nor dampen the zeal with which the men and women of that Army pursue their common aim.

The campaign began in Paramaribo in Surinam where the General paid an early call on Envoy Alvares who commenced the work both there and in Curaçao. Though now prevented by age from attending the meetings it was a continuing joy to her that her pioneering service had borne such lasting fruit – a fact to which the Minister for Social Affairs testified when presenting a government grant of 1,000 guilders for the development of the Army's social services in the area. Next day the district commissioner's launch took the General up river to the leper colony at Groot Chatillon where those who most needed constant care received constant attention.

A short flight brought the visiting party (which included Colonel John Fewster, the territorial commander) to Georgetown, Guyana (then British Guiana). Here, as elsewhere, the Army leader made a point of seeing for himself the various services to which local Salvationists were committed, and in the evening more than a thousand people gathered in the St. Andrew's church to greet him and to hear the good news of the gospel.

In Port of Spain (Trinidad) an island-wide broadcast carried a complete Army meeting – from 'O boundless salvation' to the Army doxology – from the church of the Holy Trinity, after which a new hall was opened at Tuna Puna. An even greater congregation still – an estimated 3,000 – shared in the outdoor gathering which was held in tropical heat in the shadeless sports stadium in Barbados. The people of Antigua devised their own method of welcoming a first visit by any Army General to their island. Seated in the Administrator's car the General was escorted by a cavalcade of thirty-five cars, arranged by the local trades unions, on a roundabout route from the airport to the centre of the island. As continuous loud-speaker announcements gave details of the forthcoming meetings klaxon saluted klaxon in a fervent welcome. Judging by the decibels generated the effort was worthy of the occasion. Here the Army band, uniformed in recognisably English style, testified to the past leadership of an English banding enthusiast.

Puerto Rico lies between the Leeward Islands and Haiti and could not be bypassed simply because the island was linked administratively with the United States. Commissioner and Mrs William Davidson were present to greet their international leader, and Major Paul Seiler, the regional commander, showed how a comparatively recent opening had been able to put first things first from the word go.[1]

Haiti presented a different language, a different and independent government, and a different culture – but the same basic human needs. As the Army flag had been unfurled on the island for fewer than twenty years it could have been that our aims, and our approach to those aims, were not everywhere fully understood.[2] A zealous armed guard halted the General and his party on the stairway of the presidential palace. The very word 'Army' on the visitors' cap bands was enough for him to raise his gun. But no harm came to them or to him when he realised that here was a different war waged with different weapons. Children on the island were hungry – so this Army had a school feeding programme. The blind and handicapped could scarcely work in the fields – hence the sheltered workshop. The destitute aged needed care – consequently the eventide home. Above all there was everywhere an unsatisfied desire for the bread and the water of life – which meant that the compound which housed the hall at Port au Prince could not accommodate that night the largest Army congregation ever seen in Haiti.

This particular campaign reached a climax in Jamaica which, though rated a division, possessed a range of social services of which a much larger administrative unit could justifiably be proud – schools for the blind, a home for the adult blind, a hostel, workshop and training school for the blind, a boys' training farm, a children's home, a home for children of leper and tubercular parents, a young women's residence and a night shelter. The centenary was also marked by the opening of two new halls – one in the Havendale district and the other at the Pedro outpost towards which the local comrades had raised half the cost. The street marches made a continuous picture of rows of dark faces set in an undulating sea of white uniforms and effortlessly moving by converging ways upon the ward theatre where the Sunday's meetings were to be held. The island motto – 'Out of many, one people' – provided an apt text for what the General had to say about the unifying power of the gospel. Later a memorial plaque was unveiled at the base of the flagstaff in the grounds of the Myrtle Bank hotel to mark the place where the Army's work commenced in 1887 and thence spread to other parts of the Caribbean. Two commemorative stamps were also issued – at 3d. and 1s. 6d. respectively – and were speedily sold out.

Long-term centenary plans in the United Kingdom continued to mature. Fourteen of the fifteen intended advisory boards were now established. At Birmingham the General met the advisory board and outlined the proposed development of existing social service centres in the city. In Cardiff a grant of

£25,000 from the Nuffield provincial hospitals trust enabled the Northlands maternity centre to proceed without delay on its planned extensions. In Nottingham the advisory board approved the multi-purpose social service proposals which would incorporate the Notintone Place dwelling which was the birthplace of William Booth.

The end of April 1966 saw the General en route for Hong Kong and Korea. Salvation Army work in both countries had suffered severely by reason of past events and future uncertainties cast their unhappy shadows before, but Salvationists continued to address themselves, cheerfully and resolutely, to present needs.

The unprecedented influx of immigrants and refugees confronted the crown colony with problems both material and spiritual. A resurgence of Buddhism and Taoism was inevitable in a population which was ninety-eight per cent Chinese speaking, though the practice of these ancient faiths was little more than a ritual with many. An open-air meeting in the Walled City – an area virtually immune from police control – was possibly the nearest thing which the twentieth century could show of Christian evangelism stripped to its basic essentials. At Pentecost most of the people listening to Peter and his fellow apostles were practising Jews, believers in the living God who had brought their fathers out of the land of Egypt, out of the house of bondage, and who acknowledged a moral code even if they did not always follow it to the letter. In twentieth-century Hong Kong there was not often so firm a foundation on which to build.

Take the story of the young Lau Tak Ming by way of illustration. After two months in hospital and two months in one of the Army's convalescent homes for children, this six-year-old boy was ready to return home. This for him was a fishing boat ten feet long and four feet wide where lived his parents, his grandmother and his eight brothers and sisters. A happy welcome home meal had been prepared – rice, fish, meat and vegetables – but Tak Ming paused before he started to eat. Who was going to say grace? The family paused as well. They had not heard the word before. What was grace? Tak Ming explained that grace was thanking God for the food that He had provided. But which god? In their home there were several gods – including the sun god and the god of the fishermen. But the boy was not to be put off and said the grace which he had learned while at the Army home.

Later he referred to the Sunday school which he had attended and said that he had been told that he could continue attending even when he had returned home. So on the appointed day the family put on their best clothes and went looking for such a place – though they hardly knew what they were looking for nor where they could find the object of their search. But at last they heard singing and Tak Ming recognised the tune as one which he had heard in the Army convalescent home. So in he led the way – and for the first time his family shared in Christian worship which eventually led to their conversion.

In this sense every Army activity is 'evangelical'. If the convalescent home proved to be a means of furthering the gospel, so also are the roof-top schools with their separate morning and afternoon classes and staffs; as is the Wanchai school with its enrolment of over 1,600 pupils and staff of more than forty; as are the medical clinics, the day care nurseries, the vocational training centres, the kindergartens, the night shelter, the children's libraries, the women's hostel and the youth hostel. In this sense there is no activity which is not aimed at the spread of the gospel. This does not mean the chatter of endless prayers, much less a ceaseless round of pious talk – but the discharge of every duty with a maximum of professional skill in the spirit of Christ. To the uninitiated Hong Kong may resemble nothing more than an immense swarm of busy bees, but none is busier nor more competent in their busyness than the Gideon's army of Salvationists about their Master's business.

In the jet age distances are judged by time – and so Hong Kong is nearer to Seoul than Peiping. An overnight stop at Tokyo – used to greet Japanese comrades there – was sufficient break to allow the General to commence his twelve days' campaign in the Republic of South Korea, covering the country from the demilitarised zone in the north to Pusan in the south. The costliness of the Army's past service to the Korean people was recognised by the General's visit to the Foreigners' Cemetery in the capital where flowers were laid, and prayer was offered, at the graves of the nine missionary officers buried there. The same spirit of total dedication was acknowledged

when the General visited the officer-widow of Senior-Major
Noh Yung Soo, the corps officer at Chinju who was martyred
when the town was occupied by the invading troops in the
1953–7 war.

Widespread unemployment was one reason why the Army's
social services were so greatly valued. The centenary year saw
an average of 12,000 people making a daily visit to the Army's
feeding stations in Korea. The homes for children, for women
and for the aged rarely have a single vacancy except through
death. Basic human needs reach their peak during winter's
sub-zero temperatures. This is a 'cold war' whose existence
may be regretted but whose relief is to be commended. Very
possibly this was part of the reason why President Park Chung
Hee admitted the General to the Order of Cultural Merit, the
highest national honour that can be bestowed on an overseas
visitor. This was another example of the gracious way in which
this ancient people recognised those who had been friends in
need as friends indeed – such, for example, as was the courageous woman major who was in charge of the girls' home in
Seoul at the time of the invasion from the north.

When it became clear that the capital would be occupied
she gathered her sixty-five charges about her and explained
that they would have to find a new home almost at once. This
would not be easy for they would have to walk most of the
way carrying all the rice they could, but the older girls would
look after the smaller ones and all of them would have to be
very brave. When they reached the Han river they were halted
by their own troops who explained that the bridge was about
to be blown up. But the major was determined that her girls
should be on the far side before that happened – so on they
pressed. Their long trek ended at Taegu, some 250 miles to
the south in the interior of the country. In the general confusion
the major discovered a large house which was unoccupied,
and to this she brought her homeless family without one being
lost. There is a girls' home at Taegu to this day.

Another tale involving the river Han illustrates how determined Korean Salvationists can be when involved in the
spread of the gospel. The officer in charge of a well-established
corps some distance inland made up his mind to set up an
additional post amid the assortment of shacks huddled together
on the river bank. This would enable the Army to minister to

the spiritual and material needs of those who lived in this rough and ready fashion. So a tent, bearing the sign of the cross, was erected – but attendances rose and fell according to the uncertain temper of the river. Several times during the rainy season the flood waters uprooted the tent – for it to be rescued, dried out, and re-erected – only to collapse afresh when next the river broke its banks. Then the officer who originally sponsored the project was farewelled. The local leader lost heart. For a couple of months there was no one to take charge of the meetings – until the faithful remnant besought a veteran comrade at the parent corps to come over and help them. Well that he did – for the river, in an angry mood, spilled over even a wider area leaving only the cross visible above the water. Still undismayed, some of the men swam to the rescue of the floating poles and the sodden canvas. The government then gave the harassed community a new site, but this time high winds joined forces with the turbulent waters to the collapse of the tent yet again. The faithful few then resolved that they would plan for a brick building. Mothers with babies on their backs carried stones for the foundations. Children lent a hand according to their size and strength. Faith and works at last triumphed. The river was vanquished, and it was not long before a home league, a Bible class, a scout troop and meetings for children were being held unhindered. These Korean Salvationists saw themselves one in spirit with William Booth who, in a distant land and in a very different setting, used a decrepit tent for his earliest endeavours.

The year had a mixed ending – happy for some but sad indeed for the people of the Welsh mining village of Aberfan, just south of Merthyr Tydfil.

About half-past nine on the morning of October 21, 1966, as the children were assembling for roll call at the Pantglas infants' and junior school, the base of an 800-feet-high slag heap collapsed and this immense mass of mining waste – boulders, rocks, sludge and slurry – engulfed the school and playground lying below, burying a row of terraced houses and a farmhouse as well. The corps officers of the South Wales division, under Brigadier William Fenwick, were returning home that morning from their two days' annual councils at Swanwick (Derbyshire) but, on hearing the news over the radio, made at once for the stricken village where they joined hands with other officer comrades who were already on the scene. Their activities were co-ordinated at first from one of the damaged cottages, but later they were assigned an empty house for this purpose.

It was early realised that most of the victims were children, but among the dead were also the headmistress, the deputy head, as well as several teachers who lost their lives in a vain attempt to save their pupils. The Bethany chapel in the village was used as a mortuary and, under the direction of Major Freda Eveleigh, eight officers maintained a day and night rota for six days so that no parent was unaccompanied on the heart-breaking task of identifying their child, and for a time Major Derrik Tribble (of the Men's Social Services) was responsible for preparing the children for identification. At the funeral when eighty of the children were buried in a communal grave, bandsmen from Merthyr Tydfil and Treharris united to provide music for the service.

Members of the government – including the Rt. Hon. James Callaghan (Chancellor of the Exchequer) and Mr George Thomas (Minister of State for Wales) were warm in their appreciation of the practical help given by Salvationists. When later Queen Elizabeth II arrived, the Duke of Edinburgh drew her attention to the compassionate assistance rendered at the mortuary as well as to the canteen which had been kept open continuously for five successive days and nights for the benefit of rescue workers. The Queen also expressed her personal thanks to Major Arthur Pettit and Captain Clifford Howes (the commanding officers at Merthyr Tydfil and Treharris respectively, the two corps nearest to Aberfan) for their un-tiring attention to the needs of the bereaved.

The year ended on a happier note for others – for example, for the aged in south London for whose benefit a purpose-built eventide home had been opened in the summer. Before the end of autumn Concord House in Leinster Gardens was also opened as a hostel for overseas girl students seeking accommo-dation in London. The need for this was demonstrated by the fact that in the current year the London University lodgings officer had received 4,900 applications and that, by the opening date, Concord House was fully occupied by students of eigh-teen different nationalities – with a waiting list already carrying over a hundred names. To the sum needed to acquire and transform three somewhat rundown houses into one inviting hostel the British Council made a generous grant of £38,250 – approximately one-third of the overall cost.

The same month witnessed the stone-laying of Booth House, the multi-purpose men's social service centre on the White-chapel Road, E1, so named because the site is but a stone's throw from the scene of William Booth's initial witness on Mile End Waste. The warm spring afternoon of March 27, 1968, saw the completed enterprise opened by Her Majesty Queen Elizabeth II, to whom the key was handed by the architect, Mr Martin Lidbetter, FRIBA.

In his presentation the General referred to the poverty prevailing in mid-Victorian England which moved the Founder to provide 'a basin of soup for a farthing; soup and bread for a halfpenny; soup and bread with tea, coffee or cocoa for a penny, and a warm and clean sleeping place for a penny a night as well.' Reference was then made to a white paper published some eighteen months earlier by HMSO which disclosed that nightly there were just under 30,000 homeless men in the United Kingdom, of which number the Army was 'the biggest single provider of accommodation . . . at charges which are generally the lowest'. Booth House, the ninth of the centenary projects to be completed in the land of the Army's birth, was designed to meet the requirements of the 600 residents in such a way that the satisfaction of one man's wants would not prevent the fulfilment of the needs of another.

To the total cost of £546,000 the City of London made a grant of £136,445 for the housing of the necessitous aged of the city on the third floor. Lord Rank and his family generously contributed another £45,000, and an allocation from the Army's centenary appeal brought the total income to £471,000 – leaving a shortfall of £75,000. 'I would describe this half-million', said the General before escorting the Queen around the building, 'as a calculated investment in the service of the needy which will yield an incalculable dividend in a currency which neither moth nor rust can corrupt.'

7 THE FIELD IS THE WORLD

The years immediately following the centenary celebrations provide a convenient vantage point for a selective survey of the state of the international Salvation Army. Selective it must be, for to tell the story in detail would require – as the beloved disciple feared about his gospel – more books than the world could contain. Nevertheless even a limited survey shows that Salvationists of the widest range of colour, custom and culture are one in desire to proclaim the Christian message and to meet human need in every way consonant with the spirit of that message. So on with our seven-leagued boots and let us traverse the American continent from north to south, take Australia and New Zealand in our stride, island-hop to the Asian mainland and thereafter brace ourselves to cover southern and central Africa before crossing the Mediterranean to conclude with a bird's eye view of western Europe.

To set out on such a survey from the north-western corner of the American continent is to return to what has been called 'the heroic evangelism of the Klondike' – made famous by the presence of Evangeline Booth who was then in charge of Army operations in Canada. When the gold fever began to wane it was seen that the more informal approach of the newcomers continued to appeal to the Indian people who lived in the fishing villages which fringe the south-eastern coast of Alaska. Communication difficulties accentuated by the Second World War led to the work becoming a division of the USA Western Territory – which arrangement holds good to this day.

So far as Canada is concerned Commissioner and Mrs Grinsted succeeded Commissioner and Mrs Wycliffe Booth as territorial leaders in 1964. The first 100 days of 1965 were dedicated to varied expressions of personal evangelism throughout the territory. A 'Trans-Canada Centenary Cavalcade' took the road from Newfoundland to British Columbia,

calling at all the principal cities and townships on the way so
that the aim of the centenary might become as widely known
as possible. To the celebrations in London the territory made
a notable contribution by sending the Earlscourt band, the
North Toronto youth band and the Crusaders' combo. A
composite guide company and scout troop enhanced the youth
interest, added to which there were upwards of 200 official
delegates.[1]

Over the border, from the 49th parallel to the Rio Grande,
the Army has increased in numbers and in services to such an
extent that since 1926 oversight has been shared between
four centres – New York (Eastern), Chicago (Central), San
Francisco (Western)[2] and Atlanta (Southern), with a national
office to co-ordinate their activities.[3] The accepted place of
the movement in the national life of the United States was
demonstrated by a centennial message from President Lyndon
Johnson, as well as by the ceremonial release at noon on
July 2, 1965, of the United States five cent Salvation Army
centennial commemorative postage stamp. The design was
described as 'starkly simple . . . in character with the
organisation . . . our way of saying thank you for a job well
done.'

Out of doors a marathon open-air meeting was held 'at the
cross-roads of the world' – Times Square, New York, where
for fifty-one hours a Christian witness was sustained by selected
groups of Salvationists. Similar gatherings were held from
coast to coast. For example, the good news was also proclaimed
at North Beach on the Pacific, the birthplace of the beatniks.
Halfway between a couple of night clubs which pitted the
dubious attractions of belly dancing against those of a rival
golden girl swimmer, the gospel was heard. Said one of the floor
managers about these salvation singers: 'They are respected by
the people who come here.' The audience clapped their hands
in rhythm with the gospel folk songs – as the same message,
delivered in a totally different milieu, was welcomed by an
estimated congregation of 10,000 who joined in the service of
praise and thanksgiving held in the episcopal church of St.
John the Divine in New York, Governor Nelson Rockefeller
and Lord Caradon (then the United Kingdom representative
at the United Nations) were among the speakers. Similar
celebrations were held at the other three territorial centres

– Chicago, Atlanta and San Francisco. Indeed, hardly any community, however small or obscure, but shared in these rejoicings.

The same was true of the scattered Central America and West Indies Territory. Television, radio and the press – not to mention speakers galore – joined in a chorus of appreciation of the Army's work as the General moved from island to island, beginning in Surinam and ending in Bluefields (Jamaica) where the flag was first unfurled seventy-eight years earlier.

South of the equator the witness of Salvationists in the Argentine, Bolivia, Brazil, Chile, Paraguay, Peru and Uruguay merits special mention in each instance, for the road for those faithfuls has wound uphill all the way since the first four pioneers, not knowing a word of the language, landed in Buenos Aires in 1890. Even in the centenary year there were but 100 active officers in Brazil; 150 in South America East (Argentina, Paraguay and Uruguay); and slightly less than 100 in South America West (Bolivia, Chile, Paraguay and Peru). But advances have been made – and so continue, not so much by virtue of numbers as by reason of personal fidelity.

Ignorance of the language is no longer a handicap to the leadership. The year 1963 had seen the appointment of Colonel Hjalmar Eliasen as territorial commander in Buenos Aires. He and his wife had lived long enough in Latin America to be at ease at all levels of society. One of his outstanding achievements was the introduction of advisory boards where well-wishers from business and professional life joined hands to place their specialised knowledge at the disposal of the Army.

Across the Andes, Lieut.-Colonel and Mrs Joseph Dex, who had also spent the greater part of their active service in South America and whose command of the language was nothing short of professional, had their headquarters in Santiago. Both in Chile and Peru the governments recognised our place and sought our aid. In the former country the congress had passed a law reserving the first Saturday in October for an Army street day appeal; in the latter the government besought the Army's help with the rehabilitation of prisoners.

As elsewhere on the continent the Army in Brazil is known for its readiness to respond in times of national disaster. When devastating fires raged in the state of Parana, officers and cadets from the training college in São Paulo visited the stricken villages and hamlets, distributing food, clothing, medicines and bedding. Again when extensive floods left thousands homeless in the Rio Grande do Sol as well as in the shanty quarters of the Brazilian capital, the Army – thanks to the generous aid of Oxfam – was able to provide food, clothing and shelter as well as to assist in the extensive anti-typhus campaign.

Continuing our imaginary journey across the Pacific the first land to be sighted would be New Zealand where, in spite of the division into north and south islands, the country is well served by a compact and forward-looking body of Salvationists. The territory was fortunate in having as its leader from 1960 to 1964 the thoughtful – and thought-provoking – Commissioner Alfred J. Gilliard, who was ever ready to enter into constructive dialogue with officers and soldiers alike. He was followed by Commissioner Charles Davidson whose mind and spirit had been tempered during the Second World War by the ordeal of internment.

Both leaders were in charge at a time when the government census returns showed that an increasing number of New Zealanders either made no religious profession at all or, if they did, were unwilling to state what this was. In the half century from 1926 onwards this proportion of the population rose from 5.4 per cent to 18.5 per cent. If the first-named sought to awaken his fellow Salvationists to the realities of the age in which they were living, the second provided them with a means of consultation and discussion by instituting the Advisory Council of Salvation Army Laymen (ACSAL).

Across the Tasman Sea a New Zealander, Lieut.-Commissioner A. Bramwell Cook, with headquarters in Sydney, was in charge of the Australia Eastern Territory, and a 'fair dinkum Aussie', Commissioner Hubert Scotney, with headquarters in Melbourne, was in charge of the Southern Territory.

One of the several factors which has commended the Army to the Australian public is that the movement has grown up with the country. In the year when the pioneering Gore and Saunders joined forces in Adelaide the last of the bushrangers, Ned Kelly, was captured and hanged. The 'Salvos' have shared every subsequent emergency from the hazards of the gold rush to Coolgardie in the nineties to the perils of the Kokoda trail in the forties. The centenary year saw extensive developments in the treatment of the alcoholic, the care of the aged, and the erection of new properties for both corps and social activities. Of Australia it may be said that 'a great door and effectual' stands open.[4]

More swift island-hopping would now take the reader to Indonesia, Malaysia, Singapore, Sarawak, Hong Kong and Taiwan, Korea and Japan – and then over to Burma, Sri Lanka, Pakistan and India.

For the first time since the work began in 1894 in what was then the Dutch East Indies, 1965 saw an Indonesian officer, Colonel Jacobus Corputty, in charge of Salvation Army operations in Java, Sumatra, the Celebes, Borneo, the Moluccas, Timor and Ambon, and supported by an Australian single woman officer, Lieut.-Colonel Gladys Calliss, as Chief Secretary, whose command of Bahasa Indonesian (the official language of the republic) was surpassed only by her dedication to the people. Despite the tragic hiatus of the Second World War the visitor would have seen seven hospitals and clinics working to full capacity; one had been in operation for fifty years, another for forty. Forty-four primary and two secondary schools help to meet the educational needs of children in central Celebes.

As elsewhere the work so recently begun in Malaysia, Singapore and Sarawak was brought to an untimely halt by the Second World War. Although recovery was not easy in this multi-faith area what can be said is that, in addition to the renewal of its social services, the Army soon resumed its place in the local Christian council, shares in the Christian radio programmes, holds open-air meetings where permitted and seeks to make the command *War Cry* a means of winning converts for Christ.

Though the work in The Philippines Command had suffered similar setbacks, the centenary saw marked advances. An eighty-bed girls' home, the dream of years, was opened in Quezon City. During the year over 300 new soldiers and recruits were added to the corps rolls. The command's two relief centres distributed 36,000 food parcels during the Christmas season and every Christian use was taken of the radio facilities offered by the Manila and Far East broadcasting companies. Emergencies were not allowed to pass unnoticed. Food was provided for the victims of the Taal volcanic eruption near Manila, and relief teams came to the aid of the many victims of the fires which caused such damage in Cebu City and Iloilo City alike.

The story of the opening of Salvation Army work in Taiwan is told on page 205 and some details of what is being done in Hong Kong are given on page 215, though it must be kept in mind that every need in the crown colony is accentuated by the ever-increasing overcrowding. During the centenary celebrations the Acting Chief Justice illustrated the population pressure by referring to the plight of an old lady about to be evicted from the bed space – note 'bed space' – which she had occupied for the previous twenty years. She had long lived on the left-overs from the meals of her neighbours but, as the building in which they all had lived was about to be demolished, they were all to be scattered over Kowloon. What then would this aged lady do? 'It is in cases of this kind', the speaker added, 'that The Salvation Army is able to bring help where it is most needed.' Someone must have known what our Lord meant when He spoke about the cup of cold water given in His name.

Continuing northwards, the Army in Korea would have been found about their Master's business as well. Spiralling prices had brought economic hardship to the poorer sections of the community and the DMZ (demilitarised zone) cast its shadow over all. Thanks to the generous support of Third World relief agencies, sixteen feeding stations shared in the Christlike task of relieving hardship and hunger. In addition the Army's permanent homes for the very old, the workless, and the very young were always crowded to capacity. Yet, alongside this physical relief, the pre-eminence given to the message of salvation can be judged by the fact that the 1965 Year Book reported more than a thousand hours spent by cadets in gospel visitation, and fifty-one converts won in their annual campaign.

A short flight over the sea of Japan would bring our readers to Tokyo where, in centenary year, the territorial leader had chosen as the territorial motto the Founder's words: 'Go for souls . . .'. Such evident love for God and man evoked the admiration even of those of another faith – as when a Buddhist priest, clad in his saffron robes, after offering prayer in the manner of his own religious practice, was seen to take from his personal alms and place a contribution in the Army's Christmas kettle. By setting a new record this appeal enabled relief to be distributed on a wider scale than ever before. In this connection the customary donation from the Imperial household for the Army's social services was received yet again – as has been the annual practice for nearly half a century.

The record has now to back-track geographically. Burma, India, Pakistan and Sri Lanka are near neighbours physically – but in custom and culture, language and religion, dress and diet, they are widely disparate. A stout volume would be needed to do justice to an area that – east to west – would reach from Moscow to Manchester and – north to south – from North Cape to Cape St. Vincent.[5] The Salvation Army's work in India was divided at this time into four territories; at the time of writing there are five – with Bangladesh Command added for good measure. The single illustrations of the work which follow could be multiplied many times over.

Let's make a start with Burma – where political and social changes have made it increasingly difficult for expatriate replacements, let alone reinforcements, to enter the country – but centenary year saw the first Salvation Army march of witness for over twenty years. Soldiers, friends, home league members, together with the older children from our homes, took part in this and, wonder of wonders, the band played as well. Communal life has suffered many changes. While in some country districts the Buddhist sabbath was still observed, in the larger towns the Christian Sunday is no longer a 'no work' day. Nevertheless Salvationists sought to adapt their activities to public need – and the fact that early in 1966 *The Young Soldier* (in London) helped to sponsor the visit of a five-year-old Burmese boy, living in one of our children's homes in Rangoon, to London for a 'hole in the heart' operation, caught the imagination of his countrymen and women. The Westminster surgeon, Mr Charles Drew, operated without charge, and the happy postscript is that Jothein ran in the London marathon in the spring of 1983 in order to help the work of the movement which had helped him seventeen years earlier!

Pakistan provides a first-hand illustration of the golden cord which binds Salvationists together. Over the centenary period the home leagues of the United States defrayed the cost of erecting a protective boundary wall around the territorial compound in Lahore. The Box Hill corps (Australia) paid for the erection of a brick quarters for a village corps officer. The Canada Territory met the cost of electrification at the Shantinagar farm colony and also purchased a motor cycle for the use of the farm manager. In addition CORSO helped generously with high school and dispensary projects, and Oxfam provided a Volkswagen so that the divisional officer in Karachi could more expeditiously distribute the Church World Service relief among the 10,000 monthly recipients in and around the city.

In Ceylon (now Sri Lanka) as elsewhere in the Third World, many projects were completed through generous overseas contributions. The USA Eastern Territory joined with Swiss Salvationists to underwrite the bill for repairs and renovations to the hostel for elderly women in Colombo to the tune of 40,000 rupees. The cost of a new district headquarters at Madampe was met by the USA Southern Territory. The centenary also saw the timely gift by the Canada Territory of a new corps hall at Gonapinawella in memory of the dedicated Sinhalese pioneer, Arnolis Weerasooriya, whose hometown this was.

Now to give an example of current activity from each of the Indian territories – in Bombay (Western India) the Army flag was carried for the first time into St. Thomas's Cathedral where a meeting of thanksgiving was led by the Bishop of Bombay. In Southern India one of the most spectacular events was a cycle marathon shared by more than a thousand Salvationist cyclists along the 200 mile highway from Kanyakumari to Trichur. The Indian government also marked the centenary by its first ever grant to the Catherine Booth hospital for an extension to the twenty-year-old school of nursing – a development which has changed the one-time single-room block to the present balanced complex.

At this particular stage of Salvation Army administration the North-East India Territory, with headquarters in Calcutta, stretched from Amritsar in the north-west to Manipur in the north-east, and from Kalimpong in the north to Angul in Orissa, several hundred miles south of Calcutta. During the communal disturbances in the north-east Major Robert Lesher was appointed chairman of the Oxfam Assam/Calcutta relief committee which met the needs of the homeless and the helpless in that vast area – thanks to contributions from World Vision, CORSO, the Oxford Committee for Famine Relief (Oxfam), the governments of West Bengal and Assam, the four Salvation Army American territories, along with those of Australia, Canada and the United Kingdom. This vast relief operation, here itemised in a single sentence, was spread over hundreds of miles, lasted many months, and helped thousands of people.

Finally, the Madras and Andhra Territory faced the worst flooding in its history – each of the six divisions, plus the territorial centre, Madras, being affected. Marooned villages were difficult to reach but eventually a main relief centre was established in each division and Oxfam, with characteristic generosity, backed this further relief activity with another £5,000. The main agents for the Madras mills set aside their current orders to provide 5,000 cotton blankets. Medical suppliers sent aspirins, vitamins and cholera pills for distribution. For one critical month anything that floated was used for the purpose of distribution. Nor was this assistance taken for granted by the recipients. In Macherla, where flooding was very severe and the Army has no permanent centre, the people mounted a silver Salvation Army crest on a wooden base and presented it to the divisional commander as an expression of their thanks.

For a movement which believes that in Christ Jesus 'there is neither Greek nor Jew, circumcision nor uncircumcision, Barbarian, Scythian, bond nor free,' Africa presents its own peculiar difficulties as well as its outstanding opportunities. The overriding debate in what was once known as 'the dark continent' undoubtedly centres on colour, and the Salvationist understands that the universal love of God forbids his favouring any man at the expense of his neighbour – but would have him seek the good of both. He does not expect always to please both. What he is called upon to do in Christ's name is to serve both – and this he endeavours to do. As the official Year Book for 1965 testified:

The policy of 'africanising' the missionary work continues apace. A new missionary district has been formed in the Eastern Transvaal and a capable Bantu officer has been appointed to open up this new command. With other Bantu officers now holding appointments as efficient district officers, the doyen of Bantu officers – Brigadier Ephraim Zulu (divisional officer for mid-Natal which includes the proposed semi-independent Bantustan of the Transkei) has travelled beyond the borders of the Republic visiting in recent days the United States. He also accompanied the General to Nigeria and the Congo and later, with the territorial commander and chief secretary, attended the African zonal conference at Nairobi.

As the succeeding issue of the Year Book reported, the African local officer proved himself as zealous as his officer in furthering the spread of the gospel. When Corps Sergeant-Major Nason Magali returned to his native village, Nkondweni, he himself built an Army hall in that hot arid countryside and, on his own, unfurled the Army flag. It was not until later that the divisional commander, some 150 miles away, heard a rumour of what had happened and went to investigate. Though this village was not on any Army map he first heard the sound of an Army drum, then caught sight of a trim little hall, and finally met nearly forty uniformed Salvationists – the fruit of the sergeant-major's labours. In an equally remote area a newly-appointed African district officer went exploring – to discover a flourishing Army witness among men who had returned to Swaziland after accepting Jesus as Lord and Saviour in meetings held in the mining areas around Johannesburg.

At this juncture Salvation Army service in the new independent states of Zimbabwe, Zambia and Malawi was still directed from Salisbury (Rhodesia). But the changes made to adapt to the realities of the African scene only made the African Salvationist more eager to make the good news of the gospel known to his countrymen. By this time there were more than 300 corps and outposts (African and European) in action, two major hospitals working to capacity – that at Chikankata being the largest mission hospital in Zambia. This same hospital accepted the first ever six African girls for training as nurses. In centenary year President Kaunda was congratulating a session of ten midwives and eighteen nurses on receiving their certification. Within the boundaries of the former Rhodesia Territory there were five medical clinics, a leprosy settlement,

three social service centres, two training farms, and a system
of schooling at both primary and secondary levels, plus teacher
training facilities, which was valued by government and pupils
alike.

Moving northward, the story differs only in detail in the
Congo, Equatorial Africa, East Africa, Nigeria and Ghana.
Our work in what is now called Zaire suffered an undeniable
setback because of the widespread unrest following independence. The wonder is that, despite the physical turmoil, the
main body of our people remained true to their faith and loyal
to the principles of the Army. Indeed, some expressions of
Salvation Army service were needed more urgently than ever.
At one critical period our officer-nurses maintained a round-
the-clock rota at what was then the Leopoldville airport – a
service which evoked the warm appreciation of the Roman
Catholic missionaries arriving from the interior.

Across the Congo at Brazzaville (capital of the People's
Republic of the Congo) a newly erected training college saw
the commissioning of twenty cadets – the first session ever
to be trained in the territory. Local Salvationists were also
encouraged by the fact that their principal guests, Commissioner and Mrs Samuel Hepburn, who when leaders of the
United States Central Territory had helped to finance this
project, were received by the President of the Republic, M.
Massamba-Debat.

On the other side of the continent the East Africa Territory,
which embraced Kenya, Uganda and Tanzania, was at the
moment comparatively peaceful, and the 400 active officers –
sixty of whom were expatriates – were able to continue their
evangelical, social, medical and educational work without let
or hindrance. The Kenyan President, Mzee Jomo Kenyatta,
recognised the value of these specialised services by laying the
foundation stone of the Kibos school for the blind. The decision
of the government to subsidise the work at Joytown meant
that the pupil intake could be increased to 100 from the
beginning of 1965, and the agricultural training centre – a
thousand-acre farm at Thika – attracted larger attendances
than ever from African farmers who saw that scientific instruction could help them to answer their own prayers. Small
wonder that the territorial headquarters in Nairobi was
doubled in size when an additional floor was added to what

had been a one-storey building. Perhaps the most discerning comment upon the Army's efforts was made by a new arrival at the recently opened home for destitute men in Nairobi. 'I like this place,' he said. 'It has prayers *and* hot water.'

Across to the west coast lies the republic of Nigeria with its fifty-five million people, and the spirit of Salvationists there is typified by the enterprise of the cadets who are attempting to build up a regular congregation from the people who live in the vicinity of the training college. Meetings are held in what has been called the 'bamboo citadel' – a temporary building erected in the college grounds.

The Army's main work is accomplished in the country's three southern regions, and a regional headquarters has been established in eastern Nigeria so that closer contact may be made with the population who are so far from Lagos. In the capital itself the government has erected a new primary school building costing £27,000 to replace the old cramped facilities, and at Akai both the teacher training centre and the secondary school continue to develop as the latter aims to realise its five-year plan to double all classes.

Next door lies Ghana – where the Army could not entirely escape the after-effects of the deposition of President Nkrumah, but the chairman of the national liberation council personally assured the officer commanding that the witness and work of the Army would continue to be welcome. So the new youth centre at Tema was enlarged by the addition of sleeping accommodation. At the request of the ministry of health a new clinic and children's home was set up at Anum so that the Army clinics now serve an average of 900 patients monthly. A new training college was also opened in 1965 with eight married couples in residence.

Only in Algeria did the Army have to accept the closing of a work which had begun so promisingly in 1934. This is to anticipate the story slightly but by the end of 1969 the intention of the governing council was plain. The Army's regional leader was called in for lengthy cross-examination. The sale of the *En Avant* was forbidden. No charitable gifts could be received unless the name of the donor was disclosed. The names and addresses of all officers were to be shown to the government. Evangelical work among the general population was to cease. No Algerian might attend an Army meeting. Finally even the distribution of relief was forbidden – a work which had been considered by Oxfam as one of their most successful feeding programmes. Yet the promise still holds good that the word which God speaks 'will not come back an empty echo'. The same truth applies to those countries where the Army was in eclipse during the Second World War, as well as to those where the work – though not through any unwillingness on the Army's part – has not yet been recommenced.

Homing in on Europe we catch a glimpse of Queen Fabiola unexpectedly entering an Army hall in Brussels which, in common with other centres flying the flag, had been left open on weekdays to provide warmth and shelter during a spell of intense cold. A woman Salvationist was in the act of serving hot coffee – but halted on catching sight of the royal visitor. 'Don't stop what you are doing', said the Queen. 'Please go on with your work.' That is exactly what Salvationists in Belgium had been doing – and are continuing to do.

Denmark is not one of Europe's largest countries nor is the Army there to be judged solely by its numbers, but the centenary saw the formulation of a long cherished project – the Copenhagen men's social service centre. In 1967 the dream came true for, generously subsidised by the state and the local authorities, this scheme offered four forms of social experiment. On the top floor three flats provided teenage lads committed thereto by the courts with a room of their own while sharing in the home life of a 'family' under the care of a married couple. The third floor was to be occupied by sixty men in need of rehabilitation; the second afforded the equivalent of sheltered housing for nineteen old age pensioners; the ground floor and basement housed the essential administrative offices and plant for the recycling of waste paper – a form of industrial therapy.

No wonder the Army's compassionate approach to life inspired the Danish artist, Povl Christensen, to use the line which speaks of Christ as the Christmas rose growing out of the hard and frozen soil of humanity for his design for a Salvation Army commemorative stamp.

The international centenary coincided with the seventy-fifth anniversary of the Army's work in Finland, and this was marked by the publication of a history of that period, running to 480 pages of text and 48 of pictures, past and present, by Elsa Könönen, MA, retired grammar-school mistress and soldier of the Temple Corps in Helsinki. This illuminates in masterly detail the unbreakable fidelity of the Finnish comrades, particularly during the civil war of independence in 1918 and the 'winter war' of 1939–40. The territory continued to make history as well – for over the centenary period three new wings were added to the Iltala eventide home, a youth centre was built in Helsinki, and a new corps property and a men's social service centre were opened in Turku.

The extensive social services in France were further developed by the addition of accommodation to take another hundred homeless men in the Cité de Refuge in Paris, the opening of a men's shelter in Reims, the rebuilding at Paramé of a home to take forty boys to replace the property destroyed during the war, and a new wing added to the Blanche Peyron home for girls in Nimes. An Army exhibition which was staged in the Place de la Bastille in Paris was also on show in Lyon, Marseille, Mulhouse, Nancy, Nice, Nimes, Rouen and Strasbourg.

The centenary augured well for France's near neighbour, Germany, because for the first time the territorial leader for France crossed the border to campaign there. Permanent buildings were opened to replace the wooden structures of the immediate post-war period in Berlin (Friedenau), Frankfurt/Main, Göttingen, Kassel and Stuttgart. Similar plans were also on the drawing board for Barmen, Herne and Pforzheim.

It should be remembered that for fifteen years it had not been possible to train any officers in Germany. The territory's recovery from that chastening experience can be judged by the fact that two-thirds of the present officer corps have been commissioned since the conclusion of the war.

The year 1965 was memorable for Salvationists in Italy as well. Only one-half of one per cent of the Italian population is Protestant, but in that year the President of the Republic recognised the Army as an 'Organizzazione filantropica e religiosa' and authorised Esercito della Salvezza to receive donations and legacies. Another sign of the times was that when Mrs Lieut.-Colonel Hilda Bordas (wife of the officer commanding), Brigadier Alida Bosshardt and Major Mary Scott attended the twenty-third congress of the Abolitionist Federation, they were wearing full uniform when personally received by Pope Paul VI.

To refer to a later visit to the Vatican may be slightly out of chronological order, but this is undoubtedly as good a place as any to quote from the account by Colonel Brindley Boon in *The Musician* for January 21, 1984, of the visit of the Chalk Farm band to Rome in the summer of 1967.

Carrying their instruments, the bandsmen formed up behind the colour sergeant who, the flag 'at shoulder arms', led us across St. Peter's Square towards the door indicated. The brightly garbed Vatican guard sprang to attention as we passed . . .

Contrary to expectation the band was asked to play suitable music soon after its arrival. Deputy Bandmaster Ray Todd duly conducted the playing of a number of hymns loved by all, and for half an hour this went on until the vast chapel was packed.

As the time of the Pope's arrival drew near Bandmaster Clack was asked: 'Will the band play some happy music as the Pope is brought in?' 'Why not a march?' I whispered. A march it was – and Pope Pius VI was carried in with ancient ceremony to the strains of 'The Invincible Army'.

The playing ceased . . . In excellent English the Pope welcomed the band, remembered their wives and families, and thanked them for allowing the band to come to Rome to impart their 'soul lifting' music . . . At the conclusion of the proceedings . . . the band began to sing William Booth's immortal song 'O boundless salvation'.

Before leaving the colonel presented the Pope with an Army pennant bearing the name of the Chalk Farm band and Bandmaster Michael Clack asked him to accept the LP record prepared for this particular tour.

He shook hands a second time and moved on, but then, as if becoming conscious of 'Hursley' which the band was then playing, came back again. 'That is how music should be played,' he said.

Some Salvationists in The Netherlands celebrated the centenary twice over – once in Amsterdam when, after the commissioning of the thirty-two cadets of the 'Defenders of the Faith' session, the territorial commander led a meeting of thanksgiving, and again in London when the Amsterdam Staff Band and a delegation of over a hundred officers and soldiers joined in the international celebrations.

As befits a people whose interests have long extended beyond their own shores, a number of churches, along with the Army, joined in a drive to give one per cent of their annual income to missionary work. Out of this the territory was able to send more than a quarter of a million guilders for mobile clinics to Ghana, Haiti and Pakistan, to a hospital in Java and a medical centre in the Celebes, and for the extension of medical work in Rhodesia.

Centenary year in Norway was notable for the unveiling of a plaque which marked the commencement of work on a multi-purpose men's social service centre in Oslo which was to replace a building which had been in use since 1905. Within twelve months a parallel property was opened in Bergen which, declared state secretary Kaare Kristiansen, was 'an institution ahead of its time'.

Sweden was no less happy because one of her distinguished sons, Commissioner Erik Wickberg, was at this time the Army's international second-in-command. He returned to Jönköping to lead the seventy-fifth corps anniversary, and later to celebrate the eighty-fifth anniversary of the work in Sweden. Between these events he shared in the jubilee of the Army scout movement, on which occasion 100,000 Swedish kronor were raised for the establishment of a children's clinic at the Catherine Booth Hospital in Nagercoil, South India. A similar effort by the home leagues raised over 27,500 kronor for the Army hospital in Turen, Indonesia. Not to be outdone, the young people attending their annual youth councils gave 4,500 kronor for the Army children's home in Rio de Janeiro.

It will have been noticed that the British Territory is not mentioned in this mini-survey, but further reference will be made to events in the land of the Army's birth in the ensuing pages.

8 THEY FOUND JESUS EARLY

The year 1968 – youth year – was another busy year for Salvationists, for there was still a margin of unfinished business left over from the centenary. Some items which were planned were welcome; others, whose day nor hour could not have been foretold, less so – as with the promotion to Glory of Mrs General Coutts on the evening of Tuesday, December 12, 1967, at the age of sixty-eight. Reported *The War Cry* in the final issue of that year:

As a teenager she was an active Salvationist, a keen pub boomer, and for some years the life-saving guard leader at her home corps at Warrington (the equivalent of today's Guider). After taking an honours degree in science at the University of Manchester (where she studied under Lord Rutherford) she joined the staff of the John Howard secondary school, not far from the site of the historic Congress Hall . . . When the call to officership came, the teacher returned to the classroom as Cadet Bessie Lee . . . and she was married in 1925 to Captain Frederick Coutts . . .

Ten years in corps work preceded her husband's appointment to the Literary Department at International Headquarters. By then she was mother of a young family, but that did not prevent her finding an outlet for her own particular talents . . . She played a large part in the founding of The Salvation Army Students' Fellowship, of which she was vice-president for ten years . . . and from 1945 to 1957 represented the Army on the education committee of the National Council of Women . . .

During the last four years of her life she had to depend upon a wheel chair for mobility . . . but she refused to acquiesce in her physical handicap and, with returning strength, continued to conduct her business at International Headquarters, and to speak in gatherings, large and small, from her chair. She took an active part with her husband in campaigns throughout Europe and in the United States . . . As recently as June 1967, she accompanied him to Finland for the territorial congress in Helsinki . . . But though the spirit was willing the flesh became gradually weaker, and her earthly ministry quietly ended a fortnight before Christmas.

The General resumed his overseas campaigns and left for India and Pakistan on January 11, 1968, casting a wide net from west to east over the north of the country, visiting – among other centres – Bombay and Poona and the Army hospitals at Anand and Dhariwal. Moving across to Delhi, the General was received by His Excellency, the President of India, Dr Zakir Hussain, before leaving for Calcutta where, at the invitation of the Governor of West Bengal, he attended the annual ceremony commemorating the death of Mahatma Gandhi. Here he met comrades from the Mizo Hills and was able to ask the divisional commander, Brigadier Ngurliana, to receive the Bible which had belonged to Lieut.-Colonel Frederick J. Coxhead, recently promoted to Glory, who himself had been a greatly loved leader of Salvationists in that area.

Several crowded days were then spent in Pakistan – commencing at Karachi where the distribution of the bread that perisheth goes hand in hand with the offering of the bread of life. The dedication of Salvationists to the service of God and man without regard to race or religion was recognised at the reception jointly sponsored by His Grace Joseph Cordiero, Roman Catholic Archbishop, the Rt. Revd Chandu Ray, Bishop of Karachi, and the Methodist Bishop Hobart Amstutz, as well as by the large congregation which filled St. Andrew's church.

Subsequent meetings at Shantinagar, Amritnagar and Lahore were no less cordial. The gatherings on Sunday certainly demonstrated that Salvationists in Pakistan knew full well what it meant to be loyal to 'the yellow, the red and the blue'. The talented group from the corps at Mazong who brought such blessing with their singing had been invited to 'turn professional' but had refused, preferring to offer their services freely wherever they would be allowed to sing the Lord's song in a Moslem land.

Back in London the General was present at the opening of Booth House on March 27 by Her Majesty Queen Elizabeth II, the first visit by a reigning British sovereign to a Salvation Army social service centre. Almost simultaneously came the announcement in *The War Cry* that the 'For God's sake, care' appeal, oversighted by Colonel Arnold Brown, Secretary for Public Relations at International Headquarters, had raised £2,492,776 10s. 6d. – which sum included cash and reliable promises spread over the following ten years, plus amounts in process of negotiation with local authorities. There was added a cautionary rider that this did not mean that the Army's coffers were suddenly awash with ready money. There were twenty-eight agreed centenary schemes to be financed. A further noteworthy fact was that this scheme reached such a professional level that two of the seventeen winning designs out of the 372 submitted in connection with the current British poster design competition and exhibited on the concourse at Waterloo station, were inspired by this appeal.

Youth year was marked by other events which could be described, though not in any derogatory fashion, as conventional. It was not exceptional for the Army to fill the Royal Albert Hall for three religious meetings of a Sunday, and to crowd the Crystal Palace on a Saturday from mid-morning to dewy eve. Such attendances were taken for granted. This may hardly do justice to the expertise of the practised organisers of such events though it does testify to the fact that Salvationists, young and old, find nothing incompatible between a happy social life and a deeply held spiritual experience. So for a week – and it was a week which included two weekends – the 600 accredited delegates from the British Territory to the youth congress were housed in the halls of residence of three London colleges and shared spiritual and intellectual fellowship with similar youth groups from Germany, The Netherlands, Norway, Sweden and the United States (including the New Jersey Youth band and the San Francisco tabrettes – in English, timbrellists). The week had a life-changing effect on many of their number.

If such an event was regarded as normal, youth year also provided as offbeat an enterprise as could have been found even in the Army's pioneering days.

Next door to 'World's End' in Blantyre Street, Chelsea, stood the Army hall which had once housed the Chelsea corps. This now housed a rehabilitation centre where, so reported the occupational therapist on site, the aim was 'to encourage the evolution of a therapeutic, self-run, group of drug-dependent young people, and to help individual lads and girls with their particular difficulties'.

This was no easy task. At the beginning

> most of the group were still hostile, conning everyone, secretive, aggressive, lying continually, depressed and looking sick . . . With increased supplies of methedrine available, the staff were continually hustled, fights became more frequent, thieving increased, and many had troubles at home, or with landladies, or with girl-friends. Others in the group found themselves taken unconscious to hospital, or in trouble with the police.

Later, however, when prescriptions for methedrine had come under a legal ban, there was a change for the better and the centre entered upon a new and meaningful phase. So much so that on Thursday, April 10, 1969, there was an open day and, on the following morning, sections of the London press carried a drawing of seven cardboard effigies which represented how certain patients used to feel, or still continued to feel, when hooked on the 'hard stuff'. It was, declared the *Daily Mirror*, a kind of 'public confessional'. Said a 21-year-old girl: 'Before I came here I had been on ten cures in four years. This place worked for me, and they encourage you to stay around and help other lost souls to find their way out of the torture chamber.'

In the high summer that year the centre was visited by the Duke of Edinburgh who spoke to the staff and clients with such informality as to put them all at ease. Indeed, one of the girls invited him to help himself from her brown bag of cherries – and then was embarrassed by what she had intended as a gesture of friendship. However hard the way and long back from addiction, it is worth remembering that an encouraging number of those who have passed through the centre have been re-established in the community and have begun to earn their own living.

Historians of the Second World War period were wont to dilate on the difficulties of a second front, but this army of peace and goodwill has long been accustomed to serve on many fronts at once. In June 1968, the USA Western Territory seconded Lieut.-Colonel Leonard Adams to relief work in Vietnam, and in due course he was succeeded by Major and Mrs George Collins from the USA Central Territory. Their team was made up with other American Salvationists and, from March to July 1969, the then chief medical officer from the Catherine Booth memorial hospital at Nagercoil, India (Lieut.-Colonel (Dr) Harry Williams), was released to serve as senior surgeon at the hospital, newly established in Saigon, by the Children's Medical Relief International, Inc. of New York. In addition, these Salvationists gathered around them a team of volunteers – American housewives, Vietnamese students, odd-job men – willing to turn their hand to any task as circumstances might require. Never had the varied needs of so many been treated by so few as at the Army clinics in Saigon.

Meanwhile in a second floor office at 101 Queen Victoria Street, London, there was a prolonged spate of letter-signing and envelope-addressing for by Saturday, May 24, 1969, notices had to be in the post for the forty-five members of the High Council bidding them to attend at Sunbury Court on Thursday, July 17, for the purpose of electing the ninth General of The Salvation Army. The full list was:

Commissioner Gilbert ABADIE	Territorial Commander, France.
Commissioner Frederick ADLAM	Territorial Commander, Rhodesia.
Commissioner Gösta BLOMBERG	Territorial Commander, Sweden.
Commissioner Edward CAREY	Territorial Commander, USA Eastern.
Commissioner Paul CARLSON	Territorial Commander, USA Central.
Lieut.-Commissioner William CHAMBERLAIN	Territorial Commander, Caribbean and Central America.
Lieut.-Commissioner Jacobus CORPUTTY	Territorial Commander, Indonesia.
Colonel Haakon DAHLSTRØM	Territorial Commander, Finland.
Commissioner Joseph DAHYA	Territorial Commander, Western India.
Commissioner Charles DAVIDSON	Travelling Commissioner.
Lieut.-Commissioner Hjalmar ELIASEN	On furlough.

Commissioner Francis EVANS — Territorial Commander, New Zealand.

Commissioner Frank FAIRBANK — Chancellor of the Exchequer, IHQ.

Commissioner Ernest FEWSTER — Governor, Men's Social Work, Great Britain and Ireland

Commissioner Olive GATRALL — Principal, International College for Officers.

Commissioner Alfred GILLIARD — National Editor-in-Chief, USA.

Lieut.-Commissioner Samuel GNANASEELAN — Territorial Commander, Madras and Andhra.

Lieut.-Commissioner Hubert GODDARD — Secretary for Trade.

Lieut.-Commissioner John GRACE — National Chief Secretary, USA.

Commissioner Frederick HARVEY — Territorial Commander, Australia Southern.

Commissioner Koshi HASEGAWA — Territorial Commander, Japan.

Commissioner Samuel HEPBURN — National Commander, USA.

Colonel Edward JOHN — Territorial Commander, East Africa.

Lieut.-Commissioner Paul KAISER — International Secretary, IHQ.

Commissioner Sture LARSSON — Territorial Commander, Norway.

Lieut.-Commissioner Arthur LONG — On furlough.

Commissioner Albert MINGAY — British Commissioner.

Commissioner William PALSTRA — International Secretary, IHQ.

Lieut.-Commissioner William PARKINS — Territorial Commander, USA Western.

Commissioner Charles PEAN — Territorial Commander, Switzerland.

Commissioner Carl RICHARDS — Territorial Commander, South Africa.

Commissioner Aage RØNAGER — Territorial Commander, Denmark.

Lieut.-Commissioner Leslie RUSHER — Territorial Commander, Korea.

Commissioner Glenn RYAN	Territorial Commander, USA Southern.
Commissioner Hubert SCOTNEY	Territorial Commander, Australia Eastern.
Colonel Donald SMITH	Territorial Commander, Pakistan.
Commissioner John SWINFEN	International Secretary, IHQ.
Lieut.-Commissioner Julia TICKNER	Leader, Women's Social Work, Great Britain and Ireland
Commissioner William VILLENEUVE	The Salvation Army Assurance Society.
Lieut.-Commissioner Tor WAHLSTRÖM	Territorial Commander, Germany.
Lieut.-Commissioner Harry WARREN	Territorial Commander, Scotland.
Commissioner Herbert WESTCOTT	Principal, International Training College.
Commissioner Kaare WESTERGAARD	Territorial Commander, The Netherlands.
Commissioner Erik WICKBERG	Chief of the Staff.
Commissioner Clarence WISEMAN	Territorial Commander, Caribbean and Central America.

In characteristic fashion Salvationists in London greeted the members of the High Council by flocking to the Westminster Central Hall in greater numbers than the auditorium could seat, and then by their unflagging attention to the five visiting speakers, each of whom represented a continent. The following day the world leaders commenced a measured survey of Army affairs, the main conclusions of which were listed in *The War Cry* for July 26, 1969. The steady growth of the international membership in terms of soldiers, recruits and adherents was noted, and the world community strength of The Salvation Army – that is, based on the unduplicated list of names recorded on one or other of our rolls, senior and young people's – was stated to number two and a quarter millions. Attention was directed, however, to weaknesses in certain aspects of our youth work. The implications of the relationship of the Army to the World Council of Churches, dating back to its formation in 1948, were also considered and a recommendation was made that the Army should continue its membership . . . It was widely agreed that we had a duty to maintain our witness both to the convictions which brought the Army into being as well as to the biblical principles which govern our structure and worship.

The conference gave more time to the nature and demands of Christian moral standards than to any other subject, and it was agreed that the gulf between the lifestyle required by the example and teaching of Jesus and current non-Christian practices only increased the need for Salvationists more earnestly to seek the grace which would enable them to follow the rule of Christ. The conference was equally agreed that Christian standards could be upheld only in the spirit of Christian love. No effort should be spared to restore anyone overtaken in a fault. Both individually and corporately Salvationists should hold themselves responsible for the spiritual welfare of their comrades. No wounded traveller should ever be left lying by the side of the road. So deep was the concern felt in the conference as to how best this end could be secured that it was agreed this matter be given further detailed consideration.

Conference business concluded on Wednesday, July 16; the High Council was opened by Commissioner Erik Wickberg, the Chief of the Staff, on Thursday, July 17, at two o'clock, who also led the initial devotional exercises. After the legal formalities had been completed the Council, by secret ballot, elected Commissioner Hubert Scotney as President, and the other offices necessary for the conduct of business were also filled.

No High Council wastes its time on words, but this Council was particularly expeditious because it later transpired that only two of the nominees were willing to allow their names to be put forward for the ballot – Commissioner Kaare Westergaard and Commissioner Erik Wickberg. However, the Council took all necessary time and care over its procedural structures for, valuable as precedents may be, each Council is self-governing and may approve, or reject, or amend previous procedures as the current membership may desire. A simple majority is sufficient for such action though, in practice, most changes are made by consensus.

By mutual agreement neither candidate gave a nomination address, though each replied fully to the numerous questions which were presented to the questions committee and approved for submission to the nominees. The upshot was that all this preparatory work was completed by the evening of Tuesday, July 22, and on the following day the Council proceeded to vote. Only one ballot was necessary before the chief teller, Lieut.-Commissioner Julia Tickner, was able to advise the President that Commissioner Erik Wickberg had secured the necessary two-thirds majority. By four o'clock, so reported *The War Cry* for August 2, 1969, the doors of the council chamber were opened to admit reporters, cameramen, Salvation Army staff, and such members of the world and his wife who were in the neighbourhood. The General himself made haste to come down from International Headquarters and when, with the General-elect, he entered the dining hall, the members of the High Council lifted up their voices in a chorus which is not to be found – and probably never will be found – in *The Song Book of The Salvation Army*: 'For they are jolly good fellows'. Perhaps some members of the press were astonished that so secular a refrain was so well known by so select a company. But then the press – and this is said with the utmost respect – still has much to learn about the Army, and Salvationists would not deny that they still have much to learn about the world which they are seeking to serve.

The General had eight weeks left in office. One weekend he gave to Blackpool – to which corps he had been appointed from the training college as a probationary lieutenant in the spring of 1920. The annual congress in Scotland demanded his presence – for Glasgow was the city of his youth. On his way south the comrades of the north-east had to be greeted for there was an extension to be opened at 'Hopedene', the Army's maternity home in Newcastle on Tyne, by the Countess of Tankerville. Manchester could not be passed by – for the General married a Lancashire lass in 1925, nor could Cardiff be forgotten – for was not his mother's maiden name Mary Jones and could she not read and speak Welsh to her dying day? Nottingham had also to be visited – particularly as the corporation had made the munificent gift (spread over ten years) of a quarter of a million pounds so that 12 Notintone Place, the birthplace of William Booth, might be preserved as

a permanent memorial, and the rest of the property transformed into an up-to-date social service centre. Six days were
also given to the annual congress in Denmark where the
General marched with Danish Salvationists to the reopening
of the modernised Copenhagen Temple. In another of the
many meetings the General presented Commissioner Aage
Rønager, the territorial commander, with his long-service
medal for fifty years' unbroken officership. Further promise
for the future was engendered by the stone laying – held on
the site of the first Salvation Army property in Denmark – of
the new Helgensensgade corps building and student residence,
at which the territorial commander acknowledged the interest
in this project shown by the King and Queen of Denmark,
and their generous contribution from the Queen Anne Marie
fund. Sunday's meetings in the Idraets Huset (sports palace
hall) brought the congress to a rewarding conclusion as many
seekers knelt at the mercy seat.

At this point in Salvation Army history the retirement age
for a General was seventy and keeping strictly to time, the
final farewell was held on Saturday evening, September 20, in
the Royal Albert Hall. *The War Cry* set the scene.

Seated in the arena were scores of white-shirted band members
whose gleaming instruments turned to pure silver under the spot-
lights. Behind them sat rows of local officers in sombre blue; in
front of them the pastel shades of 'Take-over bid' performers. In
the stalls was a swathe of white-bloused singing company members. On the platform echelons of songsters were massed around
the scarlet and white of the International Staff Band, above whom
were more white blouses – students of the national school of music.

There were sounds to be remembered. It could hardly be
otherwise when the International Staff Band played Eric Ball's
'Good News'. There were gales of laughter – as might be
expected when practised performers delighted the congregation with excerpts from the Gowans and Larsson 'Take-over
bid'. There were numerous speeches – perhaps more than
there ought to have been remembering the Preacher's warning
that 'God is in heaven, and thou upon earth: therefore let thy
words be few.' But far more significant than a crowded Royal
Albert Hall was a news flash which had appeared in *The War
Cry* a brief four weeks previously.

Television viewers of Sunday evening's newscast saw the Belfast Mountpottinger corps[1] (corps officers, Major and Mrs Stanley Richardson) marching away from their open-air meeting with its customary gospel message. And this in a city where, by government proclamation, the Army was the only people allowed on the streets.

During the recent outbreaks of violence the local social services had offered accommodation, food, clothing and blankets to those without shelter. The corps halls at Shankhill and Old Park, as well as the Cable Street goodwill centre, also remained open nightly. There was a PS. to all this which could have occurred only in a Salvation Army setting. The officer in charge of the Buckingham Street goodwill centre was asked to look after several barrels of beer which had been hurriedly removed from a public house which had been set on fire. 'Yours is the only place', said the landlord ruefully, 'where I know they will be safe!'

Without doubt (said the General as he concluded the Royal Albert Hall gathering) the image of the corporate life of the Army during the first half-century of its existence had been the unmistakable profile of William Booth. But our current image is not the reflection of any single person. Nowadays it is compounded of the words and actions of a multitude of recruits, soldiers, local officers and officers engaged in Salvation Army service at grass-roots level. Our image is now the sum total of the witness of all our lives. Every life, without exception, must therefore be like a city set on a hill which cannot be hid. And with this challenge, a united act of dedication, a prayer – and the familiar Army salute, the meeting was over.

PART FOUR

THE NINTH GENERAL: ERIK WICKBERG

(September 21, 1969–July 5, 1974)

1   THE NINTH GENERAL

Erik Wickberg was the ninth General of The Salvation Army but – declared his biographer, Lieut.-Colonel Bernard Watson – to some extent an 'unknown General' for he was of continental stock and a large part of his service had been spent in Europe. His predecessors had included an American and an Australian – but their first language in each instance was English. The new General's first language was Swedish though, as he moved to Berlin at the age of eight when his father was appointed principal of the Army's training college in the capital, German ran his mother tongue a close second. When there was a further change of appointment which brought the family to Switzerland, French became another spirited runner in the language stakes. None of these was of the 'pen of my aunt' variety. The General shared the view that any claim to have mastered a language implied the ability to solve a crossword in that language. Seeing that he also speaks fluent English without a trace of accent, it is clear that he long enjoyed a flying start in the art of communication.

In the pains and problems of life he was early tested. He chose for himself when and where to yield his life to Jesus as Saviour and Lord, as he did over his decision to become a Salvation Army officer. His first appointment was to Hamilton (Scotland) but he soon returned to Germany where he married the gifted Ensign Frieda de Groot, an officer-friend whom he had known for several years. This was a bitter-sweet idyll – for the young mother died after giving birth to a baby boy. The bereft father cared for his infant son as best he could until 1932 when he married Captain Margarete Dietrich. Two years later the Wickbergs were appointed to the European section of the overseas departments at International Headquarters. The most unexpected change of all still lay ahead of them.

Adolf Hitler came to power in 1933 – and soon the pressure

on a movement which was international in character, whose members were known as soldiers, whose world leader was a 'General', and whose principal headquarters was in London, began to be felt. The Army in Germany was never proscribed nor was the wearing of the uniform officially forbidden, but heightening world tensions were reflected in the restrictions which were placed on what had hitherto been accepted as normal activities. Commissioner George Carpenter was elected as the Army's fifth General on the day following the Nazi-Soviet pact and this is how General Wickberg later described the way in which he and his family were personally affected.

> Before returning to Sweden Commissioner Larsson had a conversation of much significance with the General-elect. Should war come – and it was still thought by some that it might be avoided – Larsson was to act on behalf of the General with regard to Army affairs in Germany. This was as far as anyone could think at that moment. An amount of money would be remitted to Stockholm . . . and a young Swedish officer, who had been serving in the European section of the overseas departments for nearly six years would be appointed to assist the Commissioner 'in case of need'.
>
> On the evening of the last Friday in August this young officer, married and with three children, aged nine, six and two years respectively, was told to wait for an instruction before going home. He was then told that it had been decided to transfer him *pro tem* to Sweden to assist Commissioner Larsson should IHQ communications with Germany 'and any other country' become difficult or impossible. He would need to leave immediately. A passage via Newcastle-Bergen-Oslo-Stockholm would be booked for the morning.

Next morning the family was duly waiting at the appointed London terminus. A comrade officer bidding farewell said: 'We may see you back in a fortnight when all this has calmed down. Enjoy your holiday!' It was more than twenty years before the Wickbergs saw England again.[1]

When the war was over and the need for Swedish relief work in Europe – particularly in Norway, the far north and the Baltic – was no longer an urgent priority, Brigadier Wickberg was given charge of the Uppsala division. On the sound New Testament principle that he who has been faithful over a few things is made ruler over many, he was later appointed Chief Secretary for Switzerland with the rank of lieut.-colonel. This was followed by further promotion and a similar term in Sweden. The autumn of 1957 saw him back in Germany again, this time as territorial leader – though this was a very different country from the one to which he had been transferred in the late autumn of 1925. And a very different Army as well for, despite all that had been done since the Armistice on Luneberg Heath, the work of post-war reconstruction was still heavy going. Perhaps the new leader's most significant decision was to move the territorial headquarters from the divided city of Berlin to Cologne early in 1961. But the full implications of this timely action were still being worked out when the unexpected promotion to Glory of the Chief of the Staff, Commissioner Norman Duggins, after but ten weeks in that appointment, brought Commissioner Wickberg to the post of the Army's second-in-command – an office which he filled with distinction until his own election as General in 1969.

General and Mrs Wickberg lost no time in facing up to the demands of their new international responsibilities, for three days before their public welcome in the Westminster Central Hall on October 8, 1969, they met the officers of the British Territory gathered in council at Butlin's holiday camp at Bognor Regis. Brilliant sunshine greeted this meeting of kindred spirits, and the sincere pleasure of all concerned was re-emphasised at the Central Hall meeting.

The War Cry spoke of it as 'a great night for welcomes'. It was certainly a great night for the appropriate epigram – polished as well as homely. Commissioner Gösta Blomberg, who had known the General from schoolboy days, spoke of him as a man 'with many interests but one passion . . . of many methods but one purpose . . . of many languages but one message'. Commissioner Samuel Hepburn, National Commander of the Army in the United States, was in more Lincolnesque vein when he spoke of the General as one 'who does not carry all his groceries around in his front window'. Mrs Wickberg was likened to 'our new Army mother' and as for 'the world outside', that, said the General, 'is our world, and we cannot opt out of it'.

The following week the newly promoted Commissioner Arnold Brown took up his duties as the Chief of the Staff and Mrs Commissioner Brown assumed the responsibilities which had hitherto been carried by Mrs General Wickberg. This left the General and his wife free to commence their round of public welcomes both at home and overseas. Wisely the General set up two or three markers in his first message to the Army world through the international *War Cry*. It was not his intention to make any off-the-cuff announcements of 'far-reaching changes in structure or policy'. Such decisions were never taken 'without careful research and responsible advice from experienced leaders'. It would be foolish to insist on change simply for the sake of change, but 'to adapt and adjust to meet the needs of those whom we seek to serve' would be a priority, and 'Evangelism with a capital "E" would continue to be our main concern.' Any who were attracted to any particular form of Army service could write him personally and would receive a personal reply.

With future lines of action thus defined the General and his wife set out for Paris as their first call. 'But why Paris?' asked the man from the *Figaro*. Questions of this nature are an occupational hazard for anyone holding the office of General. Interviewers are wont to turn a blind eye to the obvious in their determination to unearth the obscure. Paris was the city (explained the General) to which William Booth had sent his twenty-year-old daughter, Catherine, in 1881, and France was the first continental country where the Army flag was unfurled. He was but following the best of all possible precedents. This nice point satisfactorily settled, the General addressed the luncheon meeting convened by the *Comité d'honneur de l'Armée du Salut*. This was followed by a more unbuttoned gathering in the capacious restaurant of the Palais de la Femme, and a still more tumultuous welcome in the evening at the Salle Centrale.

Like Caesar's Gaul – though with far more pacific intentions – Sunday was divided into three parts. The morning was given up to a lucid exposition, heard in respectful silence, of the experience of Christian holiness. In the afternoon the meeting in the Maison de la Chinie was devoted to a resumé of the Army's manifold activities – evangelical and social. In the evening in the basement of the massive Cité de Refuge the truths which had been proclaimed in the afternoon were put to a practical test as many of the dejected and defeated in the congregation accepted the Christian offer of salvation.

A further two days were given to engagements in Paris and

then, in one of those changes which an Army leader has to take in his stride, Der Regierenden Bürgermeister Klaus Schütz was greeting the General 'as one Berliner to another'. As a sign of the regard of the city in which he had lived as a boy, the reception for the General was held in the senate chamber of the Berlin-Schöneberg town hall where he signed the Golden Book – an honour last accorded to the Apollo 11 astronauts. In the exchange of courtesies the General presented the Mayor with a German edition of Richard Collier's *The General Next to God*, and the press conference which followed lasted over two hours, so unflagging was the interest of the media and so fluent the replies they received in their mother tongue.

From the beginning of the century William Booth had conducted Repentance Day meetings in Berlin in the Circus Busch, and his eldest son, Bramwell, had followed his example. The custom had been maintained though the venue had been changed – and 'Busstag, 1969' was held in the Ernst Reuter hall, less than a mile from the notorious wall. Nevertheless there were those present in the meetings whose age allowed them to cross into West Berlin and to warm their hearts again at the fellowship of Die Heilsarmee.

This was how the General felt. 'My dear Berliners,' he said, 'I belong to you.' And Mrs Wickberg strengthened the faith of the beleaguered Salvationists when she quoted Luther's '*Ein feste Burg ist unser Gott*' ('A safe stronghold our God is still'). As a girl she had sung those lines. As a mature Salvationist she had proved their truth. 'The God of Luther [she said] is still our refuge.' Twenty-eight of those present agreed with her as they knelt at the place of prayer.

With Christmas duly celebrated in the land of the Army's birth, the New Year found General and Mrs Wickberg again in Germany – this time sharing in Salvation Army day in Stuttgart. The hazards of a bleak mid-winter diverted their plane to Munich – which meant the hastiest of scampers over almost 150 miles of snow-bound roads in order to be in time for the reception planned by the state government of Baden-Wurttemberg. A lively exchange of news and views then continued at such length that it could have been that some of the General's admirers had forgotten that his day had begun at five a.m.; that the morrow was earmarked for three weighty conferences with officers from all parts of Germany;

and that there were another three public gatherings scheduled for the day following! But the word of promise is – as thy day so thy strength shall be. The programme went through as planned – and not long after the Federal Republic recognised the ties between the General and their country, as well as the post-war care shown by the Army for the German people themselves, by bestowing on him the Grand Cross of Merit.

In spite of these crowded days it would be wrong to describe the engagements of the Army's international leader as a relentless treadmill. In its day that was a purposeless task which sapped the victim's morale. But a General's round of appointments, tightly packed though they may be, generates its own inspiration – both for him who speaks and those who listen. This is what a line in the Army song book calls 'blessing, and being blest'. So Birmingham, Alabama, was gratified because for the first time they had received a Salvationist General in their city. New York – and particularly the Scandinavian community – rejoiced because the General, himself a Swede, graced the eighty-third anniversary of the Scandinavian work in the States. This particular campaign was completed by public meetings in the bilingual city of Montreal and, on the next day, in Toronto.

Meanwhile the Army had been making headlines in the French press by protesting against certain scenes in 'Hair' which was being played at the Théâtre de la Porte Saint-Martin – in particular, an indecent profaning of the Cross. *The War Cry* for January 21, 1970, carried a press photograph of Commissioner Gilbert Abadie, the territorial commander, rising from his seat to make one such protest. As might be expected, this provoked the fury of some and the support of others. One charge was that the commissioner had taken money from the Christmas collections for the poor to pay for the tickets which enabled the Army demo to be staged within the theatre itself. This unfounded allegation enabled Commissioner Abadie to reply that he had received more than twice the cost of his protests in unsolicited contributions from friends and supporters. Indeed, members of the public had joined of their own free will in manning some of the collecting points. In one instance the organist at a Roman Catholic church in the capital offered to take his turn at the harmonium which was used at the Gare St. Lazare to accompany the carols, and a group of nuns had joined the Army singers.

Following the annual week of prayer for Christian unity, a mass meeting was convened by the Army in the Palais de la Mutualité to call attention to the need for Christian standards in public life, over which the Auxiliary Bishop of Paris presided, supported by M. Claudius Petit (deputy for the Loire) and Pastor René Chateau. Some two hundred interrupters did their best to break up the meeting but *The Times* Paris correspondent gave full marks to the chairman and speakers for refusing to be intimidated. The regular 'Letter from Paris' in the London *Daily Telegraph* said:

> The substitution of vituperation and personal violence for rational argument is becoming an alarming commonplace in French life, particularly when small groups of youthful extremists object to the views of anybody of any prominence. The rowdy obscenities which marked a Salvation Army meeting called last week to protest against widespread pornography was perhaps only to be expected.

Two days later a procession numbering more than 500 – headed by the Army flag, marched through the main boulevards of the capital carrying such placards as 'Yes to love, no to filth'; 'Silence equals complicity'; 'Yes to liberty, no to libertinage' (dissipation). The fact that this witness was made by the participants in complete silence and with great dignity made a powerful impression upon all who saw it. One Swiss weekly wrote:

> Courageous as was the action of Commissioner Abadie, it is not his courage one admires the most but his love of his neighbour. More than any other religious society, *l'Armée du Salut* is free from rites and symbols. Thus the profaning of the Cross or the parody of baptism could have been a matter of indifference to the Commissioner. But he could not accept that the profoundly religious sentiments of his compatriots should publicly be mocked.

Said *Christianity in the Twentieth Century:*

> There are those who say that this is a secondary matter. There are more grave problems in today's world – war, the atomic bomb, racialism. Of course, but are they not all linked? Are not eroticism and violence closely related? . . .

I think it is courageous that Christian believers have attacked
at least once, other than by petitions and resolutions, and not in
church buildings but in the temples of pornography themselves
. . . Without doubt the protests of Salvationists themselves in
France against the debasing of human dignity will not be lost.

On the other side of the English Channel an equally powerful
weapon was about to be launched – Commissioner Catherine
Bramwell-Booth's full-length study of her grandmother, entitled *Catherine Booth, the Story of Her Loves*. Some sighting shots
had already been fired when the commissioner was interviewed
by Magnus Magnusson on Sunday evening, February 15. The
full weight of this (nearly) 500-page biography was felt when
the commissioner made a pulpit of Mowbray's book shop
gallery during 'Hodder week'. She disclosed that her typescript
had undergone five separate revisions. Otherwise it would
have been much longer than it now was – so much had this
distinguished Victorian to say to her own generation, and to
ours as well. It was soon plainly apparent that this was no
commercial puff, aimed solely at sales and profits, but a
restatement of the Army's first purposes as exemplified in the
life of a wife and mother in whom Christian zeal was rooted
in Christian integrity. Deep spoke unto deep. The chairman
of Mowbray's board of directors said that never before had he
seen his bookshop crowded with so diverse a variety of people,
from Catholic nuns to Salvation sisters, gripped by a word of
the Lord.

The name of Catherine Booth was again part of the present
when General Wickberg led the centenary celebrations of
Corps No. 6 at Hastings – a Christian Mission station which
the Founder's wife herself had opened in the Old Market Hall
in George Street. All had not been smooth sailing since, for
from 1909 to 1912 the Hastings magistrates had made repeated
attempts to curtail the holding of Salvation Army open-air
meetings by either fining or imprisoning both officers and
soldiers for conducting such meetings. With delightful uncon-
cern for public relations *The War Cry* of that day described
the action of the authorities as 'a most trumpery, paltry,
pettifogging piece of superfluous interference'. Happily public
memories are not sixty years long. The corps sergeant-major,
Alderman Dengate, was content to summarise the history

of the corps in four words: 'Rejected, tolerated, accepted, respected'.

Afterwards General and Mrs Wickberg crossed the North Sea once again to celebrate Good Friday in Malmö with a congregation approaching two thousand in the city theatre, and on Easter Sunday evening with over a thousand comrades and friends in the community hall in Oslo. Back in Salisbury the General participated in the ninetieth anniversary of a corps whose name is writ large in Army history. Here the Bishop of Salisbury, the Rt. Revd J. E. Fison, turned a delicate compliment when he drew the General's attention to the fact that the Noah's ark which was sculpted in the cathedral had a Viking prow. 'If ever', he added, 'there is a time for internationalism in the Christian church, it is now.'

As no man can be in two places at once the General could not attend the final public meeting to be held in the Clapton Congress Hall on May 14 to mark the end of eighty-eight years of literally daily Salvation Army activity centred on Linscott Road, Clapton. With Mrs Wickberg he was meeting the people of Japan – first in the persons of the Emperor and Empress who were pleased to accept a copy of the newly published biography of the Army Mother; then with the children in the newly opened Kiekoryo Memorial Home; then with the officers of the territory; last of all with the Salvationists and friends assembled in the Kanda central hall.

Each minute of the weekend was filled with sixty seconds' worth of distance run. Saturday saw a march of witness through the Ginza in Tokyo, leading to a rally in the Hibiya Park, followed by a public meeting in the spacious Kiyoritsu hall. Whit Sunday was occupied by three meetings attuned to the spirit of the day, and the Monday was shared between a women's rally and a youth demonstration – after which the international visitors left for Osaka, Japan's second largest city, where a round of engagements was fulfilled within the context of 'Expo 70'. What is of more than passing interest is that, after the General had left for Korea, twenty of the seekers who had knelt at the mercy seat during the weekend voluntarily attended a counselling class and were introduced to the officers in charge of the corps which operated in the areas where they lived.

From Japan to Korea was to move from one ancient land

to another, but the fact that the flag was not unfurled in Korea until 1908 meant that historically the Army there was but a thriving youngster. For more than half of that time the alien authorities were very suspicious of any challenge to their rule, so that the presence of more than two hundred national officers and the eager attention of thousands of soldiers testified to what God had wrought. One reason for the Army's growth may have been – according to the Minister for Culture (who represented the President of the Republic and, in that capacity, invested the General with the Order of Moo-Koong-Wha) – that 'no other group had identified itself so completely with the people of the land'.

The same could be truthfully said of most countries where the Army is at work, for the General had not long returned to International Headquarters when he was called upon to preside at the opening by HRH Princess Alexandra of a purpose-built hostel for men in Shadwell Street, Birmingham. From some reporters *The War Cry* gathered the information that the Princess was wearing a matching suit of white and beige embossed cotton with white accessories; from others that part of the hostel's overall cost of £300,000 was being met out of a grant of £212,000 from the Birmingham corporation towards the three major social service schemes which were being undertaken in the city during the Army's current extensions programme. Both items were newsworthy.

Before the year had run its course there were two areas, hitherto unvisited by the General, which were to benefit from his presence – one was the Republic of South Africa, the other was its northern neighbour still called Rhodesia. Both had problems peculiar to themselves, but in both the Army sought as far as possible to honour its basic principle of meeting human need, whatever form it might take and wherever it was to be found. This was exemplified by the nature of the crowds which gathered from the Saturday morning open-air meeting which was led from the vantage point of the city hall steps in the modern industrial city of Johannesburg, to the bonfire meeting held on the slopes of Mountain View – the Army settlement in the far north of Natal, forever associated with the name of Major Mbambo Matunjwa, converted in the first Army meeting to be held in his native Zululand and admitted to the Order of the Founder in 1942.

Ten days in South Africa were followed by a further ten days in Rhodesia where, wrote the Australian Salvationist reporter:

> The Army is almost entirely African. It is a well-groomed Army, wearing attractive biscuit-coloured uniforms which can be – and are – well laundered, with the womenfolk wearing white hats.

The Army in Rhodesia, like the Army in other parts of the continent of Africa, has much to make glad the hearts of all Salvationists everywhere. Around 1,200 men greeted the General in one welcome rally; 250 women greeted Mrs Wickberg in another. In Bulawayo Salvationists marched a thousand strong to greet the visitors. This time the congregation in the men's rally numbered 350; in the women's there were 550. But all totals were eclipsed by the 3,000 fires which burned during the day and lit up the night sky at Ciweshe where the main rally was held. The subsequent day's march of witness numbered over 10,000 officers, local officers and soldiers – everyone, men and women alike, in uniform. Rightly to estimate the influence of the Army in this part of Africa one must add the 180 day schools with their attendance of 32,000 children, not to mention the increasing part played by Salvationists in the government of their own country.

To give a single illustration – *The War Cry* of June 27, 1970, carried the story of Aaron Mungate who attended the village school which boasted but three grades – sub-A, sub-B and standard one. By 1946 he had become head boy at Howard where the school motto is 'Godliness and good learning'. At forty-seven years of age, by the overwhelming vote of the college of chiefs, he became a member of the newly formed lower house of the Rhodesian parliament.

From the same continent had come a cry for help to handle the refugee problem in Nigeria. The sudden end of the internal fighting had highlighted the plight of the homeless and the hungry, of the sick and the wounded, of lost children trying to make their way home again, and of parents searching high and low for their missing children. The instant answer to the appeal from Lagos was the dispatch of a six-strong medical team from London. The territorial commander, Lieut.-Colonel Leonard Kirby, returned from his homeland furlough, and the fourth Sunday in January was set aside in the Army world for praying and giving. Captain Hilda Fielding, SRN, SCM and Captain Honor Hutchins, SRN, SCM were at their work in Nigeria from February onwards, and Brigadier (Dr) Sidney Gauntlett followed them shortly afterwards. The 'siege' areas – that is, those which had been most seriously affected by the war – were the districts of immediate concern and, to his relief, the territorial commander found that no officers had lost their lives though, in many instances, their personal losses had been heavy due to fighting and looting. The Army team was assigned one of these areas and at one time some 150,000 refugees were receiving a cooked meal daily. Some idea of the scope of this work can be gained from the fact that 4.32 million weekly rations were distributed and 4.13 million cooked meals were served.

Nigerian officers whose links with their various headquarters had been severed for thirty-one months were supplied with food, clothing, medicines and blankets. The immediate needs of those who had no money save the now worthless Biafran currency were met. Seed was distributed to provide the next season's crop. Children found wandering because their homes had been destroyed or their parents killed were cared for at the Mrs General Coutts' memorial home or at the Army home at Akai.

Before the year was out Commissioner Arnold Brown (the Chief of the Staff) and Mrs Brown had visited Nigeria and had presented one of the district officers in the south-east state – Brigadier O. Offiah – with 'a certificate in recognition of exceptional service'. During the civil war, though unaware of the whereabouts of his wife and family, he had 'maintained the work of the Army, caring devotedly for his officers and soldiers'.

The same selfless dedication to the relief of human need was seen on the other side of the world when, on May 31 of the same year, an earthquake devastated some 30,000 square miles of northern Peru, some 70,000 people lost their lives, and an estimated 800,000 were rendered homeless. So completely cut off was the stricken area that for five days there was no word of the safety of the married officers and their family in charge of the Army work in Trujillo. Not till the end of the week did news reach the territorial headquarters in Santiago that though the officers' quarters was uninhabitable, and the hall and school were badly damaged, the officers and their children were unharmed.

In the true spirit of a Salvationist, the lone district officer for Peru, Captain Enrique Taramasco, had gained permission from the authorities to proceed northward to the scene of the disaster, and the territorial commander, Colonel Peter Staveland, working from Lima, secured a fleet of trucks for the transport of provisions and medicines. But equally quickly did it become clear that a disaster of this magnitude called for a concerted relief effort of similar size. Lieut.-Commissioner Raymond Gearing, of long experience in South American affairs, was called from retirement to co-ordinate the entire operation.[2] Within days a skilled team of officers and workers left the United States for Peru. Arising out of the visit by Mrs Richard Nixon to the disaster zone the Army's national commander in the United States, Commissioner Samuel Hepburn, along with Commissioner Edward Carey, were invited to serve on the Peru Earthquake Voluntary Assistance Group. The result was that the Army in the USA collected and conveyed to northern Peru nearly one thousand tons of medical supplies, dried foods, tinned goods, water purification units, four 1½-ton trucks, three jeeps, not to mention quantities of beds, cots, blankets, clothing, tents and building materials. Once again there came to pass the saying that where there's need, there is The Salvation Army.

2 DIVERSITIES OF OPERATIONS

The year 1971 presented the Army with new and diverse opportunities – with consequent operations which were equally diverse. In the General's forward planning, this particular year had been dedicated to the interests of children and, well in advance, Colonel William Larson had been appointed to oversee this international effort. His principal task was to explore ways and means whereby the Army's work among children everywhere could be extended and how new children, thus attracted, could be led to commit themselves to the children's Saviour. This crusade was later extended to cover 1972 as well – though it has to be admitted in advance that rarely does human need flow solely through the appointed channels, however well prepared these may be. In this respect the year just begun was to be no different from the old year nor, for that matter, from any previous year. 'Dedicated to the unexpected' continued to be the necessary motto for those who would serve God and man.

An early instance of this occurred at the 'World's End' drug dependents' centre (London) which was opened on February 13, 1967, but ceased to function on December 14, 1970. This had been an interesting return to the Army's early day willingness to experiment in the cause of righteousness. Not to experiment with righteousness, but to experiment for righteousness' sake – as when William Booth opened the Lamprell Street match factory in 1891 in order to demonstrate that workers could be paid a higher wage, and the industry still make a profit, without the employees running the risk of phosphonecrosis ('phossy-jaw'). William Booth was content to have made his point as soon as match manufacturers ceased using toxic phosphorus.

In a similar spirit 'World's End' was an effort to link the skills of medicine to the grace of God in providing treatment for the drug addict. If no universal remedy emerged from these months of experiment it did not mean that this period of trial and error had been wasted. One valuable conclusion from the study of more than a hundred young people who were treated at the centre was that 'each addict could make progress according to his individual capacity, if he willed to do so.' In other words, the staff was confirmed in the truth that their labour in the Lord had not been in vain.

With this same divine assurance the Chief of the Staff, Commissioner Arnold Brown, dedicated the new social service complex which was opened at Greenock a fortnight before Christmas, 1970. Here was to be found accommodation for eighty men, including twenty old-age pensioners on a more permanent basis, with a six-bed unit for the rehabilitation of alcoholics, plus room for another fifteen transients seeking a night's shelter.

Nor, as God is no respecter of either persons or place, would this assurance be denied to His servants – African and European alike – who, on Palm Sunday, 1971, shared in the opening of a maternity block in the Congolese town of Kavwaya (almost due south of Kinshasa) where the Army already had a primary school, a school of domestic science, a dispensary, as well as a corps and divisional offices. Help towards the cost of this most practical project had come from Switzerland and The Netherlands, while the Congolese government had funded the essential installation of electricity and running water.

Nor would this assurance be withheld from the staff at the Lyncroft maternity home and hostel where additional facilities for mothers and babies were opened on May 12, 1971, representing the third stage of development plans for the social services in Birmingham (UK).

Nor from those serving at the Amity House advice centre in Plymouth where, almost simultaneously with the Birmingham project, a four-storey Goodwill centre for women and mothers in need of emergency accommodation – with cots available for babies and toddlers – was opened, allied to which was a sheltered workshop for elderly and retired citizens.

And certainly not from those appointed to staff the memorial centre built around the house in which William Booth grew up in Notintone Place, Nottingham. The description in *The*

War Cry of the proceedings on Friday, October 1, could not be bettered, so here are some of the relevant paragraphs.

> There were elements in the crowd which would have intrigued William Booth. A Swede, ninth in succession as General from himself; his German born wife; his Canadian Chief of the Staff; his American secretary for public relations; not forgetting the director of the new goodwill centre, born in the Argentine, wedded to a daughter of an Anglo-Danish marriage and named – Booth . . .
>
> He would have nodded his head in approval at the presence of the Secretary of State for Social Services, Sir Keith Joseph . . . though he hardly could have foreseen the arrival of the Lord Mayor and the Lady Mayoress, the Sheriff and his lady, the aldermen and councillors in their gold braid and finery, all coming to the Notintone Place to honour his memory . . . along with his eldest grand-daughter, Commissioner Catherine Bramwell-Booth (R), straight-backed and soldierly despite her eighty-eight years, who was there to unveil his statue.
>
> Throughout the afternoon all went according to plan – and there could have been no better way to honour his memory than that the house where he first saw the light should operate as a day and night centre to serve the people of Nottingham.

But the Founder's dreams were continuing to come true far beyond his native land – in Spain, for example. This had been one of Railton's dreams as well. 'I wish they would let me open up in Madrid,' he had said to his wife on one occasion when sighing for fresh worlds to conquer. The Founder's one-time lieutenant actually rented a small carpenter's shop in the Calle del Oliver, and the attendances seemed to him to warrant moving to an even larger building. But Railton's uncertain health meant that he had to return home, in addition to which the authorities may have supposed that he represented a new and militant arm of the accepted church. Maybe he did – but not in the sense they imagined.

Nearly seventy years later, a girl cadet was collecting in a block of flats in Geneva when she knocked at a door where lived Enrique and Rachel Rey – a husband and wife who had already committed themselves to Jesus as Saviour and Lord, and who were seeking to learn how better to serve Him. Within little more than twelve months these two Spanish comrades were enrolled as soldiers of the Geneva 1 corps. Subsequently

Enrique became the recruiting sergeant,[1] and on Ascension Day, 1971, he and his wife were commissioned as officers by the Chief of the Staff, Commissioner Arnold Brown, and appointed to unfurl the Army flag in Spain.

Some preparatory work had still to be done. The Army's religious and legal position had to be made secure. Captain and Mrs Rey had to decide where to start, so they moved to Corunna where they had relatives and friends. A hall was rented, together with a flat which would serve as officers' quarters. Then, after further negotiations, the small block of property in which the hall was situated was purchased in its entirety for Army use, recognition was granted by government authorities in Madrid, and meetings were begun. 'Share our joy,' reported the captain. 'Jesus is the same – yesterday, today and forever!'

At the self-same Ascension Day meetings mentioned earlier, reference was made to a small group of Christian people who were eager for the Army to begin working in Oporto, their native town in Portugal. A paperback life of William Booth, written in Portuguese, printed in Brazil, and on sale in an Oporto bookshop, was the spark which set alight this flame of desire. Enquiries transmitted via São Paulo, London and Paris brought to Oporto the territorial commander for France, Commissioner Gilbert Abadie, who himself had served as the Army's leader in Brazil and who spoke Portuguese. The upshot was that two retired officers, also fluent in Portuguese through their own long service in Brazil, agreed to oversee this new opening. The work grew apace and when one of the newly commissioned local officers attended a day's meetings held in the Westminster Central Hall, London, on Tuesday, October 5 of that year, he was presented by the Lurgan band with an Army drum to take back to Oporto.

At the commencement of 1972 Major and Mrs Carl Eliasen were appointed to take charge of the work in Portugal, and later in the year a Swiss pastor, Daniel Mathez, who was being transferred to France, entrusted to the Army the work which he had begun some ten months earlier in the Pichelaire district of the city of Lisbon. The possession of both senior and young people's halls, each well furnished, at a reasonable rent, was accepted as a direct answer to prayer. Said Pastor Mathez: 'By handing over this mission to Salvationists I am only returning to them a little of their spiritual influence on my life, as it was in a Salvation Army meeting many years ago in Switzerland my mother gave her heart to the Lord – the starting point of her lifelong service as a missionary, mostly in Portugal.'

Before the year was out the General had given his blessing to yet another social experiment – one which enabled bail to be granted to young men over seventeen years of age on remand from the Bow Street and Marlborough Street (London) magistrates' courts. Hitherto the procedure had been to refuse bail to those of 'no fixed abode' even though they had no previously recorded conviction. What made this practice the more vexatious was that half the number originally charged were released without being given a custodial sentence. In other words they were found not guilty, or placed on probation, or fined, or conditionally discharged. 'We want', said the General, 'to remedy the injustice of a situation where a man of "no fixed abode" is automatically remanded in custody.' So did Mrs Xenia Field. She had repeatedly drawn the attention of the authorities to this anomaly, and the Home Office had at last agreed to a privately financed and administered experiment which could run for three years. This was to be funded by the Xenia Field Foundation, and the needful oversight and accommodation were to be provided by the Army in conjunction with the Inner London probation service.

The Home Secretary, the Rt. Hon. Reginald Maudling, MP, who took the opportunity of inspecting the facilities at Booth House, unveiled a commemorative tablet, and spoke appreciatively of the generous interest of Mrs Field and this further evidence of the practical service of the Army. This he saw as yet another way of lessening any undesirable rise in the prison population.

A parallel to this was to be seen in the way in which long-term prisoners in the Army's Eastern Territory in the United States were prepared for eventual parole and release by being allowed to take part in an Army correctional services programme. Chosen men were released to Salvation Army supervision to spend an agreed period at home or in an Army camp. Initial experiments along these lines proved their worth.

One of the most significant global events during the General's term of office was the International Commissioners'

Conference held at Ocean City, New Jersey, from September 10–21, 1971. More than fifty world leaders gathered to consider the Army's present position and future plans. Preliminary work on the thirteen main items in the agreed agenda had already been undertaken by separate study groups and submitted to the conference. Presiding over the discussions were the General and the Chief of the Staff, and the final recommendations were fully set out in the international *War Cry* for October 16, 1971.

Pride of place was understandably given to the Army's supreme aim: the salvation of the whole man – body, mind and soul, to which end all Salvation Army activities should be directed. As these largely depend upon the individual officer much thought was given to his character and work – woman as well as man, single as well as married. Equality of opportunity was to be a practice as well as a principle.

The burden of financing the world mission of the Army would continue to fall upon the Army as a whole. The willingness of the strong to help bear the burdens of the weak was deeply appreciated, as were the efforts of all territories and commands to meet their own specific responsibilities.

With regard to our relationship with other Christian bodies, the conference reaffirmed our claim to be 'an integral part and element of the great church of the living God, a living fruit-bearing branch of the true vine'. The statement continued that 'the weight of opinion was in favour of maintaining our links with the World Council of Churches and other ecumenical bodies, taking advantage of the opportunities they offer to make clear the Army's unique witness.' In brief, the conference desired to

  (i) assure the world that the Army stands firm by 'the faith once delivered to the saints' . . .;

 (ii) reaffirm the confidence of Salvationists in the empowering and guidance of the Holy Spirit . . .;

(iii) challenge Salvationists to maintain Christian standards of morality in their personal conduct and their public relationships;

(iv) call upon Army corps and individual Salvationists to provide a more effective witness to God's redeeming grace through Jesus Christ . . .;

    (v) confirm the loyalty of Salvationists to the Founder's insight
        that a Christian social service ministry is an integral element
        in authentic evangelistic endeavour; and to

   (vi) testify that Army leaders are continually seeking to be respon-
        sive to the changing patterns of society which impose new
        and challenging demands upon our movement . . .

The conference concluded by expressing the warmest gratitude
for the generous hospitality of comrades in the United States,
which 'had strengthened the bonds between Salvationists the
world over'.

    With little more than a fortnight's interval General and Mrs
Wickberg began their South American campaign which lasted
from October 7 to October 26, and in this they were supported
by Commissioner Kaare Westergaard, the recently appointed
International Secretary for Americas and Australasia. São
Paulo, the territorial centre for Brazil, was the first port of call,
and the welcome of the territorial commander, Colonel Joseph
Dex – supported by representatives of the state governor and
the city prefect – began at the foot of the steps of the plane.
Saturday afternoon saw a well-attended women's rally addressed by Mrs General Wickberg, while the General himself
shared in an act of witness in one of the central city squares.
The enthusiastic evening gathering lasted for two and a half
hours, during which Dr Emma Azevedo Castro, honorary
consultant for thirty-seven years at the Army's home for unmarried mothers, was admitted to the Order of Distinguished
Auxiliary Service. 'It is an obligation to help the Army,' she
forcefully declared, 'for they do what we cannot do or do not
want to do.'

    Sunday carried a full programme of Army meetings. There
were simultaneous open-air gatherings both morning and evening as well as a ready response to the word of truth in each
of the indoor gatherings. Monday was occupied with two
private gatherings for officers with a soldiers' rally rounding
off the day, concluding with a promise from the General –
given with a good heart yet so difficult to fulfil – that next
time, if at all possible, he would stay longer.

    The platform party at the welcome meeting in Buenos Aires
could not have been more representative. Present on behalf of
the Argentine government was the director of the department

of non-Roman Catholic faiths, the ambassadors of Sweden and Finland, the British consul, together with members of the Advisory Board as well as leaders of the Roman Catholic and Evangelical churches. The territorial commander, Lieut.-Commissioner Per-Erik Wahlström, presented Envoy Atanasio Blanco, of the Caballito corps, to the General for admission to the Order of the Founder. This recognition of the envoy's forty-four years of exemplary service was received with unanimous acclaim. A women's rally, a soldiers' rally and a youth rally completed the Saturday's events, leaving Sunday free for the message of holiness and salvation which brought many to a deeper commitment to the Father's will and others to an initial acceptance of Jesus as Saviour and Lord.

Up and over the Andes took the international visitors to Santiago where the territorial commander, Colonel Peter Staveland, with Mrs Staveland, voiced the welcome of officers and soldiers from the three countries of Chile, Bolivia and Peru. Meetings with the officers prepared the way for well-attended public gatherings. As is customary on these occasions the outdoor witness was regarded as of equal consequence with the indoor. Sunday began with three open-air meetings held simultaneously in the heart of the capital. Following the holiness meeting where the life of the Spirit was described as one which grows, matures, flowers and fruits, an afternoon march of witness culminated in an open-air rally when a number of seekers knelt at the drumhead.[2] The evening salvation meeting abounded in praise and testimony, and the mercy seat was lined with seekers.

On the following day General and Mrs Wickberg were received by the President of the Republic, Dr Salvador Allende, who expressed his thanks for the way in which Salvationists sought to meet the needs of the people of Chile, particularly in connection with the recent earthquake relief in Petorca and Chincalco.

Natural calamity is no respecter of people or place, as was tragically manifested at this time by the cyclonic storm and tidal bore which swept across the massive Ganges delta in so destructive a fashion that it was well said that never was so much suffered by so many through so little fault of their own. The fact that the area involved was first called East Pakistan and then, when man had made nature's confusion worse confounded, was known as Bangladesh, only demonstrated that rue by any other name is just as bitter. All figures of such a catastrophe can be only estimated but it was considered that an area of more than 5,000 square miles was devastated; 5,000 homes were damaged, 20,000 fishing boats were sunk; 250,000 head of cattle and twice that number of poultry were killed, and a possible half a million human lives were lost. Remembering that more than a thousand miles separated West Pakistan (where the territorial headquarters was situated) from East Pakistan, the then General Secretary, Brigadier Ernest Yendell, accomplished more than a man-sized job in assembling a medical team – including a doctor, two Salvationist nursing sisters (Captains Alina Vanninen and Vera Walker) together with other national officers – on the other side of the subcontinent and bringing them within working distance of the stricken area.

Appeals for help in Nigeria had scarcely ceased when appeals for East Pakistan began to be heard – and answered by Salvationists the world over. Lerwick (in the Shetlands) led the way so far as the United Kingdom was concerned. Relief monies from International Headquarters supplemented the response of the United States. Japan air freighted a consignment of blankets. Hard pressed by her own needs, India contributed according to her capacity – and similarly around the globe.

But within a few months the situation grew worse by reason of the swelling flood of refugees into India. What follows are extracts from an eye-witness account by our man in Calcutta – the General Secretary for the North-Eastern India Territory, Brigadier Robert Bath – and dated June 11, 1971.

I have just returned from a tour of refugee camps between Calcutta and the East Pakistan border, and have never before seen so much need and distress. Refugees from East Pakistan are everywhere – in camps by the roadside, under trees, lying in ditches, squatting in every available space . . .

At the border we already have a large relief programme which includes an emergency hospital as well as a milk distribution post for children . . . Now a request has come through for a medical team and station to be set up in one of the camps within the Barasat subdivision . . .

There are about 40,000 in this one camp which was established only a few days ago, and tents and canvas sheets are still being erected . . . The official number of refugees who have crossed from East Pakistan is now 4.75 million. They come in droves – homeless, destitute, hungry. The official figure of reported deaths among the new arrivals is now 3,642 – and is rising all the time.

At the Army's feeding centre in Calcutta some 3,500 people are given a meal daily, but there is now added to these a line-up of refugees . . . There will soon be five million people on our doorstep. With a different emphasis to that of the current play we simply gasp and exclaim: 'Oh! Calcutta!'[3]

This plea was as good as answered in the very issue of *The War Cry* in which it appeared, for page two of that self-same number carried the announcement that two qualified nurses – the experienced Major Eva den Hartog and the London-born Sallie Birnie – left Gatwick for Calcutta on Friday night, June 18, by generous courtesy of British United Airways.

The story can be resumed some weeks later, by which time Major den Hartog was serving at the field hospital at Barasat. Senator Edward Kennedy had arrived in company with Dr Nevil Scrimshaw (US nutrition expert), together with the unwearying Brigadier Robert Bath and the district representative of CASA (the National Christian Council Relief Organisation). A four-year-old boy dies from malnutrition as the visitors arrive. His 36-year-old mother explains that her husband died on the trek across the border and her remaining child is lying ill in the next bed. Nearby two young children are sitting on the end of another bed and the Senator is told that they are orphans – a boy aged twelve and a girl aged ten. Their father died on the way to Barasat, their mother after arriving at the hospital. Their total possessions are contained in a rice bag under the bed. They are to be taken to the Salvation Army children's home in Calcutta on the following day.

Stories of this kind never end because human need of this kind never ends. No family but knows their unpalatable taste. Neither the godly nor the ungodly can escape this harsh discipline. The last issue of *The War Cry* for 1971 reported the promotion to Glory of Mrs Mamie Thompson of Belfast – a life-long Salvationist who spent herself in the service of others. During the day she had been serving refreshments to those who had been working to put out an extensive fire which resulted from a bomb attack on a factory which stood close to one of the principal Salvation Army halls in Belfast. As Mrs Thompson resumed duty in the evening a dividing wall collapsed without warning. Two of her comrades were seriously injured. She herself was killed.

Said the Governor General of Northern Ireland: 'This is indeed a grievous return for all the good that The Salvation Army tries to do.' Maybe so – but this is the Christian behaviour pattern which Salvationists have followed in the past – and intend to continue to follow. They are not, as God shall help them, to be overcome by evil, but to overcome evil with good.

3 IN LABOURS MORE ABUNDANT

'Children's year has ended and Children's year has begun,' said the General when responding to his welcome at the Croydon Citadel corps on the morning of the first Sunday in 1972. What was originally planned to occupy one year had, on second thoughts, been extended to two – and this may be as good a place as any to summarise what had been accomplished so far.

There is a sense in which the whole of a Salvationist's life is one long campaign. Nevertheless, to adapt Samuel Johnson somewhat, it does help to concentrate the mind wonderfully when a specific task is given a specific deadline, together with a slogan which continually highlights the end aim. The slogan was duly provided – 'Every child matters' – and, at the first knee drill in 1971 to be held in the Bramwell Booth Memorial Hall at International Headquarters, the General himself launched the campaign.

This world challenge quickly gained a world response. In Hong Kong the Army did not need to go looking for children. There were more than 10,000 in its schools and nurseries already. The Australia Southern Territory hit on an ingenious plan to form mobile teams of company guards (Sunday school teachers) who would tour new housing estates and hold meetings for children as need might arise and facilities be secured. In the Gujerat division of western India a 'chariot tour' carried the children's charter to twenty-five different corps so that, before the journey ended, more than 2,000 new signatures had been secured. In Scotland 10,000 carrier bags were printed and distributed bearing the children's year logo. A page of pictures in the international *War Cry* showed various territories expressing their concern for children in various ways – coloured children in the United States being taught in an Army school; a Korean doctor, whose training was sponsored by the Army, treating a sick child in an Army hospital. Home leagues in the USA Central Territory distributed a wall hanging which, under the title of 'Children learn where they live', read:

> If a child lives with criticism
>   He learns to condemn,
> If he lives with hostility
>   He learns to fight . . .
> If he lives with tolerance
>   He learns to be patient,
> If he lives with security
>   He learns to have faith . . .
> If he lives with friendship
>   He learns to show love.

Japan has its own children's day each year – the fifth day of the fifth month, which the Army used to stage a march in the centre of Tokyo while loud speakers announced the purpose of children's year. In East Bengal one woman missionary officer expressed her practical commitment to the year's slogan by undertaking the daily preparation of baby food and porridge for the 600 children in the refugee camp. The year was given unusual publicity in Britain by the revival of a very old tradition at the Plymouth Barbican. The skipper of the *Kathleen and May* asked Colonel Edmund Taylor (R), who had enjoyed a long-standing fellowship with the fishing community, to dedicate his infant child on the deck of his trawler. The Army flag flew at the masthead. The band of the Plymouth Exeter Hall corps accompanied the singing. The large crowd standing on the quayside shared in the service, and the happy parents were presented with a Bible on behalf of the corps. As a television team was on hand widespread coverage was given to the Army's faith that 'every child matters'.

As was ever the case there were children – and adults – in distress at numerous points of the compass, as the continuing disorder in Northern Ireland so painfully demonstrated. Children's year had hardly begun when a bomb attack rendered unusable the Army hall in Londonderry and laid waste the surrounding property. But the spirit of Salvationists in the city was evidenced by the way in which the picture of the Founder was acclaimed when it was rescued from the debris, as well as by the outsize notice which appeared in a matter of hours:

'This hall has been destroyed but the work of God goes on!'

Only months later a car bomb extensively damaged the hall at Newry though, as the explosion occurred late on a Sunday evening, no one was injured. Salvationists were among the many who realised that only Christian grace could assuage the divisive bitterness which prevailed, and so a call to prayer was issued which read:

> Upon all our hearts these days is the burden of concern for the people of Ulster . . . for whom we intercede in such a manner as will bring us into fellowship with the sufferings of this part of our world family. It will doubtless be costly to intercede for the peace of Ulster, but we pray that political and economic functions may be reconciled in a mutual regard for that greater good which can emerge only from an acceptance of those restraints and motives implicit in a Christian society.

The children of the stricken cities and towns became an object of special care. In Belfast and Strabane twenty-two underprivileged children from Roman Catholic homes were given a Kentish holiday along with the same number of children from less fortunate Protestant homes. Some months later Salvationists in Glasgow met the cost of providing another mixed group of children from Northern Ireland with a week's holiday in Strathclyde – enriched by excursions to the Ayrshire coast, to Loch Lomond and to Edinburgh.

But there were other areas of human need which lacked even the occasional relief of natural beauty – for example, the world of the city dosser. Here is how Philip Howard of the London *Times* described what he saw during the winter of 1971/72.

> The soup run starts after midnight in the big Salvation Army shelter at Hoxton. Either Joe Burlison or Bernard North slices the loaves given by a local baker, while the other spoons the vegetables out of the seven gallons of simmering soup because if they are left in they clog the tap of the urn . . . Their first call is underneath the arches at the Charing Cross underground station where rows of solitaries sleep on the pavement wrapped in newspapers, their heads and feet in cardboard boxes, their backs turned on the world.
>
> The two men walk through the Embankment Gardens telling those lying on the benches that the soup has arrived. They do not

disturb those who are sleeping because it is hard enough for a man to fall asleep on a bench in the open without being woken up and having to start all over again. On cold nights they will blow on the ball of their thumbs and hold them on the eyes of their customers to thaw the frost and allow them to see. They have found two men dead of cold already this year.

A crowd of about fifty gather round the van, supping soup, dipping bread and talking – probably for the only time during the day. Many of the down and outs are on Christian name (or at any rate nickname) terms with the Salvation Army men. Some even trust them enough to talk about the past . . .

The next haven for the soup truck was Euston station . . . The dossers here are better dressed, less withdrawn and more talkative than those at Charing Cross. Many are from the Midlands or from the north and working, but not earning enough to pay for lodgings and to send money home as well . . .

The last call is Spitalfields market, known with reason by the denizens of this ghost town as 'the graveyard'. Men stand and sit around a bonfire of cardboard boxes and garbage that burns all night. Swarms of sparks fly upwards as sure as man is born to trouble, lighting up shadowy figures sitting on the heaps of rubbish, drinking from dirty bottles and eating from dirty tins . . .

The dossers at Spitalfields are the hardest in London to communicate with, the most disturbed and the farthest away from the ordinary world. When this particular soup run started just over a year ago they seldom accepted the soup or made any noise except a grunt. Now many drink the soup and some are beginning to talk to the men who bring it. In all there were about 200 customers for soup last night. In the summer, when more young people sleep rough, the number may be nearly doubled . . .[1]

But who cares for those who care? The 'Joe' beside whom Philip Howard sat in the soup van is a married man. He has a wife and three children. His predecessors did not often think of their future when their pledge was to live and fight *and die* in the ranks of the Army. But the passage of time has highlighted the needs of those who have borne the burden and heat of the day, and shortly after the close of the Second World War, two warm-hearted friends placed at the Army's disposal a country mansion at Bidborough among the orchards of Kent, which was originally built as a private residence for the Countess of Tankerville. 'Glebelands' then became the happy home of some twenty-five retired officers but, with the wear and tear of the years, a new property was felt to be necessary. Another site became available when Springfield Lodge, a one-time girls' home situated at the junction of Grove Hill Road and Dog Kennel Hill in south London, was demolished, and a purpose-built residence, capable of accommodating thirty-five guests, was opened by the General on Thursday, February 10, 1972. As the responsibility for retired officers was part of the concern of Mrs General Wickberg at this time, it was fitting that she should personally thank all who had taken an interest in the decor and furnishings of the new home, as well as in providing the incidental items needed to complete such a project.

But however many the inevitable transfers from the 'actives' to the 'retireds', the front line had still to be manned, and one of the by-products of the International Commissioners' Conference at Ocean Grove (mentioned in the previous chapter) was the appointment of Captain and Mrs Enrique Lalut to commence the work of the Army in Venezuela. This, in common with many another Army beginning, was a modest affair from the public point of view. As in the gospel parable, the seed that bore an abundant harvest was the least of all seeds. A garage space was rented and on June 30, 1972, the first meetings were held in E. Rincon. But in the flourishing oil city of Maracaibo in western Venezuela lived a friend whose memories of the Army went back thirty years to his youthful days as a Salvationist in Surinam (formerly Dutch Guiana).

He himself had hoped to train as an officer in The Netherlands, but the Second World War put paid to his plans and so he and his family moved to Maracaibo. Then, in a Caracas newspaper, he saw a photograph of Captain Lalut, to whom he promptly wrote inviting him to address church and business groups in the oil city about the work of The Salvation Army. This was an opening which the captain seized with both hands. Caracas, the capital, is sometimes called 'the city of perpetual spring' but, amid all its beauty, waifs and strays had nowhere to lay their heads. It was not long before two children's homes were filled.

This could have been a new event in Venezuela – though not elsewhere in the American continent where for almost a century the Army has been expected to be on hand at the least sign of fire or flood. The year 1972 provided ample opportunity to be at the ready where duty called or danger. During the summer of that year the eastern seaboard had more than its share of flooding. Relief teams were at work as far north as upstate New York providing such basics as food, clothing, bedding and drinking water. Twenty-two mobile canteens were on continuous duty rendering similar service both in Virginia and Washington, DC. Relief workers moved into the affected areas as soon as Hurricane Agnes hit the Florida Keys, and vehicles with supplies converged on the devastated districts from Louisiana, Mississippi and Alabama – their workers remaining on site until cleaning up operations had been completed.

Meanwhile General and Mrs Wickberg had been preparing for their annual round of world congresses – this time in Japan, The Philippines, New Zealand and Australia (Melbourne, Adelaide, Sydney and Brisbane), a programme which was to keep them fully occupied from mid-April until the end of May. Each of these centres would include a series of public and private gatherings which would tax the resources of the most seasoned leader, added to which were the climatic variations (even within a single continent) which would test the stamina of the experienced traveller. To make sure that there were no idle moments which could be wrongfully employed, there was also what the New Testament calls 'the care of the churches' daily clamouring for attention. In addition, in the interests of the movement itself, there would always be well-wishers to be cultivated and critics to be mollified – though not at the expense of principle.

Six weeks of this might leave the ordinary mortal longing for a quiet life but, on his return home, the General had the British congress looming ahead. This was not a hardy annual as, for example, in New Zealand or The Netherlands, but Salvationists in the land of the Army's birth could hardly be denied what was a regular feature of the life of their comrades elsewhere. These rejoicings were to be held in the Empire Pool, Wembley – a secular setting if ever there was one, but those planning to be present were long accustomed to such sites being transformed into hallowed ground.

One of the last soldiers' rallies conducted by General Bramwell Booth was in the Ring, Blackfriars Road, just south of the Thames. This had been Rowland Hill's old Baptist chapel which had sadly sunk to the level of a boxing stadium but which, on the night of January 18, 1928, was restored to something of its former glory if only for a single evening. So with no qualms but with great rejoicing that so public a witness to the reality of things eternal could be so publicly made, a 'drive-in' to the car park provided a pad from which the 1972 congress was launched. There was prayer – audible and silent – that Wembley would 'throw a light which would illuminate the rest of the country' which was greeted with fervent 'Amens'. Yet so down to earth were the proceedings that no incongruity was felt when Mr Jack Warner – acknowledged coiner of the saying that the Army was 'Christianity with its sleeves rolled up' – added the friendly greetings of the neighbourhood police-man. The Thursday evening 'Congress spectacular' which followed the senior citizens' rally earlier in the afternoon, allowed the congregation to greet the 1,200 uniformed Salvationists drawn from every division on both sides of the border. The Saturday afternoon and evening festivals each attracted a congregation of several thousands who welcomed to London for the first time since 1914 the staff band from the United States Central Territory.

Sunday witnessed three meetings – with upwards of eight thousand people present at night – which were led by General and Mrs Wickberg, the Chief of the Staff and Mrs Commissioner Brown, supported by the British Commissioner and Mrs Commissioner Albert Mingay and Lieut.-Commissioner and Mrs John Fewster. Some two hundred seekers knelt at the mercy seat in the course of the day. On the Monday afternoon the women's rally was made a unique occasion by the presence of HRH The Duchess of Kent and Commissioner Catherine Bramwell-Booth (R), and at night there was a first presen-tation, albeit an abridged version, of the latest Gowans/Lars-son musical 'Jesus Folk'.

Another epoch-making occasion was the International Social Conference held in the Netherlands training college at Amstelveen from August 21 to August 27. There had been only two such previous conferences – the first in 1911 over which the Founder presided; the second, ten years later, con-vened by General Bramwell Booth. As more than half a century had passed since then, the Army's social services could not be charged with spending more time in talking than doing. On this occasion fifty-seven officer and soldier delegates were present from thirty-one territories, and the main items on the agenda included the need

(i) for the recruitment of professional and para-professional helpers, both lay and officer.

(ii) to recognise the place of the social services as an integral part of Salvationist activity.

(iii) for constant attention to be given to government and other forms of funding, if the Army was to retain its basic purpose and organisational flexibility.

(iv) to allow for client and consumer participation in the planning of the programmes and services.

Almost coincidental in time with this conference the General issued to the British press a statement on the outworking of the Abortion Act of 1967. The extracts which follow were taken from the international *War Cry* of October 14, 1972.

We sense considerable danger in the almost facile request for abortion on demand, with its concomitant claim that only the woman herself, who may be below the legal age of consent, should determine whether or not to bear a child. We feel that abortion cannot rightly be considered in isolation from the rest of the entire field of family relationships, including sex education, family planning and contraception, and the whole complex emotional interaction involved in the termination of a pregnancy.

We agree with the opinion that abortion is almost always a sign, either medically or socially, of failure.

While acknowledging that contraceptive advice, even to unmarried young persons, is preferable to an unwanted pregnancy, we strongly affirm our belief in the Christian ideal of chastity before marriage and fidelity within marriage. Realism compels us to acknowledge, however, that many people nowadays fail to maintain these standards, some even denying their value and validity. Thus unwanted pregnancies outside marriage will continue to occur.

The experience of officers in the Women's Social Services of The Salvation Army has led them to feel that in most instances it is best to try to help the woman to accept an unplanned pregnancy and, subject to medical advice, to let it go to term, while giving supportive help.

Our concern is based on the belief in the immeasurable value and beauty of the right use of the sexual instinct which is God-given; and the truth that the unborn child is a potential person from the moment of his conception, as well as a potential member of a family and of society, with spiritual, moral and legal rights in both spheres.

The statement concluded that, in the light of these facts, the terms of the Lane Commission were inadequate, and repeated the plea, made in 1967 by General Frederick Coutts, for a full-scale study by a Royal Commission with a view to a basic revision of the existing act. If abortion was to continue to be legalised, it should be on adequate medical grounds, both physical and psychological, but not for social reasons.

One of the obvious handicaps in writing a history of this description is that to mention one name is to omit half a dozen others equally worthy of reference. To single out a natural disaster in one continent where the Army has offered service beyond the call of duty is to fail to draw attention to equally meritorious endeavours in the other four. But if names are to be mentioned from this period let the final two be of comrades who would otherwise be unlikely to catch the world's eye. One was Envoy Whang Sook Hyun who, for more than twenty-five years, gave herself to the service of orphaned Korean children. The other was Mrs Senior Field-Captain Moore who, for fifty years (since 1955 as a widow) ministered to the Indian community in North British Columbia. The former was admitted to the Order of the Founder in 1970, the latter in 1971.

Readers who have found Salvation Army ranks bewildering will doubtless be glad to be reminded that at the end of 1972 these were reduced to six in number – lieutenant, captain, major, lieut.-colonel, colonel and commissioner. But howsoever these officers might be addressed, their willingness to serve remained undiminished.

As a PS. let it be added that on September 30, 1972, the Salvation Army Assurance Society, founded in 1891, was merged with the Wesleyan and General Assurance Society. No officer involved was made redundant. In the divine economy there is always work for willing hearts and hands to do.

4   GOD GAVE THE INCREASE

World organisations may be forgiven if it takes them rather longer than most other groups to add all their figures together. It was not until the first issue of the international *War Cry* for 1973 that the results of the children's year campaign were published. But they were worth waiting for. The General described them as 'the most encouraging reading I have seen for a long time'. In 1971 nearly 25,000 children were dedicated to God under the Army flag, which means that – as near as may be – twice that number of adults promised to bring up their children in the fear and admonition of the Lord. The number of young children on the cradle roll climbed to over 160,000. The world attendance at the company meeting (Sunday school) was over 10.5 million, with nearly 30,000 company guards (Sunday school teachers) undertaking their instruction. There was an annual attendance of more than 850,000 at brownie packs, sunbeams and bluebirds; over 830,000 at the guides, girl scouts and guards; over 580,000 at the scouts and cub scouts. Last of all there were 34,000 corps cadets (mostly teenagers) seeking to equip themselves for part- or full-time Salvation Army service.

Another heart warming advance in the latter months of General Wickberg's term of office was the unfurling of the Army flag in Fiji. As with the Australian opening in Papua New Guinea, this possibility had been canvassed over many years. Soon after the turn of the century Brigadier Isaac Unsworth visited Suva to explore how far the work of the Army could be extended in the South Pacific. Between the two World Wars a further survey was undertaken and, later still, Commissioner Alfred J. Gilliard (who was territorial commander for New Zealand from 1960 to 1964) uttered a word of prophecy where such words are not often found. The minutes of the advisory board of the Army's farm at Putaruru contained a rider that, as and when profits were available, a first charge upon such surplus funds should be the extension of the Army's work in the Pacific islands.[1]

Another ten years passed – and then in August 1972, a hand-picked group of Salvationists, possessing a wide range of gifts and paying their own expenses, set out on a ten-day investigative tour of Viti Levu, the main Fijian island, under the leadership of Captain and Mrs Brian McStay. Meetings were held in a wide range of settings – from schools to prisons and from churches to night clubs. Not everyone hailed the new arrivals as heaven-sent. Some local church leaders feared lest the presumed attractiveness of the Army might adversely affect their own congregations. Again, as in Papua New Guinea, a first requisite was a happy working arrangement with existing church groups. This was mutually recognised by all concerned and on Christmas Day, 1972, Captain McStay farewelled from the training college in Wellington and the New Year saw him, with his wife and two children, house-hunting in Suva.

Only those who have actually undertaken a new opening in a new town, or a new district, or a new country, can understand what it means to step out on the seeming void and find the rock beneath. It was given to the Fijian pioneers to share both experiences. 'We learned the meaning of "simply trusting",' testified Captain McStay. Negotiations with government ministers seemed unending. Fortunately for the pioneers, while these arrangements were pursuing their slow and tortuous way, believers in Fiji welcomed the Army to their local council of churches. The Methodists made one of their own residences available to the McStays. A cottage prayer meeting drawn from various Christian groups added this new venture to their list of intercessions. Local rotary accepted the captain as one of their members. The first public Army meeting was held on April 29, 1973 and, when Commissioner Ernest Elliot visited the island later in September, eight new soldiers were enrolled. Official incorporation of the Army in Fiji was granted by the government on November 14, 1973, and the work has gone on from strength to strength.

So far as the task of evangelism is concerned, the seventies saw a marked increase in the Army's proclamation of the gospel through radio and television.

Different countries have different ways of ordering this important aspect of public life, and it was not until early in 1923 that Lord Reith invited the Archbishop of Canterbury, the Most Revd Randall T. Davidson, to listen to a radio transmission. There was widespread ignorance as to how the wireless worked. Mrs Davidson asked Lord Reith whether it was necessary to leave a window open in order to hear a broadcast. Later that year the band of the Govan (Scotland) corps was the first to go on the air from a Glasgow studio, though a group of Salisbury musicians had already broadcast over a short-distance amateur apparatus. Fifty years later, on Palm Sunday, 1973, it was estimated that twenty million listeners in Britain heard the three Salvation Army broadcasts on that day – the BBC people's service in the morning presented live from the Romford hall, plus the fully networked ITA programme, 'Stars on Sunday' at seven p.m., plus the Sunday half-hour of community hymn singing at eight-thirty p.m. which was accompanied by the Upper Norwood band.

Such activity has become commonplace. Few communities of any consequence in any country but have their radio – and even television – station, and no Salvationist but is eager to use these facilities for the furtherance of the gospel. This ministry of the air has not – and cannot – take the place of the Army street meeting which offers the possibility of the person to-person contact which neither radio nor the television can offer. But, taken together, they greatly further the Army's approach to its natural constituency – the folk who rarely darken the door of a Christian place of worship and to whom the conventional Christian vocabulary is a foreign language.

Still remaining in the old world, it should be remembered that the end of 1972 and the beginning of 1973 marked the ninetieth anniversary of the work of the Army in Sweden. On the afternoon of December 28, 1882, three women and two men stood on the stage of a Stockholm theatre and commenced to sing: 'We're bound for the land of the pure and the holy.' Nine decades later, at the same hour and in the same place, General and Mrs Wickberg opened the anniversary celebrations with the same song. Chief among the band of five pioneers was the forty-year-old Hanna Ouchterlony who had met the twenty-two-year-old Bramwell Booth in her native town of Värnamo where the young man had gone for rest and recovery after the toil of London's East End. In turn

Hanna went to stay with William and Catherine Booth for a few weeks so that she might learn more about the revival movement which had so recently assumed the name of 'The Salvation Army'. Later she paid a second visit to London which lasted seven months – during which time William Booth commissioned her an officer with the rank of major, and appointed her to commence the Army's work in Sweden.

The current rejoicings included a visit to Luleå – a town in the far north of the Gulf of Bothnia hitherto unvisited by any of the Army's international leaders but where, in welcoming the General to the cathedral, Bishop Stig Hellsten identified himself as 'a comrade in the great salvation host of God'. Next came a call at Örebro where Mr Henry Allard, the Speaker of the Swedish parliament who had been a scout in the troop belonging to the local corps, greeted the international guests with a declaration that the Army was still as greatly needed in Sweden as at any other time. At Tranås where, for the third year in succession the band gave a festival on the afternoon of New Year's Eve, the General used the occasion to reiterate the claims and the promises of the Christian gospel.

New Year's Day was spent at Jönköping where the penitent form was not large enough to accommodate the many comrades who wished to mark the day by a rededication of themselves to the service of the Lord. Then came Värnamo, the significance of which in Swedish Salvationist history has already been noted and, in a simple ceremony, the General laid a wreath on the monument of the 'mother' of The Salvation Army in Sweden – Commissioner Hanna Ouchterlony. The campaign concluded with some 1,800 people acclaiming the General in his final meeting in Gothenburg, where the chairman of the city council showed that he knew both the Army and the land of the Army's birth well enough to quote Sir Anthony Eden (later Lord Avon) when he said: 'No money is so well used and no work is so well done as that which comes from a warm heart.' Those present in the congregation showed that they knew how to apply the aphorism.

Indeed few are the countries where this saying has not been seen in action. Even as it was being repeated in the old world it was being demonstrated in the new, for 1973 had hardly begun before Salvationist relief workers were arriving in Managua (capital of Nicaragua) from the Canal Zone, from

Costa Rica and from Panama with aid and comfort to a population stricken by earthquake. At the height of the devastation the Army was caring for a tenth of the refugees. Quotes from a week's diary bring the scene to life.

> *Monday.* Major Bernard Smith, accompanied by two Christian friends whose church had generously loaned a vehicle, arrived in Managua and, after consultation with government officials, made immediate plans to commence a feeding programme.
>
> *Tuesday.* At 7 a.m. the emergency team began working in Colonia, a village near the capital, with three truck loads of sugar, beans, milk, cereals, rice and water. Distribution continued until 3 p.m.
>
> *Wednesday.* The team went on to Shick and spent the day distributing rice, beans, sardines, baby food and water. Major Maurice McCaw joined the team from Panama. Both Major Smith and he had served together in relief work during the 1972 Peruvian earthquake.
>
> *Thursday.* Repeat of previous day's operations in Shick. An American Salvationist, Ben Hart, joined the team from Lansing, Michigan.
>
> *Friday.* The Army team was assigned to take food and water to Terres Molinas.
>
> *Saturday.* Confidence in Salvationist relief team now established in government circles. Assigned to largest feeding centre in San Judas; here our assignment is to care for 1,000 families.
>
> *Sunday.* Entire day spent on feeding programme except for break for worship.

The report went on to describe how the relief work continued throughout the succeeding week with the arrival of a further five tons of supplies from 'Help the Aged'. Contact was also established with remote areas by means of short-wave radio. News of world-wide offerings from Army corps in each of the five continents was received with rejoicing for this enabled gaps in the relief programme to be filled.

A parallel situation was reported less than a month later from the sophisticated Bay Area of San Francisco. Major Ray Robinson, the co-ordinator of the Army's disaster services in that region, was sitting down to a later than usual evening meal when he heard that a US navy jet had exploded on an

Alemeda apartment building. By nine o'clock he was on the scene, collecting his team on the way. In the Oakland corps community centre a number of Salvationist musicians had gathered to greet a distinguished New Zealand composer with whom they were to rehearse. But, when the emergency call came through, the entire company ceased music making and, without waiting to change out of uniform, made for the scene of the crash. The women's singing group stopped literally in the middle of a bar and adjourned to the kitchen to prepare food. The role assigned to Major Robinson and his volunteers was to be on hand with practical help and advice for the survivors, and with food and drink for the rescue workers. Some members of the Army team worked all through the night until four o'clock the following afternoon. One distraught woman was offering a thousand dollars for the recovery of her chihuahua. Another was tearfully but thankfully reunited to her brother while all around was unresolved confusion. Salvationist mobile units from the Bay area remained on duty until the emergency was over.

Such dedication to the demands of human necessity does not always silence the suspicions of those who cannot believe that nowadays there are those who are still willing to do 'owt for nowt'. About this time these charges grew so shrill that the General authorised a statement to the effect that the support given by the public, as well as that contributed by Salvationists themselves, was entirely devoted to the upkeep of the Army's evangelical and social services. No one in Army uniform derived any personal benefit – save for the living allowances paid to Salvation Army officers, nor were there any balances left over for 'investment' in the customary financial meaning of the term. Even if there were, no monies would knowingly be invested in, or deliberately used for the purchase of, shares in the arms, tobacco or brewing industries. What surplus there might be to spare was 'invested' – for example – in such enterprises as the Changi boys' home which overlooks the site of the infamous prison camp of the Second World War. This home, opened by the President of Singapore and costing almost half a million Singapore dollars, can accommodate some seventy lads from six to sixteen years of age drawn from various racial and social backgrounds – some from broken homes, some orphaned, some on probation. The government agreed to make a small per capita grant, parents (where possible) to assist with care and maintenance; but food, clothing and training for adult employment were to be the Army's responsibility. The contrast between war-time and peace-time Changi was in itself a testimony to the power of the Christian gospel.

The practice of this gospel is often personally costly. Bonhoeffer was neither the first nor the last to experience the costliness of discipleship. The servant of the Lord who would save others cannot save himself – as was demonstrated by the two unsuspecting cadets from the Army's school for officers' training in San Francisco – Thomas Rainwater and Linda Jones – who were walking along Geary Boulevard one April evening in 1974 when a stranger who was moving in the opposite direction turned round and shot them both in the back, killing the lad and seriously wounding the girl. A senseless random action was the police verdict. Maybe so – but both these young people had already dedicated their lives to the service of God. In General Orsborn's words they were ready 'for the altar or the sword' – as was their more experienced comrade, Major Samuel Medley. When torrential floods wreaked their havoc on Rapid City (South Dakota) in 1973, the major – who was the residential officer – moved to organise rescue and relief work. But in his endeavours to help others he lost his own life, for the relentless flood waters swept him away as well. His wife remained on duty to continue the service which her husband had begun.

A like spirit was manifest in India the same year for one of the major losses in the subcontinent was that of Captain (Dr) Walter Lucas, MB, BS, FRCS (Edin.), Chief Medical Officer at the MacRobert Hospital at Dhariwal in the Punjab. This gifted Australian doctor and his wife left for India following their commissioning in Sydney and at once began to work on their plans to modernise the hospital and to extend its field of service. A family planning project was launched and mobile clinics began to visit surrounding districts six days a week. Smallpox drives were carried out in collaboration with the state government and the 'sight for the curable blind' campaign was showing great promise when, after having been involved in flood relief activities on the Indo-Pakistan border, the doctor himself was abruptly taken ill and his earthly ministry ended

on August 22, 1973, at the age of thirty-four, within three short
years of his commissioning.

His all too brief but wholly selfless life was akin to that of
Captain (Dr) Murray Stanton, MB, ChB (NZ), MRACP,
MRCP (London) – a New Zealand officer who, after complet-
ing training with his wife in London, was appointed Chief
Medical Officer at the Evangeline Booth Hospital, Ahmedna-
gar, India. But he did not complete even his first year of
overseas service for, on May 13, 1972, he succumbed to 'a
massive infection of the most virulent form of Weil's disease'.
There was yet a third loss from the mission field when Mrs
Captain Shirley Millar, wife of the hospital administrator at
Ahmednagar, was herself promoted to Glory in the following
November.

It was therefore opportune that the General should pay
special attention to the missionary scene in Africa and Asia
during the final months of his active service. Any who mis-
takenly view such campaigns as a desirable form of globe
trotting should note that the Air Force flight to Brazzaville
was timed to arrive at one-twenty a.m. and that, on this
occasion, both welcomers and visitors were singing 'O boundless salvation' outside the VIP lounge at two o'clock in the
morning, with sundry speeches and responses – not always as
brief as the weakness of the flesh might desire – to follow. A
few hours later and those travel-hardened visitors were being
received by the Cardinal Archbishop. Strangers accustomed
to more conventional modes of greeting should be warned
in advance that any disconcerting blanks fired from waving
weapons constitute a particularly warm expression of welcome.

A three-hour open-air youth festival on the Saturday evening
was followed by an equally lengthy outdoor holiness meeting
on the Sunday morning attended by over 2,000 people. Sunday
evening saw the hall at Bacongo, the largest in Brazzaville,
crowded to the doors. Nor was Monday a merciful day of
rest. There was old man Congo waiting to be crossed, more
welcomes and responses to be exchanged on the south bank,
'O boundless salvation' to be sung yet again, the national
anthem of Zaire to be played by the Kinshasa Central band,
plus such additional hallelujahs as it might seem good to
enthusiastic Salvationists to raise to high heaven. Then on
without delay to Kavwaya – an Army centre more than 100

kilometres beyond Kinshasa; afterwards back to Kasangulu and then, for the General, a speedy return to the capital to speak at the memorial service to King Gustaf Adolf of Sweden.

At five o'clock the following morning the General – with his fellow travellers, Commissioner W. Stanley Cottrill and Brigadier Sydney Woodall – were at the airport ready to take off for Kisangani, one degree north of the equator. There was a new hall to be opened at Tshopo. Work on this property had been commenced in 1959 before national independence had been gained, but the disturbances of 1964 and 1969 had delayed the completion. Hence present joys were the greater, certainly the more vociferous. Each day had its change of congregation. On the following Saturday morning the General met the prefects of the combined secondary schools in Kinshasa, together with the head teachers of the primary schools, and later in the day the cadets of the 'Blood and Fire' session were dedicated and commissioned. Sunday was rounded off by a rally of the united corps in Kinshasa, followed by a march of witness which prepared the way for the appointments meeting for the new officers held at the Kinshasa 2 divisional centre.

The next overseas engagement was on the other side of the Atlantic – the Pan American conference in Miami, attended by forty-seven national leaders from North and South America. The General, and Mrs Wickberg, assisted by the Chief of the Staff and Mrs Commissioner Brown, piloted the ten days' proceedings which

(i) gave evangelism priority in the Army's programme, and called for the acceptance of any new methods, congruous with the gospel, which might further the work of the gospel.

(ii) declared our social services to be an integral part of the proclamation of the gospel.

(iii) while retaining the Army's uniqueness and integrity, gladly linked heart and hand with other churches and Christian groups throughout the world. Some needs were so great that only a united effort could rally the required resources and personnel.

(iv) testified that our witness to the presence and power of the Holy Spirit was best expressed by a manifestation of the fruit of the Spirit as outlined in Galatians 5:22, 23.

The delegates summed up their motivation in the simple yet comprehensive phrase: 'God in Christ has saved us to serve.'

The first page of the first issue of the international *War Cry* for 1974 carried an article by the General which referred to the calling of the High Council in five months' time 'to elect my successor'. If this told the Army world that his term of office would soon be ending, it also indicated that he must soon leave for his final Asian campaign – beginning in Sri Lanka and travelling via Madras, Trivandrum, Nagercoil and Calcutta to Bombay. Outstanding among the many ministers of mercy whom the General was able to greet was Dudley Gardiner – one in spirit with Mother Teresa – who could not be persuaded to take time off from his feeding programme in Calcutta even to travel to New Delhi to be invested with the MBE. An average of 6,000 people depended on him for a daily meal seven days a week. So the High Commissioner, Sir Terence Garvey, KCMG, came down from the capital and conducted the investiture amid the pots and pans of the Army's feeding centre in the Chandra Bose Road. It had been the General's intention to visit Lahore and then return home via Japan and the United States. International complications prevented the first proposal and, though he fulfilled his engagements in Tokyo, the drastic temperature differences between latitude 20 and latitude 35 brought on a serious attack of influenza which restricted his activities in Los Angeles and required the cancellation of his visit to New York. But by the time a press conference had been called in London to mark the publication by Hodder & Stoughton of *In Darkest England Now* – a twentieth-century parallel to William Booth's nineteenth-century *In Darkest England and the Way Out* – the General was himself again and could be seen in the pages of *The War Cry* chatting animatedly to Peter Niesewand of *The Guardian* about this latest Army publication.

But Salvation Army life was never wholly immune from the hazards of the unexpected. Late one Sunday afternoon a girl terrorist planted a bomb outside the Europa Hotel in Belfast – but she was a local lass and began to have second thoughts when she saw Salvationists assembling for their customary early evening open-air meeting. Hurriedly she rang the security forces without disclosing her identity. The street was cleared and the area searched. No bomb was discovered immediately but the alert was not relaxed. When the explosion occurred casualties were mercifully limited to a damaged pillar box and a slightly injured policeman. Had the usual open-air meeting been in progress few of those taking part would have escaped unhurt.

Opposite hemispheres of the globe suffered storm damage almost simultaneously – the most serious devastation occurring in Brisbane, Australia's third largest city, where twelve people were drowned. A dozen relief centres were opened in Army youth halls, but operations at Bundamba had to be supplied by helicopter. The new building in this western suburb of the state capital which had been opened eighteen months earlier was flooded to gallery level. The local comrades who rowed into their hall by breaking an upper window, saw their grand piano floating on the face of the waters. During the period of greatest need 1,000 people were sleeping in various Army properties.

Nature is no respecter of persons or places. A few weeks later when parts of Ohio, Kentucky and Tennessee were seriously ravaged by wide ranging tornadoes, the Army quickly co-ordinated with the Federal Disaster Assistance Administrator in manning evacuation centres and providing food and clothing for the homeless. With their detailed local knowledge officers were also able to furnish up-to-date information for the benefit of those who were seeking news of their relatives in the stricken areas.

Meanwhile on Friday, March 8, Commissioner Arnold Brown, the Chief of the Staff, dispatched the formal summonses to members of the 1974 High Council to meet at Sunbury Court on Saturday, May 4 at nine a.m. The forty officers concerned were

Colonel Edmundo ALLEMAND	Territorial Commander, South America West.
Colonel Ernest ANDERSON	Territorial Commander, Scotland.
Colonel Richard ATWELL	Territorial Commander, Rhodesia.
Colonel Johan BARONOWSKY	Territorial Commander, Congo.

Commissioner Arnold BROWN	Chief of the Staff.
Commissioner Gladys CALLISS	Territorial Commander, Sri Lanka.
Commissioner Paul CARLSON	National Commander, USA.
Commissioner Arthur CARR	Chancellor of the Exchequer, IHQ.
Commissioner William CHAMBERLAIN	Territorial Commander, USA Southern.
Commissioner CHUN, Yong Sup	Territorial Commander, Korea.
Commissioner Jacobus CORPUTTY	Joint-Territorial Commander, Indonesia.
Commissioner W. Stanley COTTRILL	International Secretary, IHQ.
Commissioner J. Clyde COX	Territorial Commander, USA Central.
Commissioner Haakon DAHLSTRØM	Territorial Commander, Norway & Iceland.
Commissioner Geoffrey DALZIEL	British Commissioner.
Colonel Bramwell DAVIS	Territorial Commander, East Africa.
Colonel Raymond DELCOURT	Territorial Commander, France.
Commissioner Joseph DEX	Territorial Commander, South America East.
Colonel Jacques EGGER	Territorial Commander, Zaire.
Commissioner Ernest ELLIOT	Territorial Commander, New Zealand.
Commissioner Francis EVANS	Territorial Commander, Switzerland & Austria.
Commissioner Frederick HARVEY	International Secretary, IHQ.
Commissioner Paul KAISER	Territorial Commander, USA Western.
Commissioner Kathleen KENDRICK	Literary Secretary, IHQ.
Colonel Hesketh KING	Territorial Commander, South Africa.
Colonel Raymond KIRBY	Territorial Commander, Nigeria.

Colonel William LARSON	Territorial Commander, Germany.
Lieut.-Commissioner Fazal MASIH	Territorial Commander, North-Eastern India.
Colonel Burton PEDLAR	Territorial Commander, Pakistan.
Commissioner Leslie PINDRED	Territorial Commander, The Netherlands.
Commissioner Donald SMITH	Territorial Commander, Denmark.
Commissioner Julia TICKNER	Leader, Women's Social Services, Great Britain & Ireland.
Commissioner Bramwell TRIPP	Territorial Commander, USA Eastern.
Commissioner Harry TYNDAL	Territorial Commander, Sweden.
Commissioner Per-Erik WAHLSTRÖM	International Secretary, IHQ.
Commissioner Tor WAHLSTRÖM	Territorial Commander, Finland.
Commissioner Henry WARREN	Territorial Commander, Australia Southern.
Commissioner Harry WILLIAMS	Territorial Commander, Australia Eastern.
Commissioner Clarence WISEMAN	Territorial Commander, Canada & Bermuda.
Commissioner Shinichi YOSHIDA	Territorial Commander, Japan.

As was natural, General and Mrs Wickberg spent several of their final weekends on active service amid scenes which were familiar to them – Good Friday in Malmö, Easter in Uppsala, Ascension Day in Zurich, forty-eight hours in the last week of May in Norway – opening a child care centre and a nursing home for the aged in Oslo, a people's high school in Jeløy and a rehabilitation centre for alcoholics in Bergen. The final weekend on active service was given to Stockholm for though the General had spent thirty-two out of his forty-nine years of officership outside his homeland, he always felt himself to be a son of Sweden.

In the meantime the Army was making ready for its own future. Before the forty members of the High Council were publicly welcomed in the Westminster Central Hall they were received by Queen Elizabeth, the Queen Mother. Each occasion, the quiet elegance of St. James's Palace as well as the crowded exuberance of the Central Hall, testified to the nature of what was taking place for each was suffused with a warmth which banished all formality.

The daily 'Sunbury Court diary' which appeared in the international *War Cry* kept the general public informed of what was happening at the eighth High Council. The elected president was Commissioner Clarence D. Wiseman, the vice-president Commissioner Francis A. Evans, the recorder Commissioner W. Stanley Cottrill, the assistant recorder Commissioner Kathleen Kendrick,[2] the chaplain Commissioner Julia Tickner,[2] the chief teller Commissioner Gladys Calliss,[2] the assistant tellers Commissioners Frederick Harvey and Per-Erik Wahlström. Members who accepted nomination were (in alphabetical order) Commissioners Arnold Brown, Geoffrey Dalziel, Paul Kaiser and Clarence Wiseman. On accepting nomination Commissioner Wiseman vacated the presidency of the High Council and Commissioner Evans took his place, with Commissioner Paul Carlson as vice-president.

Over the years a pattern of procedure has grown up with successive High Councils, though this is not as immutable as the laws of the Medes and the Persians. Nevertheless council members are not treading an unknown way and so the proceedings followed past precedent until at four-thirty p.m. on Monday, May 13, 1974, the President announced: 'I present the tenth General of The Salvation Army, Commissioner Clarence Wiseman, Territorial Commander for Canada and Bermuda.'

The conclusion of General Wickberg's active service as a Salvation Army officer was marked by a *Festschrift* which was prepared under the guidance of Professor J. W. Winterhager, PhD, DD, the Revd John Stott, MA, DD, and the Chief of the Staff, Commissioner Arnold Brown. Publication was in German, French and English – with the latter title as 'Vocation and Victory'. The English language contributors included Dr William Barclay, Dr Elton Trueblood, Professor J. N. D. Anderson and Dr Charles Duthie. The Chief of the Staff and Commissioner Gösta Blomberg were also among the contributors.

An equal, if not an even more compelling, witness to the

salvationism of the retiring leaders was the presence in the crowded Royal Festival Hall on Friday, July 5, of representatives of the three European countries in which the General and his wife had served – a united string band drawn from the Bern 1 and 2 corps, the Stockholm 7 band from Sweden and a choral group from Germany.

The following morning General and Mrs Erik Wickberg left from London Heathrow. For them a long chapter had now been completed – but there were still more pages of personal service to be written.

PART FIVE

THE TENTH GENERAL: CLARENCE WISEMAN

(July 6, 1974–July 4, 1977)

1 THE KING'S BUSINESS
REQUIRES HASTE

One advantage of the way in which one international leader succeeds another according to the good judgment of the current High Council is that each in turn brings his individual gifts and graces to the service of the Army. The length of his term of office may vary because one contingent factor is his age at the time of his election. General Clarence D. Wiseman served as such for three years less two days – a shorter term than any of his predecessors. But he more than made up for this by filling each unforgiving minute with sixty seconds' worth of distance run. This he did almost literally for, with Mrs General Wiseman, he was in journeyings oft from start to finish.

Upon election he announced that they both were 'incurable Salvationists', and when it was suggested by one interviewer that, like the Archbishop-designate of Canterbury, his role could be only that of a caretaker, he replied that this was precisely what the Lord required. 'Tend – ("take care of", OED) – the flock of God', is the charge given in I Peter 5:2 (RSV). In this spirit the Army's new leaders entered upon the last but most testing period of their fifty years of officership.

The General was born of Newfoundland officer-parents in Newfoundland. His wife, Janet Kelly, whom he did not meet until he had entered training, was of Scottish extraction though entering the work from Danforth (Toronto). They were married on January 29, 1932, and were enjoying their retirement together until the General's promotion to Glory on May 4, 1985. Their service as corps officers in Canada – in London (Ontario), Toronto and Montreal – was perforce ended when in mid-1940 he became chaplain to the 2nd battalion Royal Canadian Engineers. This was followed in April 1943 by his appointment as senior representative of the Canadian Red Shield Services. When the war in Europe ended Major and

Mrs Wiseman were placed in charge of the work in Newfound-land (then the chief division of Canada) where they served for eight and a half years.

Newfoundland Salvationists were more than happy to have one of their own as their leader – especially when he visited all but one of their more than eighty corps and outposts in the first eighteen months of his command. And not a few of the leading people on the island – including the one and only 'Joey' Smallwood, first premier of the tenth province of Canada after confederation – valued the judgment and influence of one of the sons of their own soil and sea.

After holding two of the senior administrative appointments in Canada there followed two short years, 1961–62, as terri-torial commander for East Africa, which comprised Kenya, Tanzania and Uganda. Short they were – but they were seminal years when plans were laid for the preparation of the African officer for increasing leadership responsibilities in his own land and among his own people. There is a significant sentence in the General's 'anecdotal autobiography' which, referring to this period, reads: 'Major Jonah Munyi was a tower of strength in these demanding days . . . No important decisions affecting the work were taken without reference to him.'[1] Sadly his invaluable service ended abruptly in a road accident, thus depriving the Army of one of its most promising African officers. But the day was to dawn when Lieut.-Commissioner Wiseman, as General, would appoint an Afri-can to be leader of the Army in East Africa.

As yet these things were hidden from sight and the next five years were to be spent as principal of the William Booth Memorial Training College, London. There is always more than enough for a training principal to do at Denmark Hill, especially with two sessions running concurrently and the need for the principal to arrive at his own personal judgment on the worth of each cadet. But in addition General Kitching appointed the commissioner to be the Army's representative on the Central Committee of the World Council of Churches and also the Army's spokesman at the 1964 conference of European churches which met uniquely on the MS *Bornholm* when stationed in the neutral waters of the Kattegat.

It was during the commissioner's term as training principal at Denmark Hill that the first of the hits of 'The Joystrings' –

'It's an open secret' was born. In a private devotional meeting for the college staff Mrs Lieut.-Commissioner Wiseman read a paraphrase of Philippians 4:4–9 which was entitled 'The Open Secret' – and it was not long before lyrics and melody took shape.[2] Nowadays many churches across the entire theological spectrum have their 'pop' groups, but none has been more zealous than 'The Joystrings' in giving Jesus the pre-eminence.

After seven years' absence from Canada it was back to Canada for another seven years as territorial leaders for the Wisemans – after which the commissioner was elected General. His name had been put forward as a nominee at the 1969 High Council – but he had felt led to withdraw it. This time it went forward – with the result that these two 'incurable Salvationists' spent their every moment until retirement on July 4, 1977, in shepherding their world flock. It was fitting that a country parish in the Surrey downs should present the General with a crosier bearing the inscription: 'Chief Shepherd of The Salvation Army'.

The new General's first administrative decision was to appoint Commissioner Arthur Carr as Chief of the Staff who, with Mrs Commissioner Carr, addressed themselves to the duties formerly undertaken by Commissioner and Mrs Arnold Brown who succeeded to the territorial leadership of Canada. As every officer in the Army is 'under orders' these changes were effected as expeditiously as usual – leaving the General and his wife to commence their round of welcomes – first in London, Birmingham, Cardiff and Glasgow, and then with a Sunday at the ninth Holiday-plus-Fellowship camp at Bognor Regis. The comprehensive cross-section which Butlin's provided obviated the immediate need for any further visits around the British Isles and left the new international leaders free to be greeted in New York (at the retirement from active service of the National Commander for the United States, Commissioner Paul Carlson with Mrs Carlson) and then in Berlin on Repentance Day.

The mutual regard which quickly developed between the General and Dr Coggan made it almost inevitable that the Archbishop-designate of Canterbury would express his desire to see something of the Army's services to the alcoholics and addicts who were sleeping rough in Central London. The

officer who had made these unfortunates his flock was Captain
Joe Burlison who had already been on the three nights a week
soup run from the Hoxton goodwill centre for four years. On
this occasion the Archbishop-designate and the General helped
to load the van with its cargo of steaming soup, bread and
warm clothing. To the captain the route was familiar. It was
the same which had provided Philip Howard with material for
his descriptive article in *The Times*. So round he went again
– the Embankment, the arches underneath Charing Cross
station, the plot of grassland near to Euston station and then
Spitalfields. Here is how the General described what was
possibly their last contact in the early hours of the morning.

> Like phantoms in the eerie light we moved through narrow dim
> streets, past deserted buildings whose broken windows looked like
> empty eye sockets, while the captain poked into deep doorways
> for signs of life. In one place there was a sudden stir in a bundle
> of dirty rags. A poor shivering creature lay beneath them. Burlison
> knew who it was. He seemed to know everybody. He called out a
> name and the response was immediate. 'That you, captain?'
>
> First a head, then a thinly clad torso, finally legs emerged, and
> with our combined assistance the figure struggled to his feet like
> Lazarus shedding his grave clothes, volubly grateful for our help.
> We led him to the van, plied him with soup and bread, and then
> captain tried to persuade him to enter an Army hostel for some
> comfort and care. But he would have none of it. Instead he insisted
> on returning to his solitude in the doorway where he pulled the
> rags over his poor body once again and went to sleep. This was
> his inalienable territory. He would allow no one to deprive him of
> it.[3]

On Friday, January 24, 1975, General Wiseman attended
the enthronement of Dr Coggan as the 101st Archbishop of
Canterbury – the first Salvation Army General so to be invited.
On the morning of Monday, March 17, the Primate visited
International Headquarters – the first Archbishop of Canterbury to do so – to share with General Wiseman in the launching
of a popular paperback history of The Salvation Army entitled:
No Discharge in This War, by General Frederick Coutts, who
was also present.

But Salvationists were even busier making history than
writing it. At the beginning of 1975 as at the close of 1974

the indefatigable Major Eva den Hartog and her team were treating a daily average of 500 out-patients at Jessore. At Dacca an emergency hospital was caring for refugees suffering from such diseases as cholera and infectious hepatitis. An Indian doctor, a Dutch nursing sister and an Australian Salvationist were typical of the polyglot staff whose sympathies were expressed by their skills. Four and a half tons of wheat biscuits were shared among the needy in the town of Dacca itself. A children's feeding programme was in operation at four separate centres and over 1,500 of them visibly benefited thereby. Of even greater value were the fourteen tons of vegetable seed which was distributed throughout the country-side and which, given reasonable weather, would guarantee the next year's harvest.

But this news was barely off the press when the story of how Cyclone Tracy devastated Darwin in Northern Australia was being pieced together. For this cause an emergency meeting of Salvationist leaders was held in the territorial headquarters in Melbourne on the evening of December 25, 1974. Next morning the territorial commander, Commissioner Henry J. Warren, was on his way to the scene of the disaster and Commissioner Leslie Pindred, of the Eastern Territory, was preparing back-up support. A relief team left Alice Springs for Darwin by road, and planes were chartered in the state capitals to fly in additional personnel and food supplies.

In coping with what was regarded at the time as 'the greatest natural disaster which Australia had ever suffered' there was the closest possible collaboration with the federal government disaster relief organisation, the defence forces, the police and the airport authorities. The general public showed its confidence in the Army in the money and goods which were channelled through the movement. Accredited Salvationists were allowed to board the aircraft arriving at the various state capitals from Darwin and, in addition to meeting the needs of evacuees for food and clothing, assisted them to reach their relatives and friends, or the government centres where accommodation was being provided.

The news of this national calamity 'down under' had barely been digested when, on the morning of February 28, 1975, a London underground train, packed with commuters, crashed at speed into the concrete wall at the end of a tunnel at

Moorgate station. Forty-three people died and eighty-six were
injured as 118 feet of train was telescoped into sixty-six feet of
space. The alert sounded at the Hoxton goodwill centre at
nine-forty a.m. and once again Captain Burlison and his team
went into action. They remained on duty above and below
ground at Moorgate until midday on Wednesday, March 5.
When, three weeks later, there was a reception at 10 Downing
Street for representative relief workers the Prime Minister, the
Rt. Hon. Harold Wilson, said to Captain Burlison: 'We took
it for granted that you would be there.'

The same could have been said to the relief teams who
established four camps in the Aguan valley in Honduras to
repair the damage caused by Hurricane Fifi – only they were
there, from first to last, for nearly seven months. Both Canada
and the four American territories joined in this co-operative
effort, and Corps Sergeant-Major and Mrs McBride left their
contractor's business in their home town in Kingston, Ontario,
to give their professional help just when and where it was
needed. Before these relief operations were finalised they had
been able, with local help, to provide the temporary field
hospital with a water and sewage system, a water tower,
shower rooms and toilet facilities. A requisitioned building
was partitioned into wards, examination rooms, an operating
room and a pharmacy, and Lieutenant Margaret Harper,
SRN, who had helped to prepare the wards for occupation,
was able to instruct the local staff in their use of their new
equipment.

One more hospital story must be added to these crowded
months. With apologies to Robert Browning, the title could
appropriately be: 'How we brought Captain Ann Powell's
X-ray equipment from London to Turen.'

The captain was a former member of the WRNS who, after
discharge from the service, qualified as a radiographer, became
a Salvation Army officer, and was appointed to the Army
hospital in Turen (Eastern Java) where she was to open an
X-ray department. The difficulty was that though a new X-ray
camera had been sent from Japan to Java the essential ancillary
equipment, weighing approximately half a ton in all, was 9,000
miles away in London. The needful transportation was likely
to be slow and costly.

While serving in the WRNS the captain had become a

member of the Navy Christian Fellowship by whom she had subsequently been adopted as a missionary. Through this link and the good offices of Flight Lieutenant M. T. Holdsworth, contact was made with the Royal Air Force Christian Fellowship – principally with Squadron Leader M. E. Cole and the Revd Patrick Goodland, officiating chaplain at Stanmore Park. The upshot was that it was agreed in principle that the two crates of equipment could be flown by RAF freight to Singapore. (In passing, the same plane was to carry material for a Christian discovery school serving Chinese youth in Hong Kong.) An RNZAF plane took over between Singapore and Jakarta and the final stage to the airfield at Malang – half an hour by road from Turen – was by a Devon aircraft. Once the RAF equivalent of 'Dirck, Joris and he' had reached Jakarta, they caught a commercial flight to Singapore and thence were driven, as furiously as Browning's trio, to join their precious cargo at Turen. Officially this was part of their annual leave and was so granted and accepted. The costs were met in part by the trio personally and partly by a Trenchard memorial award. To show how totally the trio regarded themselves as committed to this Christian enterprise, they spent an additional couple of days at Turen, in temperatures of over 90°, personally preparing and painting the room which would house the X-ray unit.

Meanwhile General and Mrs Wiseman were moving at their own speedy pace. Their engagements in early 1975 in the British Isles were followed by the leadership of the Eastern Caribbean congress, after which they conducted meetings in Atlanta (Georgia) and Birmingham (Alabama) and, on returning to Europe, recognised the long and faithful service of Commissioner and Mrs Haakon Dahlstrøm by conducting in Oslo their retirement from active service. This led on to a prolonged intercontinental campaign in which these ardent evangelists campaigned in Lahore, Shantinagar and Karachi, moving on from there to the Australian congresses in the six state capitals – after which there was a similar round of meetings in Wellington, New Zealand. On this particular itinerary the General broke his journey to spend Good Friday and Easter in Singapore, but among the outstanding events of this prolonged campaign were the Whitsuntide meetings in Korea where pentecostal gatherings lived out the pentecostal theme, and where in four days General and Mrs Wiseman addressed a dozen meetings, several of which filled the largest buildings which were available in the capital.

On their return home General and Mrs Wiseman shared in the third anniversary of the unfurling of the Army flag in Portugal. 'We're going to turn the world upside down' was the chorus with which they were greeted by Major and Mrs Carl Eliasen and their youthful comrades at the airport in Lisbon. The fellowship in Christ shared by those who believe in His name was evident from the very opening of these anniversary proceedings. The third Baptist church in the Portuguese capital was filled with wellwishers eager to identify themselves with the Army's mission. One of the church pastors translated the General's message and a rhythm group from Geneva added their own musical flavouring. Sunday allowed the visitors to share in the intimacy of the morning holiness meeting, after which the entire officer strength of the command enjoyed a fellowship meal together. The same could be said of the dinner meeting shared by the international visitors with their soldiers.

At the Sunday evening open-air meeting copies of the gospel of Mark were distributed so that listeners might read for themselves the passage on which the General's message was based – after which a number of hands were raised signifying a desire to accept Jesus as Saviour and Lord. Nearly 200 people packed the hall for the indoor meeting which followed. Salvationists in Portugal do not usually wear Army uniform until they have been enrolled under the flag – so the three young comrades standing on the platform looked what they were: new soldiers. By British standards Portuguese night meetings begin late and end later still – so it was twenty minutes past eleven o'clock before the long day closed and the last of the twenty-three seekers had been counselled concerning their committal to Christ. But that did not prevent an even larger company filling the Presbyterian church and spilling out on to the street on the Monday evening. Clearly there was no holding back the Exército de Salvação!

As a PS. to this report it will be recalled that, some months later, world events brought about the flight of thousands of refugees from the former Portuguese colonies in Africa and Asia. Their plight was no different from that of other expatriates who, through no fault of their own, lost both present possessions and future prospects and found themselves strangers in their native land. By this time the Army had been working in Portugal for only four years, but recent converts were ready to aid the needy after the manner of Salvationists born and bred. Through the distribution centre passed more than fifteen tons of clothing, blankets, shoes and crates of powdered milk. This was collected in conjunction with the Caritas Portugesa as well as other government and charitable agencies. Fellowship gatherings were also held at centres where refugees were being housed.

Refugees from Timor were welcomed at Salvation Army centres in Indonesia. Those who had been evacuated to Australia were assisted by two resident officers who spoke fluent Portuguese, one of whom acted as liaison officer between the immigration department and the new arrivals. Salvationists in the Republic of South Africa also sent substantial food parcels to Portuguese families stranded in Mozambique.

The summer of 1975 also saw two of the Gowans/Larsson musicals presented in quick succession in London – 'Spirit' at the Royal Albert Hall on May 31 and 'Glory' at the Mermaid Theatre on July 7. These were the fourth and fifth of the musicals which began with 'Take-over Bid' in 1967 and also included 'Hosea' and 'Jesus Folk'. Contrary to the Preacher's words, it is not true to say that 'there is no new thing under the sun'. These musicals were. The co-authors struck the rock of biblical lore and Salvation Army history and there gushed forth a fresh and sparkling stream of popular Salvationist song. In this setting popular does not mean cheap or puerile. A tune which demands to be sung is a work of art. And when the words match the melody the combination is a gift of God. That is why the musicals have already made their own contribution to the recognised body of Salvation Army song.

What is more, the musicals seen so far – and there are others to follow – give the lie to the notion that only the morose are holy. Part of the miracle of these productions is that the story line which raises a laugh also leads to the mercy seat. A sense of humour is recognised as a gift of the Spirit in which tasteless vulgarity has neither a lot nor part. It is not hard, for example, to imagine what some contemporary producers would have made of the story of Hosea – the decent country man whose wife tired of him and who shacked up with any corner boy who would have her. There would be nods and winks and salacious innuendoes galore. Not in this production, however. To those in the cast, and the larger number in the congregation, who had never read Hosea, chapters I to XIV, the musical came as a revelation of the eternal love that would not let men go.

2   NO EAST OR WEST

By midsummer 1975, the Army's tenth General had all but completed his first year of office and had travelled an estimated 60,000 miles. It was a happy coincidence that, at this juncture, Mrs Wiseman and he received an invitation to luncheon at Buckingham Palace. Seated next to the Queen he was able to reply freely and fully to Her Majesty's enquiries concerning the work of the Army at home and overseas, and afterward both the General and Mrs Wiseman conversed at some length with the Duke of Edinburgh and the other guests in a friendly and relaxed setting.

East Africa next claimed their attention – which meant that Mrs Wiseman could not be present at the United Nations women's year conference which was being held in Mexico City. However, Mrs Commissioner Chamberlain (national president of women's organisations in the USA) and Mrs Brigadier Whitehead (who held a parallel office in the Republic of Mexico) took her place. 'Yamamuro' murmured three Japanese ladies who spoke but little English, as they touched Mrs Chamberlain's uniform – but the one word was enough. When, at the same convention, Mother Teresa was being praised for her devotion to the welfare of the needy, she answered: 'Do not speak to me of my dedication. It is the Salvation Army sisters in India who are truly dedicated.'

The climax of the General's visit to Nairobi was the announcement that Colonel Joshua Ngugi would be the new territorial commander for East Africa – the first African to be given such a responsibility. From there the campaigners moved south to Zambia where the congress meetings were held amid the rolling hills about Malala, and the long awaited and greatly enlarged song book in the Chitonga tongue was used for the first time. On their way to what was still known as Rhodesia the international leaders called at Blantyre, capital of Malawi.

Army work had begun here in 1967 but owing to political difficulties in southern Africa, it was not until 1979 that the presence of the Army in the republic was officially recognised.

Rhodesia itself was passing through a period of tension from the consequences of which the Army could not hope to be exempt – especially when all but two of the corps in the territory were African. For example, the training college for African officers, the teacher training college, the secondary school and the hospital at Howard were all part of a 'protected village' operating under a dusk to dawn curfew. Nevertheless the General visited the remote Tshelanyemba hospital and the Semukwe district headquarters. At the latter centre the district officer felt that, however unsettled the countryside might be, the red carpet should be rolled out for this occasion, and so it was – hessian sacking dyed red! But no one had the least hesitation in taking the will for the deed!

On entering the Republic of South Africa the General and his wife began by dividing their attention between Johannesburg and Soweto. Large and responsive congregations gathered in both areas to greet them. On the Monday morning the General addressed a multi-racial gathering of clergy, ministers and Salvation Army officers drawn from the greater Johannesburg region. In the afternoon he spoke to a group of Christian students at the University of Witwatersrand, and this was followed in the evening by a women's rally at which Mrs General Wiseman was the principal guest. The following day was spent in council with the officers of the territory, after which the visiting party travelled to Mountain View, Zululand. Here the General was received by Chief G. M. Buthelezi, BA, and his mother, the Princess Constance Magogo ka Dinizulu. Afterward Chief Buthelezi addressed a well-attended open-air rally, and later presented his boyhood teacher, a Salvationist, to the General.

Back in London the General gave himself to the leadership of an international conference of commissioners and territorial leaders at Sunbury Court which lasted from September 26 to October 6, 1975. After campaigning at various centres in the British Isles – including the 'Holiday plus Fellowship' camp at Bognor Regis – the delegates from forty territories representing fifty-six countries, applied themselves to the conference theme, 'Growth and Mission' in the light of the biblical promise: 'I

have set before you an open door which no man can shut'
(Revelation 3:8).

Emphasising the Army's unity amid a diversity of races,
languages and cultures, the General declared that Salvationists
are undeniably one in Christ. In our primary work for evangelism we are of one heart and mind though making use of
diverse methods to secure our common aim. For this purpose
it was the duty of the officer to see that his soldiers were well
trained, demonstrating the experience of holiness based on
sound biblical teaching in everyday living. In an age of increasing polarisation it was essential to maintain our political
neutrality while always recognising the necessity to obey God
rather than man. The report continued:

> Long and prayerful consideration was given to the Salvation
> Army's place in the World Council of Churches before the con-
> ference recommended that the Army should continue its member-
> ship . . . There is clear evidence that its presence is valued, and
> encouragement has been expressed that this should be maintained.
> It is not considered that certain political attitudes and actions
> which appear to have been supported by the Council, but which
> the Army deems to be undesirable, constitute a sufficient reason
> for its withdrawal. On the contrary, it is felt that such influences
> make the Army's presence the more desirable.[1]

A further testimony to the Army's willingness to be one with
the people of God in furthering the work of God was to be seen
at the International Conference on World Evangelism held in
Lausanne in the summer of 1974. Among the 3,500 delegates
present was an Army contingent drawn from twenty-six countries, headed by more than forty officers under the overall
leadership of Commissioner Raymond Delcourt, territorial
commander for France. With the rest of the company, Salvationists sought to learn how better to promote the spread of
the gospel as well as meeting with their comrades in the
fellowship of prayer and praise. Outstanding in a memorable
programme was the Sunday afternoon gathering in the
Olympic stadium where an Army band led the united singing.

Shortly after the conference concluded, the General and his
wife crossed the Atlantic to open Heritage Hall in New York,
planned as a setting for memorabilia concerning the inception
and growth of the Army in the United States. This was

followed by a weekend's public meetings and, seeing that the international visitors were but 400 miles from Bermuda – sometimes described as the second loneliest community in the world – there seemed no reason why they should not be the first Army world leaders to visit this cluster of islands. So they shared in the seventy-ninth anniversary of the opening of the work in Bermuda and the only mishap was that as Mrs Wiseman was leaving she slipped, fell heavily and injured her knee. To add to her serious discomfort Heathrow was fogbound and the plane was diverted to Manchester, adding another five hours to the journey. Mrs Wiseman was taken straight to hospital and, though the General had to fulfil the remaining long-distance engagements for the year on his own, such was the care and attention she received that the fixtures for 1976 were fulfilled as planned.

Earlier in the autumn the General had announced that Commissioner Harry W. Williams would lead the Army delegation to the fifth assembly of the World Council of Churches at Nairobi from November 23 to December 10. The other six members would be Commissioner Gladys Calliss (Sri Lanka), Colonel Joshua Ngugi (East Africa), Colonel Ernest Denham (International Headquarters), Lieut.-Colonel Thorsten Kjäll (Sweden), Mrs Grace Lodge (USA) and Miss Anwyn Dumbleton (UK). The paragraphs which follow are from the detailed report submitted by Commissioner Williams and which appeared in *The War Cry* dated January 17, 24 and 31, 1976, respectively.

As on each occasion since 1948 in Amsterdam the Army was represented . . . We are a tiny fraction of the millions of Christians and our delegation of seven reflects that fact. But, as always, our presence was magnified by our distinctive uniform, be it white or grey or blue . . .

On the second Sunday this had world impact for, in the beautiful setting of Uhuru Park, I have never seen so many cameras trained on the Nairobi Central Band with its tall African bandmaster holding his baton aloft to signal the drums. The step was perfect and the beat of the drums impeccable, but the discerning eye would have seen in those battalions many signs of poverty and toil. The (marchers) were numbered in their hundreds . . . a revelation to the men and women from Chicago, Zurich, Delhi and Tokyo . . .

What wisdom when the Founder decided in 1910 that the Army should be involved in this new attempt to bring Christian people together.[2] We remain a tiny minority in this now vast company ... a decimal point of dissent within this eucharistic church, yet once again our distinctive ministry made delegates ponder the fundamentals of the Christian faith ... The call to evangelism and community development went forth loud and clear from this assembly. How poor would we be were we not involved in this dialogue with all the world ...

Leaving Mrs Wiseman in nursing care in London the General flew to Tokyo to share in the Army's eightieth anniversary in Japan where he was able to meet a broad cross-section of the nation – ranging from the imperial household, via one of the world's largest rotary clubs, to a group of young Salvationists who presented a drama featuring an early-day Japanese officer who built a bridge across a river in the northern part of the country. This made it possible for the children of the district to reach their day school more easily and also provided a short cut to the Army hall. Over the years this particular bridge has been strengthened and widened but it is still known as the 'Salvation bridge'. The application which the General made of this story to the lives of his hearers hardly needs spelling out.

As it was ten years since a leader from International Headquarters had visited Indonesia, the presence of General Wiseman evoked the warmest of greetings from the Salvationists who crowded the grounds of the training college in Jakarta to greet him. The same could be said of the 4,000 Salvationists in Sulawesi – formerly known as the Celebes – for whom General Wiseman was the first international leader they had ever seen. The story was one of meetings, meetings all the way – first at Palu on the coast, then at Kalawara in the highlands, then back to Java for a call at Surabaya with its 240-bed hospital, a babies' home, a boys' home and a students' hostel, and finally westward to Bandung where the impressive territorial headquarters is situated and the final campaign meetings were held.

The General arrived back in London two days before Christmas, which allowed Mrs Wiseman – now recovered from her accident – to share with him in the annual carol service in the Bramwell Booth Memorial Hall at International

Headquarters. The Chief of the Staff and Mrs Commissioner Carr undertook the customary visits to social service centres in the Greater London area for on Saturday, January 10, the indefatigable travellers left on their forty-six-day campaign in the sub-continent of India. This began the moment the plane touched down in Bombay and did not end until the beginning of March when the return flight left the Bandaranaike international airport in Sri Lanka on the fourteen-hour flight to Heathrow.

Between these two points they faced some of the largest congregations ever assembled to greet them during their term of office, as well as the handful of the faithful who gathered at a village crossroads where no official halt had been announced. At creches for babies and homes for boys smiles had been answered with smiles. They visited homes for the handicapped in the lofty foothills of the Himalayas and sweltered in the bustees of Calcutta – 'that most despairing city' according to James Cameron – where Dudley Gardiner fed the hungry seven days a week, fifty-two weeks in the year.

The General had been so moved by the relief programme in Bangladesh that he cabled his commendation to the international *War Cry* in London. This was the best thing he could have done for independent research undertaken at the beginning of 1976 showed that *The War Cry* headed the British religious periodicals sales table by a handsome margin. But while the masterly medical improvisations practised in Bangladesh excited wonder, love and praise, the regular services of the established Army hospitals from Dhariwal in the Punjab in the north to Puthencruz in Tamil Nadu in the south went on unresting, unhasting. And if the international visitors had been made welcome as they viewed the historic treasures in the golden temple at Amritsar, they had made themselves no less welcome at the sheltered workshop for the physically handicapped at Aramboly.

The General was in the midst of this campaign when word reached him that Mrs General Wickberg had been taken into hospital at Stockholm and, shortly afterward, that she had been promoted to Glory. In a discerning appreciation of her life and work the international *War Cry* for March 26, 1976, remarked that she 'preferred the more personal approach to the glare of the public spotlight,' but that 'called to serve in three European countries other than her homeland, Germany, she applied herself to the difficult task of learning a new language with such success that she was able to minister, in public and in private, without the aid of a translator,' finally carrying the highest of offices with dignity and grace.

But, as was universally expected, every Salvationist whatever his rank or responsibility, continued to do his duty. For example, at three o'clock in the morning on February 4, 1976, the most violent earthquake hitherto experienced in central America ravaged Guatemala. Thousands of people were killed and a much larger number were injured or made homeless. The town and neighbourhood of Tecpan were literally flattened. At the height of the relief operation sixteen officers – drawn from Mexico, the Caribbean and the four territories of the United States, supported by numerous other helpers – were wholly occupied in meeting the needs of the stricken population. The cost of reconstruction was estimated at a million dollars. But money was not all that was needed – and offered. One night, when there were several subsidiary tremors of an unusually severe nature, the head of one of the repair sections came to the Army officer on duty. 'Captain, this is terrifying my men. Would you come over and speak to them?' This the captain did and led a reassuring service of prayer.

The arrival of General and Mrs Wiseman in the Philippines where Lieut.-Colonel Nancy Hulett was officer commanding coincided with the unwelcome advent of heavy monsoon rains which would have quenched the spirit of comrades less ardent than the Filipino Salvationists. Nevertheless 'Jesus Folk' – the first full-scale musical to be produced in the command – was welcomed by a capacity congregation, and more than a hundred of those present signified their desire to serve Him in whose praise the musical was both written and presented. Continuing heavy rain meant that indoor activity had to take the place of any outdoor witness, but this allowed the General and his wife to enjoy a more intimate fellowship with the officers and soldiers present at the congress.

Within nine months Salvationists had proved their worth to their own countrymen when an earthquake savaged the island of Mindanao in the south of the command. At the request of the authorities half a dozen teams of from five to seven members each were assigned to the hardest hit areas –

particularly where it was difficult for government forces to operate. These teams were given an open pass to all parts and specialised in food distribution which, where necessary, was cooked at centres where the homeless were gathered. Thanks to the Army's international network financial aid was immediately made available while both Oxfam and Action in Distress agreed to co-operate in this relief service.

While in this area the General and Mrs Wiseman made a special visit to Taiwan where the Army's work had been recommenced ten years earlier and was currently a division of the Hong Kong Command. This enabled renewed contacts to be made with the administration, as well as the media and the public at large, concerning the aims of the Army and the service which could be rendered. There was a willing response from people of all ages to the mercy seat.

If the people of Hong Kong, the next port of call, used the visit of the General and his wife to express their appreciation of the Army's services on their behalf, no less did the visitors use the occasion to recognise the loyal service of Salvationists in the colony – chiefly by the admission of one of their best-known local officers, Envoy Chu Suet-King, to the Order of the Founder. This was in recognition – first of all – of her service at the King's Park refugee camp during the Japanese occupation, then of her timely aid for the Vietnamese refugees, and latterly of her specialised work as superintendent of the Kwai Chung girls' home.

Before the month was out the General had accorded the same honour to Lieut.-Colonel Henry Rostett (R) for his work in Haiti in financing the erection of Army halls and quarters, travelling at his own expense to supervise their construction and/or repair. Subsequently returning to London the General acknowledged the fifty years' ministry of hospital visitation by Salvationist Lucy Riches, expressed in her concern for the spiritual as well as the physical welfare of those for whom she cared.

The climax of the General's second year of office found expression in his leadership of the largest of the four area congresses held in the British Territory. The London celebrations centred mainly on the Royal Albert Hall during the first week in July. The other three were held in Bristol, Newcastle and Sheffield respectively, with the British Com-

missioner present at each event, the Chief of the Staff and
Mrs Commissioner Carr as the principal guests in Bristol,
Commissioner (National Commander for the USA) and Mrs
Chamberlain in Newcastle, and Commissioner and Mrs Orton
in Sheffield. The infectious spirit of these several occasions was
reflected in the fact that, when timbrel playing broke out
spontaneously, a St. John Ambulance nurse on duty joined in
and, at the close of the day, there was an old-fashioned 'glory
march' around the Royal Albert Hall.

Without doubt this meant as much to the General as the
news, which appeared on the same page of *The War Cry*, that
with the approval of the Queen, Sovereign of the Order of
Canada, he had been appointed an Officer of that Order.

3   THE TRIUMPHS OF HIS GRACE

Before the last chapter of this volume is completed it should be emphasised that, though successive Generals play a large part in the overall story, all would be agreed that the work of the Army could not continue without the unwearying devotion of individual officers, local officers and soldiers, both men and women. Reference has already been made to the Order of the Founder which recognises this fact, and during the final year of General Wiseman's leadership three women officers were so honoured. Their service indicates the scope of the Army's operations.

On November 4, 1976, the Harry Margolis hall in what was then known as Salisbury (Rhodesia) was filled to capacity with government and civic leaders, church leaders, Salvation Army officers, soldiers and friends for the public admission of Brigadier Mrs Lilian Nhari to the Order of the Founder. The brigadier was born into a rural home, attended a mission school and later qualified as a teacher. In 1938 she became a Salvationist and in the following year entered the Army's training college at Howard with her husband. In addition to sharing his vocation as an officer Mrs Nhari became a Guide Commissioner and later Assistant National Commissioner. She served twice as chairman and convenor of the Rhodesian National Council of Women, was a moving spirit in the federation of women's clubs, represented African women on the National Commission of Inquiry into racial discrimination and, after her husband's promotion to Glory and her own official retirement in 1971, continued to oversee the Army's 'vision village' at Howard – a pioneer centre set up to combat malnutrition among African children. Full of age and honour, Mrs Nhari was promoted to Glory in December 1982.

On the other side of the Atlantic a young Swedish officer, Hulda Jansson, arrived in the South America East Territory in 1928 where she was destined to spend twenty-five years as 'directora' (administrator) of Hogar Evangelina at Quilmes, a short distance out of Buenos Aires. She also held other similar appointments in the course of the years but it is for her work at the Evangelina, where love and laughter were never far away, that she is principally remembered. The brigadier returned to her native land on her official retirement from active service, but found it impossible to settle at ease in the more affluent Scandinavian society. At her own request she returned to South America and, for a further fourteen years, served in corps and children's work in Paraguay.

In the same year that Hulda Jansson arrived in South America, Captain Laura Gale landed in Colombo. In 1936 she was appointed to 'The Haven' where her forty years' service for unmarried mothers, little children, mentally retarded women and girls in need of care and protection more than justified her Sinhalese name of *Premawanti* – 'woman of love'. For nine years she organised a clinic which cared for people who were waiting to enter hospital or who had come to Colombo for medical treatment, and when in 1956 the clinic was incorporated in a government scheme, she was awarded the Cancer Society gold medal for her work. She was a pioneer member of the Ceylon Cancer Society and also one of the first voluntary probation officers on the island, for which service she was admitted a member of the Order of the British Empire.

Though the brigadier officially retired from officership in 1971 she continued to serve as Matron at 'The Haven' for another five years, returning to England only when she had completed fifty years as a Salvation Army officer and forty years at 'The Haven'. General Wiseman personally admitted her to the Order of the Founder on Tuesday, November 9, 1976.

That particular year, no more than any other, saw no lessening in the demands of human need. The fact that every earthly prospect might please did not save the tourist paradise of Bali from natural disaster. Without warning some forty villages, in a mountainous area where terraced rice fields were fringed by coconut palms and banana trees, were destroyed in as many seconds, during an earthquake. In one of the larger villages the entire main street was reduced to ruin from end to end. The junior school fell in on itself burying the pupils in the rubble. Nearly 600 people were killed. Another 900 were seriously injured. A further 21,000 suffered hurts of various kinds – and all in a region lacking modern medical resources. The 2,500 families in the fifteen villages in Kelemantan were assigned to the Army to feed and clothe, to provide medical care and temporarily to rehouse. Most of the people of Indonesia are Moslems, but Salvationists had no hesitation in ministering to them in the name of Him to whom a man's need matters more than his creed.

The same spirit could be seen at work on the opposite side of the Pacific in an industrialised urban community. Salvationists in Los Angeles had set up their 'Manhattan' project which kept open house for up to forty-five young people between the ages of sixteen and twenty-five. Some of them had already been in trouble with the police. Some were students. Some were unemployed. A minority were working. Many came from broken homes. All had one or more problems.

Some had heard of the 'Manhattan' project and thought it might help them. But would the project have them? The applicant had to appear before a board composed of residents who were there for the same reason that he wanted to be there – a personal problem. So it was small use any newcomer trying to put it across his peers. They were not likely to be taken in by any old yarn. But they would hear him out and, if he were admitted, he would have to accept the responsibilities of acceptance. He had to look after himself, to help prepare his own meals, to pay his share of the overall upkeep. In short, to work out his own salvation in the company of his age group who would chasten or encourage, correct or commend, reprove or praise as might be deemed most helpful. Of course, this approach where a spade was not knowingly called anything other than a spade proved too strong a medicine for some, but there were others for whom it proved to be a means of grace. Please let no reader discount this approach because it was not besprinkled with conventional religious phrases. The spirit was that of the New Testament.

In the meantime General and Mrs Wiseman were bestriding the South American continent – Lima to Santiago, to Asuncion, to Montevideo, to Rosario, to Buenos Aires, and thence to the principal Army centres in Brazil. But however crowded the calendar, no engagement was treated superficially. There was time for the young folk to put their questions to the General, and he took time to answer them. There was time to counsel wisely and well the many seekers who knelt at the mercy seat. There was time to share with the President of Paraguay the annual ceremony commemorating the country's heroes – only this meant being on site at seven o'clock in the morning. More comfortably the reader can now savour the story of the rescue operation undertaken by Bolivian Salvationists when Santa Cruz was flooded.

When the two relief teams which had been organised in La Paz arrived at the scene of the disaster, they were informed that everything was under control. 'Well organised' were the actual words. One group of volunteers had been assigned to attend to the morning meal, another to the evening. Admirable – and doubtless supplies for both meals were on hand? The inaudible question mark was justified. It was well that the new arrivals had brought with them food for the hungry – not to mention mattresses to soften the hardness of bare boards, medicines for the sick, various drinks for the thirsty and games for fretful children. Nor had prayers for the despondent and fearful been omitted.

Once back in England, the General and his wife faced one of the most demanding series of gatherings in their engagement schedule – the annual councils attended by the officers who staff the more than 800 evangelical centres south of the Tweed. This calls for a master of assemblies, who is also a master of the Word, as well as a master of administrative detail. Some of those who listen are as seasoned in the holy war as the speaker, but are nevertheless equally eager to hear what the Spirit has to say to His people.

The year drew to a close with Reformation Day in Hanover (Germany), followed by the European zonal conference of Army leaders at Lunteren (The Netherlands), the carol service in the Westminster Central Hall, and the customary visits to the Army's social service centres in the Greater London area during the Christmas season. What the turn of the year emphasised afresh was that it was not only the Third World countries who were glad of the Army's help. A superpower could be grateful as well.

Early in 1977 the city of Buffalo (USA) was struck by a blizzard. Forecasters had warned of this eventuality and had advised prudent families to stock up – but the storm stole a march on the weathermen and hit the city two or three hours in advance of the predicted time. As a result hundreds of harassed shoppers were stranded in downtown Buffalo and forced to abandon their cars. As the scale of the crisis became plain, all Salvation Army centres opened their doors to offer shelter and hot meals. As these centres habitually carried emergency stocks more than 2,500 people were thus accommodated.

As the first fierceness of the storm abated, calls began choking the Army switchboard for food to be delivered to homes that were snowbound. An appeal over the news media resulted in a mobilisation of snowmobiles and four-wheel-drive vehicles. Soon 150 of these with several hundred drivers were mustered and, before this emergency had ended, more than 50,000 food parcels had been delivered. This operation was so successful because Salvation Army centres in Toronto and in the state of New York as well, shared in the work of distribution.

When the region was declared a national disaster, Salvationist personnel joined hands with the federal authorities while maintaining that flexibility which seeks to meet human need whatever its nature. For example, at the height of the storm an officer in Buffalo received a call from a distracted woman in California concerned about the plight of her diabetic father, aged eighty-five. In course of the conversation she mentioned that she had a brother who lived in Buffalo but father and son had not spoken to one another for many years. The officer took food to the father, visited the son, and soon there was a happy reunion.

During the emergency the Army was able to provide shelter, clothing, food and other forms of assistance to more than 175,000 people in the nine counties principally affected.

On Monday, March 7, the Chief of the Staff, Commissioner Arthur Carr, dispatched to the Army leaders listed below the formal notice summoning them to be present at Sunbury Court on Friday, April 29, 1977, for the High Council which would elect a successor to General Clarence D. Wiseman. The forty-one members were:

Colonel Edmundo ALLEMAND	Territorial Commander, South America West.

Colonel Ernest ANDERSON	Territorial Commander, Scotland.
Colonel Richard ATWELL	Territorial Commander, Rhodesia.
Commissioner Arnold BROWN	Territorial Commander, Canada and Bermuda.
Colonel Eva BURROWS	Territorial Commander, Sri Lanka.
Commissioner Gladys CALLISS	Special Service, IHQ.
Commissioner Arthur CARR	The Chief of the Staff.
Colonel Robert CHEVALLEY	Territorial Commander, Switzerland.
Commissioner CHUNG Yong Sup	Territorial Commander, Korea.
Commissioner W. Stanley COTTRILL	International Secretary, IHQ.
Commissioner Geoffrey DALZIEL	British Commissioner.
Commissioner Raymond DELCOURT	Territorial Commander, France.
Colonel Jacques EGGER	Territorial Commander, Central America and Mexico.
Commissioner Ernest ELLIOT	Territorial Commander, New Zealand.
Colonel Caughey GAUNTLETT	Territorial Commander, Germany.
Commissioner Panureth E. GEORGE	Territorial Commander, South-western India.
Commissioner William GOODIER	Territorial Commander, Australia Southern.
Commissioner Ernest HOLZ	Territorial Commander, USA Southern.
Commissioner Richard HOLZ	Territorial Commander, USA Western.
Commissioner Arthur HOOK	International Secretary, IHQ.
Commissioner Paul KAISER	National Commander, USA.
Commissioner Kathleen KENDRICK	Literary Secretary, IHQ.

Commissioner Hesketh KING	Territorial Commander, South Africa.
Colonel Leonard KIRBY	Territorial Commander, Nigeria.
Colonel Edwin MARION	Territorial Commander, Indonesia.
Commissioner John NEEDHAM	Territorial Commander, USA Central.
Colonel Joshua NGUGI	Territorial Commander, East Africa.
Commissioner Harold ORTON	Chancellor of the Exchequer, IHQ.
Commissioner Leslie PINDRED	Territorial Commander, Australia Eastern.
Colonel Arthur PITCHER	Territorial Commander, Caribbean.
Colonel Jean-Pierre SECHAUD	Territorial Commander, Congo.
Commissioner Donald SMITH	Territorial Commander, Denmark.
Commissioner Karsten SOLHAUG	Territorial Commander, Norway.
Colonel Eliseo STEVEN	Territorial Commander, Brazil.
Commissioner Bramwell TRIPP	Territorial Commander, USA Eastern.
Commissioner Harry TYNDAL	Territorial Commander, Sweden.
Commissioner Cornelis VERWAAL	Territorial Commander, The Netherlands.
Colonel Jarl WAHLSTRÖM	Territorial Commander, Finland.
Commissioner Per-Erik WAHLSTRÖM	International Secretary, IHQ.
Commissioner Harry WILLIAMS	International Secretary, IHQ.
Commissioner Shinichi YOSHIDA	Territorial Commander, Japan.

Meanwhile consideration was being given to a merger of the Men's and Women's Social Services in Great Britain and Ireland. Each had been separately administered since their pioneering days and each was well staffed – 194 active officers and over 1,000 employees in the men's wing, and 186 active officers and 760 employees in the women's. The actual merger did not take place until the spring of 1978 but a statement of intent appeared in *The War Cry* for April 2, 1977.

Another step in the right direction was the preparation and publication of a new edition of the *Orders and Regulations for Soldiers of The Salvation Army*. To mark the occasion *The War Cry* for March 26, 1977, carried a photograph of the General presenting a copy of this new paperback to Mary Starrs (of New Barnet) and Konrad Halls (of Edmonton). The format and language of these regulations had been radically revised for this new edition but the aim and spirit remained unchanged. This is not the place for any theological appraisal of this new manual but one of its most valuable insights is the use of the term 'Christlikeness' as an overall description of the life of holiness. The man/woman relationship is dealt with frankly yet delicately and, in this context, the observance of Christian standards is shown to be the way to highest Christian happiness. The place of the Army is firmly set in the universal fellowship of Christian believers and the lifestyle of the Salvation soldier is set out in detail. When this paperback was first published in 1977, the selling price in the United Kingdom was thirty-five new pence. Sadly, costs have risen steeply since then but *Chosen to be a Soldier* remains value for money.

The General and his wife undertook one more campaign in Africa before welcoming the ninth High Council to London. This was to the Congo (formerly French Equatorial Africa), Zaire, Ghana and Nigeria.

Exactly forty years earlier, in March 1937, Salvationists from Kinshasa crossed the river Congo to hold meetings in a building bought from a Senegalese trader in Poto Poto, Brazzaville.[1] The changing fortunes of the Second World War put a brake on traffic across the Congo, but this was only temporary. Medical work began in 1947, an officers' training school was opened in 1965 and shelters for the aged were started in the following year. The fortieth anniversary saw fifty-three corps in operation staffed by 135 officers.

Salvationists from many parts of the country travelled to greet their international leaders at the Maya-Maya airport, and beneath the stars there followed a musical festival that lasted near to midnight. The following day an estimated congregation of 5,000 gathered at the Moungali Ground – an open-air stadium – for the Sunday morning holiness meeting. In the afternoon a characteristic march of witness – rank upon rank of white-uniformed soldiers – preceded the opening of the new hall at Poto Poto which stands alongside the original Army property. The congregation for the salvation meeting filled every nook and cranny of the building, overflowing into the surrounding streets – and the mercy seat was crowded many times over.

Next day the President of the People's Republic of the Congo received the visiting leaders who, after seeing the local Army dispensaries at work, journeyed some 150 kilometres into the bush to open a new hall at Boko. This was largely the fruit of the witness and work of Sergeant Baloubets, the headmaster of the local secondary school.

From the warmth of the fellowship of Brazzaville the inter-national visitors crossed the Congo to be greeted with equal warmth in Zaire where, in addition to addressing several well-attended rallies in Kinshasa, they made more than one excursion into the bush – to the huge delight of the comrades who lived outside the closely packed centres of population. Medical dispensaries, settlements for the aged and homes for children situated off the beaten track were included in the itinerary.

Air traffic delays in the General's forward journey to Ghana meant that the welcome meetings in Accra had to proceed without him! Thus when the overdue travellers touched down the following day there was hardly a moment's respite before they were sharing in a festival of music and drama. To help make up for lost time Sunday's programme began at eight o'clock in the morning – though without any compensating curtailment at the other end of the day.

A brief night's rest, and the visitors moved up country to Begoro where the local office of the Department of Social Welfare and Community Development presented twenty new beds to the Army clinic in recognition of services rendered to the people of the district. But delays still dogged the travellers whose resolute spirit alone sustained them against the weari-ness of the flesh. The onward journey to Kumasi, the Ashanti capital, had to be rerouted because of the breakdown of the scheduled flight and the disruption of communications at both ends. But thanks to the perseverance of the visitors and the patience of the visited, the divisional rally in the Prempeh assembly hall worthily crowned the day.

With the travel jinx finally shaken off the General was greeted outside the Lagos city hall by the divisional band, and Mrs Wiseman delighted the welcoming crowd beyond measure by donning the Nigerian wrap-around with which she had been presented. There were no further delays on the flight to Port Harcourt where another congregation numbering several thousand assembled for the holiness meeting. Nor could there be any mistaking the pleasure with which Salvationists greeted the General's announcement that Lieut.-Colonel Edet Barrika would be joint territorial commander with Colonel Leonard Kirby. On World Health Day the General and his party visited the Oji River Home for handicapped children, and on the Good Friday the comrades of the East Central division met them at Umuchu.

The concluding stage of the General's Nigerian campaign saw him at Ibadan in the Western Division where Easter Sunday commenced with a march of witness on what the General called 'the happiest morning in the Christian year'. This was followed by a holiness meeting in which the thirty-two years' unbroken service of Corps Sergeant-Major David Abayomi of Lagos Central – who was linked with the Army's pioneering days on the west coast of Africa – was warmly recognised.

The public welcome to the forty-one members of the 1977 High Council was held in the Westminster Central Hall on Thursday evening, April 28, 1977. At nine-thirty the following morning the Council entered into private session and, after a period of devotional fellowship, the following officers were appointed:

President	Commissioner Bramwell Tripp
Vice President	Commissioner Leslie Pindred
Recorder	Commissioner Kathleen Kendrick
Assistant Recorder	Commissioner W. Stanley Cottrill
Chief Teller	Commissioner Arthur Hook
Assistant Teller	Commissioner Gladys Calliss
Assistant Teller	Commissioner Donald Smith
Chaplain	Colonel Eva Burrows

The structure and procedures of the High Council were

discussed in detail and attention given to the membership of the working committees. Proposals were then received for nominations for the office of General and, from the names submitted, two members of the High Council agreed to go forward to election. In alphabetical order these were:

Commissioner Arnold Brown
Commissioner Harry Williams.

Both answered a list of questions on Salvation Army policy prepared by the High Council and both addressed the Council. At the first ballot Commissioner Arnold Brown secured the required two-thirds majority. After the result had been announced the General-elect was reported as saying:

All I can say at this moment is that, as far as I am concerned, the aims of the Army remain the same. The Salvation Army is dedicated to proclaiming the saving grace of God as the only salvation for this world, and to spending all its powers in the care of the poor and needy throughout the world . . .

I follow in a distinguished succession. I can never hope to be a William Booth or a Bramwell Booth, or indeed any of their successors. But I remember that after the assassination of Dr Martin Luther King, somebody said to Dr Ralph Abernethy: 'Will you be able to fill Dr Martin Luther King's shoes?' To that he replied: 'I am afraid not, but I have a pair of my own.'

I am not sure that I will be able to fill the shoes of any of the great leaders who have gone before, but I have some sandals of my own.[2]

General Wiseman was fully aware that his term of office ended on July 4, but he was determined not to be a 'lame duck' leader for the next sixty days. Prior to the assembling of the High Council he and Mrs Wiseman had campaigned in Belgium where, among other engagements, he opened a five-storey multi-purpose social service centre in Antwerp. In Italy he led public meetings in Florence and in Rome with such élan that a Protestant minister who attended one of the rallies declared that it would be a good thing for the church if the General could visit the country once a week! Even the public disturbances which caused the cancellation of the open-air witness in Rome did not dampen the ardour of Salvationists and Christian friends in the Italian capital.

With the business of the High Council ended, General
and Mrs Wiseman completed their final round of European
engagements by leading the traditional Ascension Day meetings in Switzerland. Even before reaching Zurich they met
the Blackpool Citadel band at Neuchâtel and, during the
well-attended festival in the Temple au Bas, announced the
promotion of the territorial leaders, Colonel and Mrs Robert
Chevalley, to the rank of commissioner.

At the beginning of June the General led the eighty-eighth
territorial congress in Finland where the President of the
Republic, Dr Urho Kekkonen, confessed his 'closeness to the
Army' through his mother's membership of the Home League
– first in his native town of Kajaani and later in Helsinki.

During the full-length congress which followed in Norway,
the General laid the foundation stone of the building which
would house both the territorial headquarters and the Oslo
Temple corps in the capital.

Back in London Mrs General Wiseman, accompanied by
Mrs Commissioner Carr and Commissioner and Mrs Geoffrey
Dalziel, greeted Her Majesty the Queen Mother as she
attended the seventieth anniversary of the commencement of
the Home League. The Queen Mother said:

> During the twenty years which have slipped past so quickly since
> you welcomed me to your golden jubilee, I have kept very much
> in touch with your movement. When the Home League began in
> East London, sixteen members attended the first meeting. Today
> there are more than 325,000 members active in 82 countries. What
> a power for good they must represent . . .
>
> Then in 1974 I received the delegates to the Army's eighth High
> Council who elected the husband of your World President to be
> the Army's international leader. It seems fitting that I should
> be here today to wish them well as they are about to enter
> retirement . . .
>
> Your history books suggest that when the Home League move-
> ment began on January 26, 1907, it was called by that name for
> want of a better. I suggest that it was so called because a better
> name could not be found.
>
> Home is synonymous with shared happiness, laughter, love and
> a sense of serenity. And a league, devoted to nourishing and
> encouraging these attributes and qualities, must surely have its
> place in the divine purpose . . .

With its fourfold emphasis on worship, fellowship, education and service, the international home league has a major part to play in helping to establish Christian standards and principles where they matter most – in the home.

A week later, on Monday, July 4, General and Mrs Wiseman attended their final public meeting in the Westminster Central Hall before leaving for their retirement home in Scarborough, Ontario. There was a crowded hall and many speeches. The Chief of the Staff, Commissioner Arthur Carr, announced the presence of the High Commissioner for Canada, the Hon. Paul Martin. The Hon. (Bandmaster) Walter Dinsdale, a member of the Canadian Parliament for more than a quarter of a century, conveyed greetings from the Governor General (His Excellency Jules Leger) and the Prime Minister (Mr Pierre Trudeau). Members of the Canadian armed forces brought a reminder of the days when the General was a chaplain on overseas service with the second battalion of the Royal Canadian Engineers. An African officer recalled the missionary service of the retiring leaders and, headed by their training flags, officers from five sessions witnessed to the years spent by the General as Principal at the William Booth Memorial Training College. A group of converts from the 'Share your faith' campaign testified to the General's undiminished interest in personal evangelism.

It was of the world's Saviour that the General spoke as he rose to his feet, and Mrs Wiseman concluded her response by ascribing all praise to God for the opportunities of service which had been granted them – whereupon the congregation rose to join in singing: 'Give to Jesus glory!' There could have been no better benediction on twice fifty years' active service as officers of The Salvation Army.

NOTES

PART ONE

Chapter 1
1. *The War Cry*, May 18, 1946.
2. For fuller details of the fourth High Council see *The History of The Salvation Army*, Vol. VI, pp. 283 ff.

Chapter 2
1. The father of Victor Haines, Lieut.-Commissioner William J. Haines, had been the Army's financial secretary in Germany for ten years prior to the First World War.
2. 'And God Came', Major Mina Russell, the *Officer's Review*, Jan.–Feb. 1948.
3. For this information the author is indebted to *Salvation Patrol* by Winifred Gearing (The Salvation Army, 1424 Northeast Expressway, N.E., Atlanta).
4. A Salvation Army order of merit which was instituted in 1917 to recognise the work of those whose service, in spirit or achievement, would have specially commended itself to the Founder.
5. *Marching to Glory*, E. H. McKinley, p. 135.
6. The open-air meeting coincided with the day that Atlanta, breaking the tradition of a century, sent uniformed Negro policemen into the area in lieu of white officers.

Chapter 3
1. Until his retirement the commissioner was the Army's permanent representative and latterly served on the executive committee of the WCC.
2. *By Love Compelled*, Solveig Smith (Salvationist Publishing & Supplies), p. 156.

3. 'A bunch of silver bangles', *All the World*, Jan.–March 1949, p. 156.
4. *It Began With Andrews*, Miriam Richards (Salvationist Publishing & Supplies), p. 61.
5. *The War Cry*, April 2, 1949.

Chapter 4
1. 'Wish to be affiliated with you. Have 350 members. Reply urgent. Carrie Guillaume.'
2. The equivalent of the refrain of 'Onward, Christian soldiers'.
3. *The White Castle*, Cyril J. Barnes (Salvationist Publishing & Supplies).
4. *The War Cry.*

Chapter 5
1. *The History of The Salvation Army*, Vol. VI, p. 36.
2. Much of this information is based upon an article 'God Works in Silence' by Lieut.-Colonel Charles Sowton in the July–Sept. 1953 issue of *All the World*.
3. From the personal report of the territorial commander, Commissioner Ernest Bigwood, published in the international *War Cry* for May 29, 1954.

Chapter 6
1. Chapter 11, pp. 284 ff.

PART TWO

Chapter 1
1. At this date a monthly collection of largely original vocal music issued for the use of songster brigades in the Army's devotional meetings.
2. The Salvation Army in Malayalam, Korean and Lingala, respectively.
3. 'William Booth and the world of the working man.'
4. *The History of The Salvation Army*, Vol. VI, pp. 110–116.
5. *The History of The Salvation Army*, Vol. VI, pp. 117–122.
6. *The House of my Pilgrimage*, p. 189.

Chapter 2
1. *The Salvation Army Year Book*, 1976, pp. 23 ff., 'North of the Coral Sea'.
2. The Order of the Founder was instituted in 1917 to honour

such service as would, in spirit or achievement, have commended itself to the Army's Founder.

Chapter 3
1. *The History of The Salvation Army*, Vol. VI, pp. 242 ff.
2. *A Goodly Heritage* (Salvationist Publishing & Supplies), p. 191.

Chapter 4
1. For much of this information the writer is indebted to Lieut.-Colonel Margaret White, Assistant Chief Secretary, Social Services in Great Britain and Ireland, who was first introduced to this work by applying for a post on the staff of the 'Mayflower' advertised in the home section of *The Farmers' Weekly*.
2. Much of this information, as well as that which follows, is taken from *Fight the Good Fight*, Cyril Bradwell (A. H. & A. W. Reed, Wellington, N.Z.), pp. 78, 115, 133, 134.
3. *The Natural History of Alcoholism*, George E. Vaillant (Harvard University Press).
4. *Marching to Glory* (Harper & Row), p. 56.

Chapter 5
1. *The War Cry*, September 2, 1961.
2. *The War Cry*, June 30, 1962.
3. *Catherine Booth*, Frederick de Lautour Booth-Tucker, Vol. III, pp. 88–91.

Chapter 6
1. A much fuller account of this new beginning is to be found in *One Hand upon Another* by Mrs Colonel Sallie Chesham (The Salvation Army, 145 W. 15th Street, New York, 10011) to which the present writer is also indebted.
2. *William Booth* by Harold Begbie (Macmillan), Vol. II, p. 383.
3. For the story of how neither the officers nor the eighty girls in their care were molested throughout the occupation, see *Campaigning in Captivity* by Arch R. Wiggins (Salvationist Publishing & Supplies), Ch. 16.

Chapter 7
1. The captain was promoted to Glory on December 12, 1973.

PART THREE

Chapter 1

1. First published as a weekly in 1850 by Samuel Chase and Richard Cope Morgan and renamed *The Christian* in 1870. The publishers were later known as Marshall, Morgan & Scott.
2. *And This is Joy*, Major Joy Webb (Hodder & Stoughton), p. 33.
3. The title is based on a sentence taken from a paraphrase of Philippians 4:4–9. See *A Burning in My Bones*, General Clarence Wiseman (McGraw-Hill Ryerson), p. 148.
4. *These Fifty Years*, Bramwell Booth (Cassell), pp. 193, 194.
5. Born in Aberdeen in 1903, Charles Davidson became an officer in 1923 and was appointed to Japan in March 1929. When war broke out his wife and young daughter escaped to Australia but he was interned in Changi. He was freed in September 1945, but sadly his wife was promoted to Glory before he could reach her. He returned to Japan in 1947 and, apart from less than a year's break in the USA, continued to serve there where he was territorial commander from 1956 to 1964.

Chapter 2

1. *A Hundred Years' War* (Hodder & Stoughton).
2. *The Salvation Army Year Book* 1968, pp. 34, 35.

Chapter 5

1. *The War Cry*, June 4, 1966, p. 6.
2. *The Salvation Army Year Book* 1967, pp. 44, 45.

Chapter 6

1. See pp 132–134
2. See pp 46, 47

Chapter 7

1. Both here and elsewhere there is space to itemise only one or, at the most, two of each territory's characteristic activities. It goes without saying that the Army's regular evangelical work forms the basis of all its other services.
2. Since 1976 – Rancho Palos Verdes (CA.).
3. Since 1982 – Verona (N.J.).
4. Developments in Papua New Guinea are described on pp 88, 95–98.

5. Happily such a book, entitled *By Love Compelled*, has been written by Mrs Commissioner Solveig Smith, who herself has served in India, Pakistan and Burma. This appeared over the imprint of Salvationist Publishing & Supplies, Judd Street, London WC1H 9NN in 1981.

Chapter 8
1. Now known as the Belfast Temple corps.

PART FOUR

Chapter 1
1. For a fuller account of how the Army fared in Germany, see *Holy Defiance* by Hildegaard Bleik, and *The Ninth General* by Bernard Watson, the former published by Salvationist Publishing & Supplies, and the latter by Oliphants.
2. The story is told in detail in *The Clock that Stopped at 3.25* by Winifred Gearing, obtainable from 1516 Baltimore Drive, Orlando, Fla., 32810.

Chapter 2
1. A recruiting sergeant is the uniformed Salvationist whose principal task at corps level is the counselling of seekers and the guidance of converts.
2. This is a practice not everywhere seen, but the drum is laid on its side in the centre of the Army ring and serves as a place of prayer and penitence similar to that of the mercy seat in an Army hall.
3. With delicate irony a recent issue of *The War Cry* quoted the fact that the price of one black-market ticket to see 'Oh! Calcutta' at the Round House (opposite Chalk Farm Citadel) would defray the cost of carrying sufficient dried milk from London to Dacca to provide a glass of milk for each of 18,000 refugee children.

Chapter 3
1. Reproduced from *The Times*, December 22, 1971, with permission.

Chapter 4
1. *Fight the Good Fight*, Cyril Bradwell (A. H. & A. W. Reed), p. 169.
2. Each of the single women members of the High Council served as officers of the Council.

PART FIVE

Chapter 1
1. *A Burning in my Bones* (McGraw-Hill Ryerson), p. 111.
2. *A Burning in my Bones*, pp. 147–149.
3. *A Burning in my Bones*, p. 194.

Chapter 2
1. The full text of the conference report, from which the above extract was taken, was prepared by authority of the General and appeared in *The War Cry* for October 25, 1975.
2. This is a reference to the 'Life and Work' and 'Faith and Order' movements on which the Army was represented before the First World War, and which eventually led to the formation of the World Council of Churches.

Chapter 3
1. See *The History of The Salvation Army*, Vol. VI (Hodder & Stoughton), pp. 121 ff.
2. *The War Cry*, May 21, 1977.

INDEX

Note: As married Salvation Army officers are united in their service, both being officers in their own right, references to one or both are noted under the one heading which includes the first name of each.